THE TRANSGRESSION OF THE INTEGRITY OF GOD

The Transgression *of the* Integrity *of* God

Essays and Addresses

Craig Keen

EDITED BY
Thomas J. Bridges *and* Nathan R. Kerr

FOREWORD BY
Stanley Hauerwas

CASCADE *Books* · Eugene, Oregon

THE TRANSGRESSION OF THE INTEGRITY OF GOD
Essays and Addresses

Cascade Books
An Imprint of Wipf and Stock Publishers
199 W. 8th Ave., Suite 3
Eugene, OR 97401

www.wipfandstock.com

ISBN 13: 978-1-61097-130-0

Cataloging-in-Publication data:

Keen, Craig.

The transgression of the integrity of God : essays and addresses / Craig Keen ; edited by Thomas J. Bridges and Nathan R. Kerr ; foreword by Stanley Hauerwas.

xxxiv + 274 p. ; 23 cm. —Includes bibliographical references and index.

ISBN 13: 978-1-61097-130-0

1. Philosophical theology. 2. God — History of doctrines — 20th century. 3. Metaphysics. I. Bridges, Thomas J. II. Kerr, Nathan R. III. Hauerwas, Stanley, 1940–.

BT101 .K44 2012

Manufactured in the U.S.A.

Contents

Foreword

by STANLEY HAUERWAS

THERE IS A PRESUMPTION, one often shared by Christian and non-Christian alike, that being a Christian somehow makes life and thought less difficult. For those determined to hold on to that idea I urge you not to read this book. For in Craig Keen we have a Christian theologian determined to show not only how Christian convictions make the life Christians lead difficult, but also how the thought necessary to sustain Christian life is marked by hard and difficult reflection.

Keen is not suggesting that life is difficult only for Christians. Rather he is trying to help us recognize that what it means to be a Christian and what it means to be a human being are not two different projects. According to Keen, to be a Christian is to undergo the training necessary to remember that we are human beings.

That Keen would describe Christian life this way is but an expression of his central theological and metaphysical convictions. Craig Keen believes that all that is has been determined by the cross of Christ. That cross offers not a resolution to the difficulty that marks our humanity, but rather the cross forces us to recognize that our humanity is to be discovered through the gift of prayer. And prayer is but another word for remembering we are creatures destined to be friends of God.

Keen rightly worries about my use of the word "forced" to describe God's desire to have us love God as God has loved us. I acknowledge that "force" seems an odd word to use, particularly if you are committed, as Keen and I are, to an understanding of the cross as the exemplification of God's nonviolent love. But I believe that "force" is an appropriate word to describe God's unrelenting desire to overcome our sinful desire to forget that we are temporal creatures.

I have focused on Keen's understanding of what it means to re-member our humanity because I think readers new to Keen's work will find the humanity that pervades this book compelling. Put colloquially, Craig Keen is one of the finest human beings I have ever had the privilege to count as a friend. I think the reader will find that his humanity shines through the essays in a way that is both profound and challenging. Yet it is a humanity that by its very nature cannot and does not call attention to itself. It's for this reason that Craig Keen's work is not as well known as many of us believe it should be. Hopefully, the publication of this book will change that fact.

Craig, of course, is not possessed by an ambition to be a "famous" theologian. His ambition is to live and write in a manner that he may know better how to say what it is that makes his life and his friends' lives possible. It is this humble passion that leads his friends to want to share with others what Craig has taught us. He is, after all, a theological craftsman able to help us see that Barth and Wesley, whom most would consider unlikely allies, when read in relation to one another, help us better comprehend how a life of holiness is possible. In the introduction, the editors observe that Keen's work must be read as he writes. He writes slowly and thoughtfully, choosing each word with care. We must, therefore, learn to wait on his words, asking: "Why did he use this word rather than that word?" The editors note that some might be tempted, given the care with which each sentence is written, to describe his work as "poetic." They worry that such a description might suggest that Keen's work does not meet the standards associated with more academic theology that thrives on argumentative differences. I am sympathetic with their concern that the elegance of Keen's arguments should not lead readers to rash dismissals, but I do think that these essays are wonderfully poetic because they are beautifully crafted. Indeed, it is because they are beautiful that they are arguments that matter.

Those who would read and understand Keen's way of doing theology must be prepared to pay some prices if they are to understand why and how he says what he says. It is not accidental that Kierkegaard is one of his mentors. Like Kierkegaard, he is a keen observer of our fearful pretensions, which means that when we read him we should expect to gain painful insights about ourselves. In the process, however, Keen helps us see that we are not doomed to our illusions because, as odd as it may be, even in someone as unlikely as John Wesley we discover that we are not condemned to live lives of despair. We can even risk being happy.

It is, I think, no accident that this book has been put together by two of Keen's students. In the introduction, they rightly call attention to the humanity that shapes these essays because they were fortunate to know Craig Keen as the extraordinary teacher he is. I should like to think that a good teacher will be known through the students he or she teaches. It is, therefore, a fitting tribute to Craig Keen that his students are determined to make clear the difference he has made in their lives with the hope that these essays can make a difference for the rest of us. With this book we can begin to learn what this great human being has to teach us about the difficulty of being human.

Acknowledgments

THE EDITORS WOULD LIKE to thank the following people for permission to reprint essays.

Thanks to Point Loma Press for permission to reprint, with minor editorial modifications:

> "The Human Person as Intercessory Prayer," in *Embodied Holiness: Toward a Corporate Theology of Spiritual Growth*, edited by Samuel M. Powell and Michael E. Lodahl (Downers Grove, IL: InterVaristy, 1999).

Thanks also to the *Wesleyan Theological Journal*, especially editor Barry Callen, for permission to reprint the following essays, with some editorial changes:

> "(The) Church and (the) Culture: A Little Reflection on the *Assumptio Carnis*." *Wesleyan Theological Journal* 24 (1989).

> "Homo *Precarius*: Prayer in the Image and Likeness of God." *Wesleyan Theological Journal* 33 (1998).

> "The Transgression of the Integrity of God: The Trinity and the Hallowing of the Flesh." *Wesleyan Theological Journal* 36 (2001).

> "The Resurrection of the Body: The Liturgy of Martyrdom and the Hallowing of the Flesh." *Wesleyan Theological Journal* 40 (2005).

"The Root from Which They Spring: Presidential Address."
    Wesleyan Theological Journal 42 (2007).

"Holy, Holy, Holy: The World Need Not Have Been." *Wesleyan
    Theological Journal* 44 (2009).

Abbreviations

THE FOLLOWING ABBREVIATIONS WILL be used for frequently cited titles.

Works by Karl Barth:

CD   *Church Dogmatics*. Edited by G. W. Bromiley and T. F. Torrance. 4 vols. in 14 parts. Edinburgh: T. & T. Clark, 1936–1977.

KD   *Die kirchliche Dogmatik*. 4 vols. in 14 parts. Zollikon: Verlag der Evangelischen Buchhandlung, 1932–1970.

Works by John Wesley:

WJW *The Works of John Wesley*. Begun as "The Oxford Edition of the Works of John Wesley." Oxford: Clarendon, 1975–83. Continued as "The Bicentennial Edition of the Works of John Wesley." Nashville: Abingdon, 1984–.

WJWJ *The Works of the Rev. John Wesley, M.A.* Edited by Thomas Jackson. 3rd ed. 14 vols. London: Wesleyan Methodist Book Room, 1872. Reprint, Grand Rapids: Baker, 1998.

Introduction: A Theological Life

THOMAS J. BRIDGES *and* NATHAN R. KERR

"In the dark, when we all talk at once, some of us must learn to whistle."[1]

—WALT KELLY

A Life's Story

CRAIG KEEN ONCE ATE nineteen bowls of tomato soup. He did this just *after* eating a full supper, and just *before* drinking three glasses of milk. True story. One can only imagine that this occurred, probably on a bet, just after he had watched his all-time favorite film, *Cool Hand Luke*. "Nobody can eat fifty eggs." Of course, that *Cool Hand Luke* might be somebody's favorite film is no extraordinary thing. But this is the favorite film of Craig Keen, the teacher of theology who describes what he does as "listening and speaking." "What we've got here is . . . failure to communicate." And communicate is just what Craig Keen is always trying to do. But that Craig Keen communicates—listens and speaks—in the prayerfully subversive way that he does—well, that is, in a manner of speaking, Luke's fault.

It might help if we back up here and say where we're coming from. Craig Keen is a Christian, not by descent, but by conversion. He'd prob-

1. Kelly, *Potluck Pogo*, 181.

ably say that doesn't so much make him a Christian, as simply a follower after what another Luke, in Acts, calls "the Way." And because conversion—*metanoia*—is so central to his life story, Craig likes to begin that story with the words, "I was eighteen in 1968." For 1968 would become for Craig both the year of his conversion to "the Way," as well as a parable of the kind of work a teacher of theology is to be about.

Craig was born in Oklahoma City on October 5, 1949. His parents were both raised in abject poverty by single mothers, the descendents of Scotch-Irish ancestors whose generations-long migration in search of a New World left them languishing in the Great Depression-era Southwest. Though Craig had a transient childhood, his parents always felt that being "churched" was necessary to being a "good boy" in Middle America; thus Craig came to find his lot thrown in with the Church of the Nazarene, mostly because of the fact that, as his mother put it, "Nazarenes are good people."

And so Craig, the clean-cut son of a farmboy from Oklahoma, arrived at Bethany Nazarene College (now Southern Nazarene University) in the fall of 1967 as a good conservative kid coming to an equally conservative place. A strong proponent of the Vietnam War and Richard Nixon, he was generally convinced, like most good American-holiness folk, that what was good for America was good for the Christian American to support. He chose to major in biology, convinced that was the best option career-wise. His primary concerns were typical of a good, patriotic American Christian: self-defense, self-preservation, self-promotion.

But the fall of 1967 also saw the release of *Cool Hand Luke*. Though going to the movies was technically not allowed at Bethany, Craig found his way to the cinema. Though he shared many of their convictions, Craig came from a different world than most of his fellow conservative Nazarenes. So it is not surprising that he would identify with the film's rebelliously free "natural-born earth-shaker," Luke. Nor is it surprising that he began to gravitate towards the rebels, the counter-cultural types among his peers. ("The wildest class in the history of the college," was how President Roy Cantrell described the freshmen men of that year.) He immersed himself in the music of the most counter-cultural "folk rock" musicians of his day, and even began to write his own folk songs. *Cool Hand Luke*, Bob Dylan's *The Time's They Are A-Changin'*, and Simon and Garfunkel's *Sounds of Silence* had opened up for Craig a whole new way of seeing things. The stage was set for the summer of 1968.

Craig had returned to southwest Texas for a job, where he shared a room with Arvis Wells. He and Arvis decided to spend part of each evening that summer reading and talking through a portion of a particular book of the Bible. They decided on the book of Acts because it seemed to be all about the stories of people living out their faith in a complex political climate, and would be easier to relate to their own time and place. So Craig and Arvis set out to read the book of Acts, asking themselves one simple question: Assuming what this book says is true, how are we to live, here and now? In the here and now that was Middle America in 1968, the Vietnam War was the most pressing issue. And the more Craig read the book of Acts, the more he became convinced that no faithful character in that story could ever conceivably go to war. "As long as I stayed in the story," he says, "I could not see any of these people killing, especially in combat"—whether in opposition to imperial Rome in their own time, or on behalf of imperial America in ours.

Thus it was that a naïve, eighteen-year-old Christian—conservative, American—came to declare that he was a pacifist, a declaration that Craig describes as "my first theological act." If the book of Acts is true, if the people's stories it tells are to be believed, and if these stories command us to go and do likewise, then he, Craig Keen, could not kill, especially in combat. What was happening here was indeed a conversion, a turning to respond concretely to the command to follow in the way of Jesus Christ: "Pick up your cross daily and follow me" (Luke 9:23). Craig testifies to this theological act in terms of John Wesley's *via salutis*—as a moment of repentance, justification, regeneration, and initial sanctification.

The kind of pacifism to which Craig turned was not so much a political stance, an avant-garde strategy for success or survival. It was the kind of pacifism witnessed to in the stories of Acts: an abandonment of any presumed power over the future in faithfulness to the gospel, which yet lives and works in the vulnerable posture of waiting to receive the

Spirit's irruption—the irruption of peace—into this very life and work. In other words, Craig's pacifism was an act of *prayer*, one of a very distinct kind. Such prayer does not cease to be about a very determined and particular work, a discipline. But it is the kind of prayer that works and plans in a way that does not require the putting up of defenses, but rather the gathering of one's goods so as to give them away. It is the kind of prayer that exposes one to being altered, unsettled, and overwhelmed by the neighbor whom one is given in each new moment to love. It is the kind of prayer by which the Spirit continually cuts off one's repeated attempts to construct one's own inner life of personal piety by continually turning one to welcome the voice, the hand, the face of the other. This is the kind of prayer that Craig would come to call "eucharistic"—the kind of prayer that continually, in the face of everything, "gives thanks" (see 1 Thess 5:17–18).

Craig tells a painful yet beautiful story that speaks to this kind of conversion in prayer.[2] Just months into their marriage, Craig and Elesha lived in a small one-room house that included a tiny kitchen with a small table for two. Craig had sat down at the table for lunch, a bowl of slow-boiled pinto beans before him, and had commenced praying a long, silent prayer over his food. Elesha could not see Craig well from where she was sitting and spoke to him, interrupting his prayer. Craig snapped in response: "Can't you see that I'm praying!" He apologized, of course. But the reason he snapped is that he had been trying to be especially devout, and his own personal prayers were a matter of immense importance. "I found that being married was complicating my personal piety," Craig says. "I kept thinking that I was trying really hard to be godly, but Elesha kept getting in the way." That phrase—"getting in the way"—would come to have special significance for Craig. He would come to realize that in prayer people are always getting in the way, coming between himself and God—"especially Elesha," he says. He would come to realize that to pray is to find joy in the interruption of the other, to give thanks for the other person that I am given to love. Prayer is, you might say, to be constantly turning away from that personally pious, self-righteous jerk alone at the table in turning in thanksgiving to welcome the other, the neighbor that is always right there before me—the

2. Thank you to Christina Smerick for first recounting this story for us.

neighbor that is always breaking in, interrupting. "That moment during a pinto bean lunch became a rather sacramental one for me and my theology—and also for my teaching."

And so it is that the two "Lukes" he encountered in 1968 opened up a whole new, wild imagination about how one might come to live and work in the world. The student and worker protests of 1968, for example, suddenly took on new significance for Craig. He now saw in these movements not the kind of self-defensive, self-preserving impulse that drives so much of Christian and American politics. He saw in these protests a parable of the kind of uncertain but expectant hope that he found in the stories of Acts and in *Cool Hand Luke*, in Dylan and in Simon and Garfunkel. He saw in these protests a parable of the freedom with which one is given to work and to wait when all of the world is crumbling around one, the freedom to smile joyfully ("that ol' Luke smile") as one shares one's body with other dying prisoners in disdain for the system, the freedom to dance so viscerally and euphorically (to dance, Craig would say, as only Elesha ever could) as to shake off all demons, the freedom to prophesy while the religious elite stone you to death ("just like they said they would"), the freedom to forgive as one is being strung up on a Roman gibbet. And so, Craig found himself resonating with these voices of protests not because he wanted to be a part of some alternative political movement, but because he didn't know how to be faithful to the call that he was hearing in the stories of Acts without also finding a way to be faithful to the call to which he heard these students' and workers' voices witnessing. He found in these voices an echo of the prayer that he himself had been given to pray.

And so Craig put an end to the childish ways of self-promotion and survival, to what we so politely refer to as "professionalism" and concern for one's "career." "What mattered to me at that time was not what I was going to do with the rest of my life; what mattered to me were the issues of personal and existential significance that had arisen in light of reading the book of Acts in the summer of '68." He changed his major from biology to philosophy, transferred briefly to West Texas State University, only to return to Bethany in the fall of 1970 to complete a degree in philosophy and religion.

The Craig Keen who returned to Bethany in 1970 was a completely different person than had first come to that place just three years earlier. Now he had become the longhaired hippy in class with the clean-cut "preacher" types. He had become that precocious student whose questions seemed always to be interrupting the long, pedantic march of some professor's lecture. He had become that hard-to-figure out religion/philosophy major whose closest friends seemed always to be making trouble and getting kicked out of school, the kind of religion major who preferred writing folk songs to composing sermonic monologues. Everything was up in the air. Everything was to be abandoned to the way in which he had felt himself called. Marriage, school, career—everything. So much so that when asked to state his "vocational plans" upon entering the department of religion at Bethany, he simply wrote: "Apostle." "I didn't know what else to write," he says. "I certainly had no plans of being a preacher, or a missionary, or anything like that."

In all of this, Elesha kept insisting that Craig had an obligation to keep studying, to do this work. And so Craig threw himself into his classes. He threw himself into the writings of Kierkegaard, Wesley, and Barth, into the novels of Hesse and Dostoevsky, and into albums like *The Times They Are A-Changin'* and *Bookends*. Through it all, as scrambled as his theology became and as mired as he was at times in the most gut-wrenching doubt, Craig found a way to move down that path which faithfulness to his calling required. And so, when his theology teacher and mentor at Bethany, Rob Staples, encouraged him to do so, Craig left for Kansas City with Elesha and their young daughter, Heather, to pursue the MDiv degree at Nazarene Theological Seminary. And when teachers like Ken Grider, Oscar Reed, and Paul Bassett pushed him to go even further in this work, he left for California with Elesha and their daughter and newborn son, Stefen, to study for the PhD in Theology at Claremont Graduate School (their son Bryan was born just days before Craig sat for oral exams). Since that time, Craig has spent thirty-three years teaching philosophy and theology to mostly undergraduate religion majors—first at Point Loma Nazarene University, then Trevecca Nazarene University and Olivet Nazarene University, and now Azusa Pacific University.

Craig doesn't remember ever having made a distinct decision to pursue a career in teaching. His decisions to continue with his studies were always driven by the encouragement of his professors, and even more so as a way of alleviating Elesha's worries as to how they were going to feed three children for the rest of their lives. Craig never intentionally set out to be a "teacher." It happened, you could say, almost by accident. The image Craig likes to use is that of someone walking down the street, slipping on a banana peel, falling awkwardly down a flight of stairs, bouncing through a window, falling headlong into a long dark chute, and flying out onto one's feet in front of a classroom. It could have been otherwise. And yet, Craig will just as readily tell you that he has been called to where he is, that his vocation is nothing less than to communicate the gospel in the university classroom—to serve the work of this ecclesial people as *teacher* of theology. (It was in light of this calling that Craig came, in 1995, to give himself to ordination in the Church of the Nazarene, as a deacon.) However it is that he got here, teaching is just what Craig does. Better, it is who he is. In everything that Craig Keen says and writes, he is above all a teacher.

So what is it that makes Craig the teacher, the communicator of the gospel that he is? When faced with this question, Craig doesn't give answers so much as point to events in his life that testify to the ways in which God has (nevertheless) given him to live faithfully—if unknowingly—into the work to which he is being called. One of those events occurred in the fall of 1973, his first year in seminary. Craig was going through what you might call a severe crisis of "belief" (not "faith"). As he confessed to Paul Bassett at the time: "I don't know what to believe! I don't even know if I'm a Christian anymore." (Bassett told him to read the Apostles' Creed. And Craig says it actually helped.) It was during this time that Craig had what he calls a "vision." One evening Craig found himself standing before the pearly gates of heaven, facing Saint Peter, who told him that, alas, he could not enter heaven because he was an idolater, that he worshipped Jesus *as if a creature*. You see, the "crisis of belief" that was killing Craig at the time was christological—he couldn't find any way, intellectually, of affirming the deity of Jesus Christ. Every passage of Scripture that was supposed to prove the deity of Jesus struck him as easily interpreted in some other, more credible way. And even then, were a credible argument to be mustered up by Christianity's cultured defenders, the doctrine of the deity of Jesus Christ—the teaching that *God* becomes, in fact, not just flesh, but the flesh of *this* man, this human transgressor, Jesus—seemed so outrageous that those other ways of interpretation would always be more palatable and so preferable.

All of this was paralyzing to Craig, and not just intellectually. And once again, that night, Craig underwent a *metanoia*—an overturning of the mind. It suddenly occurred to him that he had been thinking things backwards, that things needed to be turned upside down. It occurred to him that what he had been doing all along was hunting—"exploring"[3]—for some kind of way to make Jesus fit into his already constructed way of understanding, to assimilate Jesus to his world without creating any difficulties for that world. "I was insisting that 'Jesus' fit me," Craig says, "when suddenly I realized that the exact opposite was to happen. The task was rather to give myself to him. And when that happened, the world that I had created for myself came crumbling down." And so Craig came to confess that everything is to be situated in Jesus Christ. The point of the vision, to Craig, was precisely that he is to worship this man, this human being Jesus Christ, with everything that he is. That even if worshipping Jesus sends him to hell, that that is where he is to go—while yet giving everything in worship to Jesus as God. Accordingly, Craig once again testifies to this event in terms of John Wesley's *via salutis*—as a moment of entire sanctification.

Theologically, it was important for Craig that this Christic event was a distinctively trinitary event. Whatever we mean when we say "God," our speaking must emerge out of following the crucified man Jesus into the darkness of hell with such audacious hope that we can only now live by continually receiving the gift of new life that comes by the Holy Spirit's work of resurrection. For Craig, this meant that the prayer of repentance that he had begun to pray back in 1968 was here

3. In the use of the language of "exploration" and "communication" here and in what follows, we have in mind a distinction that Nicholas Lash makes in his essay, "Considering the Trinity." Lash describes the distinction between theology as exploration and theology as communication in this way: "The function of theology, as 'exploration,' is to try to find out what God is like. The function of theology, as an aspect of Christian communication, is to facilitate acquaintance by checking our propensity to go whoring after false gods" (187).

and now to be prayed anew. All of the hope and joy and freedom that he had heard in the voices of protestors, that he had seen in the character of "Cool Hand" Luke, and that he had read of in the stories of Acts—all of that was to be situated within this trinitary event of Christ's cross and resurrection.

And what all that means, finally, is that the kind of communication with God that Craig had found his earliest prayers of conversion finally to be about—the kind of communication where people are always "getting in the way"—happens only in Christ. The very possibility of communicating is grounded in the prayer that is Jesus Christ; if Jesus is the Word of God, then "Jesus" is the one word that is always to be communicated. And if everything is to be situated in this Jesus, then one cannot give witness to this word—one cannot speak—without listening to the way in which I hear every single one, the neighbor, witnessing to that word in her own sighs and cries for new life, hope, freedom. I am a communicator of the gospel only as I am given to hear witness to the human being Jesus Christ that I am to worship in the voices and faces and bodies of others, and only as I speak out of and in response to that hearing. One's worship of and witness to Jesus is always to happen as a shared work carried out in solidarity with the voices and faces and bodies of every single other I am given to live with and to love. That is to say, communicating Christ is always and everywhere to be a liturgical act, the real, hard work of particular persons, an event of what one might call church.

To be a teacher of theology is just to be involved in the struggle of continually learning anew with one's students how so to communicate Christ whenever one comes to say the word "God." In other words, teaching theology comes down to how one prays, how one cries out and gives thanks, how one lives in embodied solidarity with the particular bodies in this particular room, how one intercedes and lets the other intercede for—interrupt—one's self, how one works and how one waits. And so, to be a teacher is finally not to impose a certain set of ideas on people, but it is to work with one's mind with them, to wait with one's body with them, to communicate with them in a way that expects something new to arrive that no work of any of our bodies or minds could have constructed. And so, Craig says, "While I walk into any classroom with lots of things to say, I say those things in a way that listens and waits for what I could not have prepared to say, for what may in fact unsettle and overwhelm what I had to say." Anyone who has heard Craig pray in the classroom, and who has witnessed the long, seemingly endless em dash of a silence that comes before he is able even to get out more than one word ("God———————————————————

———————————Teach us. Amen.") can testify to the kind of waiting of which Craig here speaks. And any student who has ever witnessed Craig smile wryly (the smile only Craig can smile) in response to something she has just said, only to have Craig step back and let another seemingly endless em dash of silence ensue before he responds, knows of the joy Craig finds in being unsettled and overwhelmed by the voice of another, by the other's witness to Christ. And anyone who knows of the vulnerability with which Craig walks into a room of waiting students and silently hangs a simple pewter crucifix from the wall before turning to pray, knows that all of this communication happens for him through the word of the cross—the crucified *Logos*. This is Craig Keen, the teacher. This is his life, his work.

It is this life, this work out of which Craig Keen's distinctive theological "voice" emerges. And it is that voice which we would like the reader to hear as she works through the essays in this volume. That voice, to one who has ever heard it, is singularly unmistakable. As one person put it upon hearing him read a paper at a recent American Academy of Religion meeting, "He sounds like nothing I've ever heard from a theologian. He sounds almost like a person crying out, alternately, in pain and in joy when he speaks. He sounds . . . like a person praying, inviting you to listen, certainly, but also inviting you to laugh and to cry, to pray, with him."

To hear Craig Keen speak—and speaking is just what he's always doing—is to hear one speak out of a deeply profound sense of personal urgency. But the urgency with which Craig speaks is so profoundly personal precisely because he has listened so intently to the voices of the particular persons whom he has been given to love all his life. "All of this stuff is to be lived," Craig says, "and you have to live it towards the ones right there before you—towards your wife, towards your children, towards your elderly parents and the single mothers who raised them in abject poverty. The voices of these persons are to be heard in it all, in everything I say and do." Perhaps that is why, when Craig turns his attention to thinking a certain set of complex theological ideas, as he does in the essays that follow, what one hears sounds a lot less like that of an academic setting out on some expedition to discover what God is like, and a lot more like that of a kind of folk artist giving sound to—communicating—the one word of God he has heard in the voices of those particular persons he has been given to listen to and to love his whole life. It is that kind of personal urgency that has always driven Craig's lifework—the kind of personal urgency that emerges from attending to the cries of pain and joy, of death and of hope, of the particular neighbor there before him. And it is that kind of personal urgency alone out of which Craig teaches and writes, listens and speaks, works and waits.

A Life's Work

And so it is, as a work of this life's love, that each of the following pieces came to be written. Regarding their contents, we would like not so much to add something to them as to draw attention to what is already present, by giving a broad map of the journey they will require the reader to embark upon. These are demanding pieces to read: if one reads them with the patience that they deserve, one will not be able to stand and observe ideas from a distance—one will be continually confronted by the Christian gospel, through a theologian who writes as one wounded and enlivened by that same gospel.

Though many have described Craig's written work as "poetic," these pieces have come about through an intense labor. Every word has been agonized over, and each sentence has been constructed with prayerful intentionality. This is not mere "theological poetry"; this is theological work, and is in this sense liturgical theology (an *ergon* of the *laos*). Much toil has gone into these projects, and we think reading them also ought to require the work of following each sentence, listening to each voice and paying attention even when the "poetics" of the text tempts you not to. Craig did not pick these lines because they fit together conveniently, but because he wrestled with these ideas for so long. And so when Craig's prose causes you to pause and wonder what a particular phrase might mean, we humbly ask that you the reader do just that—pause, and let the words carry you somewhere strange.

We have chosen to name the first portion of this book's essays "Metaphysics." This section will especially interest those paying attention to theological method, as well as Christology and Trinitarian theology. Of "metaphysics," Craig says such questions as those about Being, for example, "do not lie outside the theologian's purview." But such questions are not the ones she first asks. "If she takes up such questions at all," Craig says, "she does so freely from the outside—with passion, perhaps with desire, but without need." We have nevertheless chosen to name this portion of the book "Metaphysics," because the way in which Christian dogmas such as the Trinity and the two natures of Christ are often discussed is in a metaphysical manner, because—*God bless it*—the Western philosophical tradition found at its height that the Supreme Being is actually Jesus! Having built a bridge from its hierarchical ontology all the way up to the Christian God, philosophy is now an ally of Christian theology. To do theology is to do philosophy. But the Supreme Being that is at the top of the Western world is not the God that meets flesh in Jesus Christ. Thus, when theology meets such questions as typically fall under "metaphysics," "ontology," or "ethics," one might—with astonishment—find that such categories as *physis* (nature) are transgressed, such categories as Being are surpassed, and that the morals of a society guided by justice are violated by God-come-near. And theology lives in this encounter, and works from the broken body of this particular God, who became a very particular Jewish man, Jesus of Nazareth, who still holds fellowship with the damned. And although this God-man does not fit easily within traditional metaphysical categories, it does not follow that deeper questions—such as the way in which Christ might change the way we think about *physis*—should not be pursued; it rather means that these questions will be pursued without a desire to evacuate the mystery, with an openness to the ways in which Christ exceeds ideas and continually breaks them open to what they cannot contain.

Chapter 1, the essay that shares the book title, "The Transgression of the Integrity of God: The Trinity and the Hallowing of the Flesh," exemplifies how Craig carries out this theological method. He inhabits the history of Trinitarian doctrine, showing us through his engagement with various thinkers why the christological and Trinitarian dogmas the creeds witness to are important. They are important not because they mark the time when the church defined God properly, but because they witness to a story in which God touches flesh and flesh touches God, explosively, without God's otherness being compromised. The Trinity is the doctrine to which this story—this double violation of integrity— gives rise. It is because all that is Holy touches all that is unholy in this particular man from Nazareth, that this man goes all the way to hell, that the Father sends the Spirit to the abode of the damned to resurrect this man and to open a way for all the sick, dying, and dead to be with the Holy One of Israel, that we have the doctrine of the Trinity. To say "Father, Son, and Holy Spirit" is to remove the quarantine on "God" by subverting those human hierarchies erected on the idea of a Supreme Being, calling humans instead to enter into a theosis that, in Wesleyan fashion, means going where God goes—to the unholy ones of history.

Craig is thus not diminishing the importance of doctrines typically labeled "metaphysical"; he is guarding against their use to domesticate the wild freedom of God by dulling the edge of the gospel, or by explaining away the awe and wonder that ought to accompany an encounter with the story of Jesus of Nazareth. One cannot simply say an abstract word like "God," and plug the concept of a Supreme Being into an algorithm that will overcome dissonance. Commenting on Barth (and displaying his method as well), Craig says, "Rather, 'God' here is that which happens as one is drawn in a very particular way into the very particular history of Jesus."

Chapter 2, "After Crucifixion: Unhanding Metaphysics in the Liturgy of the Eucharist," continues this approach to metaphysics by weaving the narrative of an immigrant crossing the desert into a discussion of the eucharistic community called "the church." Her faith means that she has been gathered into the Eucharist, she who has no place to lay her head in the grand, integrating visions of those who would imitate the Greeks in finding a system "specifying in some detail *God's* relation to all the goods (*ousia*) their inquiries have surveyed, goods that come into their hands as their inquiries grow more and more ambitious." Craig is critical of such attempts to map out the integrity of the cosmos because the story of Jesus Christ is the event par excellence that violates every effort to keep the sacred and profane, the rich and the poor, the healthy and the sick, the divine and the human separated. Metaphysics are to be thought differently, in an "uncanny, irrevocably prayerful" way, "a way, say, not out to apprehend, overpower, deport, or naturalize the alien, but rather to defer to her," a way that "would undo the thinker" and "open wounds through him out into the ground that had hitherto so well supported him, wounds possibly undoing integrity, well-being, wholeness; [even] *physis* itself," causing the thinker to "undergo a kind of passion." Such passion is that of the theologian gathered into the Eucharist along with the poor, a passion that requires the thinker, in a manner similar to the rich young ruler, to give all one's (intellectual) capital away to the poor and to follow Jesus. This is not a call for theologians no longer to think structures, but to think them in a way that is open, as the body of Christ has been opened to the neighbor.

The final chapter in the metaphysics portion of the book, "The Resurrection of the Body: The Trinity and the Hallowing of the Flesh," discusses grace and works. Here grace is not the fulfillment of any human potency or a gracious completion of nature; it is the resurrecting of bodies and the hallowing of flesh. And works are not something that could put humans in competition with God, for works are what humans are "given to do" (as Craig likes to put it).

In order to approach grace and works in this manner, Craig enters into an intense conversation with John Wesley. Although Wesley's work is often located within the Augustinian and Lutheran-Reformation trajectory that led to pietism, Wesley himself is not so easy to nail down. Craig Keen's Wesley "finds that the coming of salvation is wrapped in a mystery that no intent theological gaze can master even by the most complex idea," and we see in Wesley's theology a tension in which God is sovereignly responsible for all of salvation, even our works, so that there are no impermeable boundaries around our works that make them "ours." Moreover, works of grace are bodily, for the work of the Spirit comes to people entangled in a bodily world. This work forms a pattern—the means of grace—and the church is the form this pattern takes. After arguing that a eucharistic logic pervades Wesley's account of the means of grace, Craig moves beyond Wesley to discuss the eucharistic nature of theology, drawing upon the work of Jean-Luc Marion, Alexander Schmemann, and William Cavanaugh. The essay concludes, returning to grace and work, that "human faithfulness and works are thought to conflict only when human faithfulness is thought to be a deep inner experience in one's private soul, an experience that is then perhaps to be expressed in some external form." The work to which the people are called is rather a shared ecclesial work that is given by God to be done. Such work is "comparable to what comes on Easter Sunday morning to the Jesus who lay dead in the tomb all of Holy Saturday," and it is therefore a bodily event, the hallowing of flesh. Thus, "'Faith without works is dead,' because only the dead do not work . . ."

The essays in the second section, gathered under the name "Creaturehood," approach questions of creation, human being, the image of God, and nature from within the event in which God becomes fully human without ceasing to be everything that God is. Chapter 4, "Holy, Holy, Holy: The World Need Not Have Been," restores the doctrine of *creatio ex nihilo* to its very particular liturgical roots in Israel's history, and in the resurrection of Jesus. In so doing, Craig argues that the heart of this doctrine of creation is not an efficient cause for the universe ("God"), but God's free power to elect the poor and weak of this world in the face of the powers that would ruin them. Thus, it is in Deutero-Isaiah, when Israel faces certain destruction at the hands of Babylon, that "God is most forcefully announced in the Old Testament to be Creator." This announcement does not found a cosmology, but is doxological in nature, having its theological significance in the memories (exodus) and hopes of Israel (rescue from Babylon). God, in electing Israel, elects the weak, poor, blind, and lame, and brings salvation to them. Similarly, in the New Testament, it is to the lifeless corpse of the crucified man in the tomb, the defeated Jesus, that the Holy One of Israel moves, and from this corpse makes all things new. From out of this locus, the church lives in the liturgical rhythm of baptism and Eucharist, for baptism is entry into the nothing that swallowed Jesus in the tomb and participation in the singular act of new creation that is Jesus' resurrection, and Eucharist is "to live in the glorious moment of the one unprecedented creation which has called into 'existence the things that do not exist' (Rom 4:17)."

Craig engages the often scrutinized passage that speaks of the *imago dei*, Genesis 1:26–27, in Chapter 5, "*Homo Precarius*: Prayer in the Image and Likeness of God." Drawing upon the exegesis of Claus Westermann while engaging Barth and Wesley, Craig argues that the image of God is not a unique human quality, or an aspect of being human, but is rather an event between God and humanity. The image is not in the human, but between God and the human: it comes as God's address, which calls for a response. The human being is thus one who prays. Insofar as Westermann favors Barth's account of the *imago dei*, Craig goes on to say that for Barth "human life lends itself precisely to the notion that the human being is prayer, that is, is an openness to the openness of God." Barth thinks through human being at the place where the outgoing God becomes human, that is, in Jesus Christ. What Jesus reveals is that God has always been outgoing, and that human beings are themselves called out into the coming of God.

Although Wesley's explicit account of the image of God appears on the face of it to conflict with Barth's, there is something more at play in Wesley: he directs our attention to God, not the self, and what he says of the self is that when sanctified it is a living hunger, a capaciousness waiting to be filled by God. It is not wholly passive, but has the rhythm of breathing: "a continual inspiration of God's Holy Spirit: God's breathing into the soul, and the soul's breathing back what it first receives from God; a continual action of God upon the soul, the reaction of the soul upon God."[4] Craig therefore concludes that the human being in the image and likeness of God is a person living in the posture of prayer, exposed and vulnerable, wholly open to God.

Chapter 6, "The Human Person as Intercessory Prayer," is a two-part essay: a response to Stanley Hauerwas on the nature of holiness, and then an intense engagement with the idea that the human as a person is by definition opened to the other by the Wholly Other, and so is a living, breathing intercessory prayer.

Craig finds hope in Hauerwas's doctrine of holiness, especially his rejection of the autonomous, dualistic Cartesian self in favor of a bodily self shaped by a storied community. But Craig questions why holiness

---

4. Wesley, "The Great Privilege of those that are Born of God," in *WJW*, 1:442 (III.2). This is quoted in broader context in chapter 5.

must be forced—by habits, by a community, and by grace, which, in Hauerwas's words, "often is but another name for necessity."[5] Here Craig insists that "grace is God, not a force" and questions why a tight, storytelling community surviving the negotiations of being human is a proper description of the church. Christ's story, he reminds us, opens boundaries; it does not close them. It is what "the most far-reaching and flexible narrative cannot get its arms around," and it contains and reproduces (in the church) a holiness that is perfection "because it is a kind of ek-stasis that unravels every communitarian fabric, every story, every virtue, every habit."

The second part of this chapter continues to question the modern self in engagement with Barth and Wolfhart Pannenberg. With Barth he argues that the meaning of "Person" within Trinitarian theology determines what the human is called to be as a "person": as God turns to face and go out in love to the lost, poor, dead, dying, and damned, so we are to go out to those whom God faces. To be a person is to follow the journey of Jesus, the one most fully human, which occurs as the journey of the Son into the far country; this is the outgoing of God, and it is the path to which we are called. From Pannenberg's stress on the priority of the future, Craig emphasizes the way in which we are not yet persons, even as "now we are united to each other in anticipation of that day." What results from this theological synthesis is a vision of the human who is not only open to the coming of God and so lives as a prayer, but also is open to those whom God faces, and is therefore an intercessory prayer.

Craig delves more into the relation between church and culture in Chapter 7, "(The) Church and (The) Culture: A Little Reflection on the *Assumptio Carnis*." Instead of offering another typology that assumes the church is primarily a culture, Craig reminds us that Jesus Christ is the reason that the church exists and that its activity in the world must always be measured by Christ. But Christ is not an ideal, balanced human being who offers a model for health and wholeness—"The whole of the life of Jesus Christ is not a fullness; it is an emptying in which He does not assert himself, but rather asserts the other." Because he relates

5. Hauerwas, "The Sanctified Body," in Powell and Lodahl, eds., *Embodied Holiness*, 37.

to humans, including those at the bottom of the pile, he is rooted in culture, but he does not leave things the same; rather, in him they are *aufgehoben*. However, this path of renewal through Christ also follows his path through humiliation and suffering, and thus the apocalyptic rhythm of Christ's encounter with culture is that of nihilation and redemption. Craig does not offer a formula for the church's interaction with culture (nor does he think one is needed), but he does offer considerations for how the church ought to relate to institutions.

Chapter 8, "Toward a Theology of Nature," assesses the modern theological situation and argues that it is time for the concept of *physis* to be rethought. Contending that Heidegger offers the most inviting rethinking of nature, he expounds Heidegger's account of the early Greek view of nature, in which *physis* is an event of unconcealment, the revelation of Being, an "opening up and inward-jutting-beyond-itself." Though there is no direct route from Heidegger here to Christian theology, theology itself cuts across all disciplines and opens them to the revelation of God. Theology takes such notions as *physis* and offers them up in doxological discourse, as early christological and trinitary thinking show. After showing how early Christian thinkers like Cyril of Alexandria and Leontius of Byzantium transformed such concepts as *physis*, *hypostasis*, and *prosōpon* in their intellectual adoration of the Trinity and the two natures of Christ, Craig asks how we are to think these concepts today in a way that neither abstracts them from the world nor subsumes "God within a comprehensive network of relations that would deny God's transcendence." His response draws upon Wesley's vision of God as sanctifying love, which is not so much an attribute of God as it is a movement of God, who goes out to what is not God, being a "yes" to it. God sanctifies what is by definition "not God," allowing creatures to partake in the divine nature, without compromising the otherness of divinity. *Physis*, then, is that which may yet come to be hallowed by God.

The third portion of the book is titled "Teaching Holiness." Each of these pieces was an address given in front of a crowd of people—and we have left the first person language of Craig's lectures intact, because we hope readers of this volume will imagine a body, standing at a lectern, carefully pronouncing these carefully selected words. But what really constitutes the teaching here is that it is the teaching of how holiness—the holiness of God, into which Christians are called—ought to influence how one thinks of justice, the complicity of intellectual progress (even of the Christian kind) with colonialism, academic striving for excellence, and the vocation of a scholar. Craig declares a radical holiness here, one that calls not only the rich to go to the oppressed, but also the oppressed to go to the oppressed; one that does not call us to merely go to the poor in order to elevate them to the middle class, but to dwell there in solidarity with them and not insist that they cease to be poor. In these chapters, what Craig takes to be the task of theology becomes hauntingly clear: it is to answer the same call given to the rich young ruler, "Give all your [intellectual] possessions to the poor, and come follow me."

Chapter 9, "The Just Shall Live by God's Faithfulness," challenges the traditional view of justice as equilibrium, pointing instead to Jesus as the source for all that should be learned about justice, because he is the just and holy One. We see in Israel's history that justice meant traveling aright, that is, going where God goes. God guided a people into a promised future while prodding them to go to the widow, orphan, and alien—those like their ancestors, to whom Yahweh went in Egypt's slave camps. Israel's plight through various exiles and occupations culminates with the coming of the Messiah, who came heralding the promised "reign of God" that was to bring justice. So Jesus goes out to the unclean, the oppressed, and the outcast, calling them to run into the reign of God with all their might in order to be "just." But since God's reign "breaks out on the bloody hill outside the gates of Jerusalem that dark Friday," we learn that justice is not about getting even, getting your due, or getting to keep what you have. Rather, "we become just by grace through faith because it is by faith that we follow Jesus to the arrival of God's gracious reign where life seems most certainly to be crashing and burning." Such is the call of justice, which is holiness.

Chapters 10 and 11 are two lectures on holiness given in succession, and they each invoke commonplace academic ideals and contrast them with Scriptures declaring the sovereignty of God. The first lecture, "I Am the Lord and There Is No Other: The Allure of 'Faith Integration,'" borrows a portion of its title from Isaiah 45, a declaration that Yahweh is sovereign that came at a time when it seemed that Yahweh had been defeated by the gods of Babylon (who currently had Israel crushed under her feet). To be holy meant for Israel to understand "that there is no other god besides Yahweh," and "to turn to this one particular God and there be saved, to find in Yahweh alone all righteousness, all justice, and strength—to live out into the coming of this wild, particular God—and do so both with abandon and with hope." When this holiness is contrasted with the colonialism accompanying the modern project, with the sort of learning "that launched a thousand thousand slave ships to make those colonies the kinds of resources that would keep the glow of Enlightenment bright," the latter is brought under judgment, along with the allure of the integration of faith and learning. What is called for instead of such integration is holiness, which means going where God goes—to the poor.

The second lecture, "My Lord and My God: The Allure of 'Excellence,'" contrasts the confession of Thomas in John 20 with the supposedly highest of virtues—excellence. Thomas' exclamation further ratifies the sovereignty of the Holy One of Israel, as well as the nature of such holiness: "What it means for God to have embraced the crucified Jesus and for Jesus to remain crucified even in his resurrection life, is that God is holy precisely as the God who rushes to the poor, the sick, the dying, the dead, the damned—and bathes them with God's own holy life." As day in and day out we are hauled before the court of excellence, and our effectiveness is assessed, what the doxological words of Thomas witness to is something different, namely, holiness. This holiness is not achieved, even by the highest excellence, but is a gift. And this gift sets the church to working, but it is a work without anxiety; for the church is to learn that before the radical holiness of God we have nothing to lose or gain.

The final chapter of this book, "The Root from Which They Spring," is a difficult piece to read, not because of dense argumentation, but because of its frankness. It is also a fitting essay to conclude the collection, because it demonstrates how Craig is inspired by figures such as Wesley, Kierkegaard, and Barth, but to an extent that does not compare with the influence of the holiness of Scripture, that is, the otherness of holy writ. Craig insists that the God spoken of when Job cries "violence!"

(Job 19:7), and to whom Jesus commits his spirit after crying out in godforsakenness (Matt 27:46), cannot fit into any universal system of thought. Craig does not see a "worldview" in Scripture; he sees contextualized particulars, people with particular stories, and a particular, peculiar God. The "argument" of this address is fairly simple: that to be a theologian is to have an apocalyptic vision, in which one realizes that "the reign of God is coming—for you!" "To be thus God-struck is to face what Kierkegaard's pseudonym, Johannes Climacus, points to when he says that the passion of the thinker is to think what cannot be thought." The faithful response to this call, Craig concludes, is to offer everything that one is—especially one's intellect, one's mind—as a sacrifice of praise before the mystery of the crucified and resurrected of Jesus.

Part I Metaphysics

1

The Transgression of the Integrity of God
The Trinity and the Hallowing of the Flesh[1]

As HISTORIANS OF IDEAS are quick to point out, philosophy in the Western world was for millennia *the* driving force moving all serious intellectual labors. A thinker thought hard not in the first place to discover courses of action likely to have cash value in a world where success is all about counting. Hard thinking was worth the trouble because of the intrinsic value of the love of and quest for wisdom. Even disciplines that in our time have become proud of being non-philosophical were born for the sake of knowing the good, the true, and the beautiful: biology, physics, psychology, astronomy, music, rhetoric, mathematics, among them. It is for this reason that so many fields have attached themselves to the PhD degree. To have a PhD degree in biology, for example, once meant that years of education had fitted one to teach the particular mode of loving wisdom that is peculiar to the study of living things. That philosophy has become one among many disparate compartments within the so-called modern university shows how far it has

1. A paper delivered to the thirty-fifth annual meeting of the Wesleyan Theological Society, Azusa Pacific University, Azusa, CA, March 3–4, 2000. An earlier version of the present essay was first published in *Wesleyan Theological Journal* 36 (2001) 73–102.

fallen. But in its heyday it had no rival. To think unrelentingly in any field was to philosophize; and since all fields were grounded in the good, the true, and the beautiful, to philosophize in *any* one of them was to be on the way to philosophizing in *every* one of them. To philosophize was finally to think comprehensively: to leave out nothing—no stray entity, no stray flash of light, no stray quantity or quality—but to bring everything, however ephemeral or unobtrusive, into its stronghold, to establish everything on solid ground. Philosophy in its most unrelenting and revered form was metaphysics; and metaphysics in its most unrelenting and revered form was ontology, the concerted inquiry into what it is to be.

Of course, there is an earlier history to all of this, a history that *begins*—a history with a *first* philosopher. However, what has characterized this history from before the time of Heraclitus and Parmenides to our own time—which make no mistake is the history of the very soul of the West—is a dogged insistence on unity. This is *one* sphere with a center, *one* city with a wall and a standing army, *one* tower with a foundation. That foundation may be called simply "the One" or "the Logos" or "matter" or "form" or "substance" or "spirit" or "praxis" or "will" or "the will to power" or "energy" or "creativity"; but it is also not at all uncommonly called "God." For anything to be deemed real it must be grounded on this ground. Unless it rests here, unless there is no question of parentage, unless differences are ultimately resolved in this identity, this "same," then "the falcon cannot hear the falconer" (Yeats), the world is not the world, A≠A.²

The name of Jesus began to be attached to this foundational *modus operandi* as his story was translated into the propositions of second-century defenders of the faith. A century earlier the same thing had happened to the stories of the ancient Hebrews. Of course, "Jesus," as a human, all too human, name, is ambiguous. Human life is irregular, fraught with accidents. It lacks the necessity of strict identity. It could have been otherwise and sooner or later it *is* otherwise: human beings die. Fortunately, however, this name "Jesus" is attached to no ordinary human being. This Jesus is the Christ, the Son of the living God. This

2. See Schüssler Fiorenza's critique of "the logic of identity" and "the Man of Reason" in *But She Said*, 139–44, 150–58; cf. 186–94.

Jesus is God with us. In this Jesus the whole fullness of deity was pleased to dwell. And so, what came to be increasingly important from the second century on were not the accidents of this history, but the Supreme Being who is *shown* to be supreme particularly here. (Of course, the Supreme Being is uniformly supreme *a se*. There is no more and no less to a Supreme Being.) Thus the name of Jesus became a password for entry into the kind of foundational thinking that the Greeks and then the Romans had been practicing for centuries; and, of course, when one gains entry, a password is no longer needed. It is now the One-God—the Supreme Being—that matters.[3]

And what of this Supreme Being? The greatest intellects of the Christian era gave their time and enormous powers to its conception. They built an idea by comparison to which all that had preceded it paled, an idea that laid claim to the tested philosophical heritage, mining that heritage for usable materials, putting those materials to use.[4] But these great intellects also remembered the strong language used of Yahweh and Abba in the Holy Scriptures. And so, they translated anthropomorphic doxologies that recounted the mighty deeds, the watchful care, the extravagant love, and the untiring faithfulness of that God into metaphysical propositions about omnipotence and omniscience and benevolence and immutability. "God," it is well argued, is a pure unity;[5]

3. This is not to say that any of this ever became unambiguous. Indeed, it is above all the point of this little essay to argue that in the doctrine of the Trinity that figures so largely in Christian tradition there moves an energy that calls the integrity of the Supreme Being into question. However, it seems no exaggeration to say that for centuries there was in the history of Christian thought a steady movement from the flesh-and-blood earthiness of the New Testament Jesus to the ethereal Perfection of perfections that stands at the apex of a great hierarchy of beings.

4. "Like the treasures of the ancient Egyptians . . . which on leaving Egypt the people of Israel . . . surreptitiously claimed for themselves . . .—similarly all the branches of pagan learning contain not only false and superstitious fantasies and burdensome studies . . . , but also studies for liberated minds which are more appropriate to the service of the truth about monotheism to be found in their writers. . . . We can see, can we not, the amount of gold, silver, and clothing with which Cyprian . . . was laden when he left Egypt; is not the same true of Lactantius, and Victorinus, of Optatus, and Hilary, to say nothing of people still alive, and countless Greek scholars?" Augustine, *On Christian Teaching*, 64–65 (2.40.60). See also Gregory of Nyssa, *Against Eunomius*, 193 (7.1).

5. "God therefore must . . . be a simple intellectual existence, admitting in himself

the highest, unchangeable being and good from whom all else that is and is thus good is created *ex nihilo*;[6] thus lacking no power, containing all things, untouched and undefiled by its creatures' "wretchedness," inherently compassionless, without need, though needed by all else;[7] "absolutely perfect" and thus without rival;[8] loving itself first and only then

---

of no addition whatever, so that he cannot be believed to have in himself a more or a less, but is Unity, or I might say, Oneness throughout, and the mind and fount from which originates all intellectual existence or mind." Origen, *On First Principles*, 10 (1.1.6).

6. "The Supreme Good beyond all others is God. It is thereby unchangeable good, truly eternal, truly immortal. All other good things derive their origin from him but are not part of him. That which is part of him is as he is, but the things he has created are not as he is. Hence if he alone is unchangeable, all things that he has created are changeable because he made them of nothing. Being omnipotent he is able to make out of nothing, i.e., out of what has no existence at all, good things, both great and small, celestial and terrestrial, spiritual and corporeal. . . . Therefore, all good things throughout all the ranks of being, whether great or small, can derive their being only from God. Every natural being, so far as it is such, is good. There can be no being which does not derive its existence from the most high and true God." Augustine, *The Nature of the Good*, 326 (i).

7. "Therefore, Lord God, You are the more truly omnipotent since You can do nothing through impotence and nothing can have power against you. . . . In fact, You are [merciful] according to our way of looking at things and not according to Your way. For when you look upon us in our misery it is we who feel the effect of Your mercy, but You do not experience the feeling. Therefore you are merciful because You save the sorrowful and pardon sinners against You; and You are not merciful because You do not experience any feeling of compassion for misery. . . . You, though nothing can be without You, are nevertheless not in place or time but all things are in You. For nothing contains You, but You contain all things. . . . And you are life and light and wisdom and blessedness and eternity and many suchlike good things; and yet You are nothing save the one and supreme good, You who are completely sufficient unto Yourself, needing nothing, but rather He whom all things need in order that they may have being and well-being." Anselm of Canterbury, *Proslogion*, 90 (vii), 91 (viii), 98 (xix), 100 (xxii).

8. "God is absolutely perfect, lacking no perfection. If, then, there are many gods, there must be many such perfect beings. But this is impossible. For, if none of these perfect beings lacks some perfection, and does not have any admixture of imperfection, which is demanded for an absolutely perfect being, nothing will be given in which to distinguish the perfect beings from one another. It is impossible, therefore, that there be many gods." Thomas Aquinas, *Summa Contra Gentiles*, Book One, 158 (42.i).

loving the reflection of itself and its perfections in its creatures;[9] the One without which there is not even fragmentary creaturely perfection—no goodness, truth, beauty, life, wisdom, blessedness, intelligibility.[10]

The world of beings stands in relation to this Supreme Being as a system of more or less goodness, truth, and beauty—of more or less being.[11] Every entity has its place in this great class system. The divine Ground gives every entity what integrity it has. It is the divine Ground that thus makes this a system. Entities stand together only because each stands on the absolutely unshakeable solid rock Foundation without which no entity could be at all.[12] To rise in the direction of this One is to rise away from insecurity, wretchedness, disease, disorder, disintegration, evil; and to rise toward security, blessedness, rest, wholeness, integrity, goodness—in short, it is to rise toward purer and purer, greater and greater, higher and higher *being*. To rise in the direction of this One is to find *oneself*, what one was created to *be*; it is to find one's *home*, where one was created to *reside*. This God who is an inher-

---

9. "Whoever loves something in itself and for its own sake consequently loves all things in which it is found: for example, he who loves sweetness for itself must love all sweet things. But God wills and loves His own being in itself and for its own sake, as shown above. Every other being, however, is by way of likeness a certain participation of His being, as appears from what has been said. It remains, then, that God, in that He wills and loves Himself, wills and loves other things." Ibid., 246 (75.iv); cf. 152–53 (38.i–vii), 204–5 (60.i–vi), 277–82 (91.i–xviii).

10. "Thee I invoke, O God, the Truth, in, by and through whom all truths are true; the Wisdom, in, by and through whom all are wise who are wise; the True and Perfect Life, in, by and through whom live all who live truly and perfectly; the Beatitude, in, by and through whom all the blessed are blessed; the Good and the Beautiful, in, by and through whom all good and beautiful things have these qualities; the Intelligible Light, in, by and through whom all intelligible things are illumined; whose kingdom is this whole world unknown to corporeal sense; whose kingdom gives the Law also to these mundane realms; from whom to be turned is to fall; to whom to be turned is to rise; in whom to abide is to stand fast; from whom to depart is to die; to whom to return is to revive; in whom to dwell is to live; whom no [one] loses unless [she] be deceived; whom no [one] seeks unless [she] has been admonished; whom no [one] finds unless [she] has been purified; whom to abandon is to perish; to reach out to whom is to love; to see whom is true possession." Augustine, *Soliloquies*, in *Augustine: Earlier Writings*, 24 (I.3).

11. Augustine, *Nature of the Good*, 327 (iii).

12. Cf. Augustine, *Trinity*, 434 (14.12.16).

ent Integrity—who in perfect self-sufficiency is untouched by all and each—effortlessly grants to its creature (if the proper conditions are met) an integrity undisruptively derivative from its own, an integrity that makes the creature *untouched* as its "heavenly Father" is *untouched*. However, even the creature who is plummeting into the dark abyss of disintegration, who has turned its petals and leaves away from the nourishing rays of the bright sun, who has braced itself against the pull of the *actus purus*, who has closed its mouth to the medicine of immortality, even this creature yet participates in the integrity of the Supreme Being—to the extent that it *is*.[13]

The Abasement of God

How different this orientation upward is from everything one reads of the history of Jesus in the Gospels. When the Gospel of John, for example, speaks of the incarnation of the Word (1:14), it directs the reader's attention to a movement downward. The word *flesh* in John's prologue carries with it a heavy Hebrew ancestry.[14] In the Hebrew Scriptures, *flesh* (*basar*) most commonly signifies human frailty, weakness, helplessness, ephemerality, vulnerability, mortality. *God*, on the other hand, is never spoken of as flesh;[15] God is not flesh, flesh is not God.[16]

13. Feminist theologians have very effectively critiqued such hierarchical thinking. See, e.g., Ruether, *Sexism and God-Talk*, 53–54, 85–92, and passim; Schüssler Fiorenza, *But She Said*, 114–20.

14. There are several shades of meaning of the word *flesh* (*basar*) in the Old Testament. It can signify skin and muscle, tissue and organs, what clothes the bones. It can signify the body as a whole. It also can signify the relationship between human beings. One's brother or even the human being as such is one's own flesh. However, even here it is not inappropriate to understand human vulnerability to be implied. Wolff, *Anthropology of the Old Testament*, 26–29.

15. "Before God in his holiness . . . [the human being] as *basar* is not only one who is frail, but also one who is liable to sin and for whom, therefore, the voice of the living God is unendurable (Deut. 5:26): 'For who is there of all flesh, that has heard the voice of the living God speaking out of the midst of the fire, as we have, and has still lived?' Under the scorching wind of God's judgment all *basar* withers like grass (Isa. 40:6). . . . Thus even in the Old Testament *basar* does not only mean the powerlessness of the mortal creature but also the feebleness of his faithfulness and obedience to the will of God." Ibid., 30–31.

16. Schnackenburg, *Jesus in the Gospels*, 290. Schnackenburg adds this: "The ab-

This is not to say that flesh as such is evil. Even as frail and vulnerable and exposed to the constant threat of death, even as radically other than God, the human is flesh precisely *in relation to God.*[17] The life, the soul, of the flesh is "God's breath." Indeed human being is human being not in itself, but *vis-à-vis* God, *coram deo*. In this sense "flesh is [the human's] situation before God."[18] Yet this does not in any sense diminish its difference from God. God's sustenance holds flesh to what it is not and cannot be. Thus, for this flesh to be held together with this God is for its difference from God to be intensified. God is consistently above. We are consistently below. Isaiah's encounter with God in the temple highlights the human condition (Isaiah 6). In the face of God one can shout, "woe is me!" or one can shout, "here am I, send me," but one cannot aver that "there is between God and us a common essence."

Therefore, with the affirmation in the prologue of the Gospel of John that "the Word became flesh," the tension between fallible human being and God is heightened enormously. God does not cease here to be Wholly Other in relation to the flesh and yet this God *dwells* with us *as* the flesh that is this Jesus Christ.[19] The movement here is a descent from above to below, from the sufficient to the insufficient, from the immortal to the mortal, from "to be" to "not to be." Yet this movement does not lead simply to a kind of external relation in which the integrity of opposing poles remains intact. God and flesh touch—explosively.

One finds this tensile movement at play throughout the Gospel narratives. Jesus—"the one who will save his people from their sins"

---

solute term *flesh* is not merely a circumlocution for *human being* . . . but in Johannine thinking an expression for what is earthly and limited, frail and transitory (6:63), the typical, purely human way of being, so to speak, in distinction to everything heavenly divine, divinely spiritual."

17. Thus *basar* is not used of a corpse. See Wolff, *Anthropology of the Old Testament*, 29.

18. Schweizer, "Sarx, Sarkikos, Sarkinos," 7:123. Schweizer continues: "When he is viewed in this way, he can no longer be split up into a divine part and an earthly part [as in Platonism]. If there is a distinction, it can only be between God and man, heaven and earth."

19. Brown, *John*, 1:33. Cf. Schnackenburg, *Jesus in the Gospels*, 290: "Here, however, the element of the flesh that is sinful, inclined toward sin, or imprisoned by sin (I John 2:16) is not present."

(Matt 1:21)—begins his short life a poor peasant girl's helpless baby, a baby of uncertain legitimacy (Matt 1:18). He is, from the first, homeless (Luke 2:7). His parents have no power, no property, no prestige worthy of note (Luke 1:46–55). He is brought up. He grows (Luke 2:40). He presents himself to a wild man, living and working at the margins of proper society, to be baptized, "to fulfill all righteousness" (Matt 4:15), as he says. He is moved by a Spirit other than his own out into the wasteland where he is to suffer (Mark 1:12). He hungers and thirsts (John 4:6–9). He is thrust into the flame of the temptation to lay hold of power and property and prestige (Luke 4:2–13). He gathers around himself a motley crew of misfits and laborers and political radicals and Roman collaborators and women (Luke 6:14–16).[20] He touches the sick, the blind, the lame, the poor, lepers, prostitutes, the demon-possessed, corpses (Matt 8:1–3; 21:31–32; Luke 4:18; 6:20, 24; 7:22; 8:26–42; 14:12–14, 21). He touches them and they touch him (Luke 8:42–48). Indeed, in a system in which the holy and the unholy are separated by an untransgressible line, to touch them is to be touched by them, and to be touched by them is to touch them.

Of course, this Jesus is acutely aware of his *heavenly* Father. It is his Father that he makes known. And yet he looks to his Father as an *Other* who is incomparably free in relation to everything creaturely; an *Other* who cannot be exploited by anyone, however propertied, powerful, prestigious, or pure; an Other who "for human beings is new, surprising, and challenging . . . totally different from what people imagine and want to be true. It is this very God, in his grandeur, superiority over the world, and incomprehensibility to human beings, that Jesus proclaims."[21] This is the oddity of Jesus above all else. He proclaims and he performs and he *is* Immanuel, God with us. Yet God with us is no less God, Wholly Other.

---

20. "Jesus raised women above an androcentric view and placed them on the same level as men. He masterfully breaks through the barriers of contemporary Jewish society: we have only to think of his intervention for the sinful woman, who invaded a dinner for men, or the women whom he received into his following." Schnackenburg, *Jesus in the Gospels*, 207. See also de Jonge, *Christology in Context*, 63–64, 102–3.

21. Schnackenburg, *Jesus in the Gospels*, 314.

In the life and ministry of Jesus one comes to us who is what we are, who has what we have. But also in the life and ministry of Jesus One comes to us who is in every respect what we are not and cannot be, what we have not and cannot have. Things do not stay in their place in or about this Jesus. There is a concurrence of what cannot concur. What cannot touch, touch. Thus Jesus violates the standards of propriety and shocks and disturbs those whose identity it is to preserve and defend the integrity especially of things holy. "The extraordinary appearance of Jesus is based on the fact that he is God's representative and agent, who brings the otherness of God close to humankind; he is the man who goes against all human standards."[22]

In the Gospel stories the urgency of Jesus' message and of his broader ministry has everything to do with the imminence of God's coming rule and reign. Jesus' urgency is offensive, because the God he announces is offensive.[23] This Wholly Other God is on the move, breaking into this closed world from beyond it, like a bombshell hurtling down from above. Jesus moves because God is moving. The coming of this *basileia* is what Jesus is about to such a degree that he proclaims it no less with his hands and feet than with his throat and lips. He goes where the *basileia* is going. He goes where God is going. It is his unbridled faithfulness and obedience that make him finally transparent to the coming of this God.[24] Thus one can equally well say that the reign and rule of God go where he goes, that *God* goes where he goes. To look to him is to look to the God who is coming. To touch him is to touch and to be touched by the Wholly Other God who is coming.[25]

22. Ibid., 315.

23. "The religious message that Jesus Christ brought can be understood in its aspect of confrontation with earthly, human thinking as the pervasive concern of the Gospels. . . . [He] is always the stranger, the one misunderstood in many ways, the messenger from God witnessing to a completely different kingdom, who lifts up as an urgent appeal the otherness of God and his claim on human beings closed up within themselves. This center of Jesus' religious message is recognizable in all the Jesus pictures and christological designs and is independent of the historically conditioned interests of the evangelists." Ibid., 314.

24. "Who is Jesus? Simply *the kingdom of God in person.*" Moltmann, *Jesus Christ for Today's World*, 7.

25. "The particular dynamic of Jesus' message of the *basileia*, then, is that the rule

How radical this is emerges most disturbingly only with the passion narratives. That Jesus was a constant affront to the given order meant that already far before the last week of his life he was on a collision course with the powers of his world.[26] And yet even the successful plots to put his life to an end do not separate him from the coming of God. He enters boldly into Jerusalem, he chooses his last week; it is not thrust upon him by high priests and governors as if their actions rob him of his destiny.[27] His feet and hands proclaim the coming of God all week long. Where he goes this week, God goes. What he touches this week, God touches. What touches him this week, touches God. The passion of Jesus is the passion of the Wholly Other.

As troubling as it is to consider such a transgression of the integrity of God, saying that this is God's passion week is an extension of the testimony that is spoken all over the Gospel narratives that the *basileia* is coming—and it is coming for the poor and diseased and outcast and frail, for the lost and forgotten, for the dying and the dead and the damned. The orientation of the Gospel narratives is downward. Jesus is in those narratives nothing but a drawing near to God that goes precisely where God goes; but this Jesus, "though he is in the form of God, empties himself, taking the form of a slave; humbles himself and becomes obedient to the point of death—even death on a cross" (Phil 2:6–8; translation altered slightly). The movement is from God outward. It is from exaltation to debasement.

of God is imminent but that it also emerges from its futurity as present. . . . Jesus in fact claimed unheard of authority for his own person, even if his attitude . . . can be understood in terms of the content of his eschatological message. As he maintained that in his ministry the coming rule of God was present already to the salvation of those who received his message, he knew that he was not only in agreement with God but that he was also the mediator of the inbreaking of the rule and forgiving love of God. With this awareness he was not afraid to oppose freely the tradition that was sanctified by God's revelation to Moses, trusting that in the process he was in harmony with the will of God. It is not surprising that in this regard he caused offense to devout Jews and that his person became the subject of violent controversies between adherents and opponents." Pannenberg, *Systematic Theology*, 2:330, 334.

26 See Schnackenburg, *Jesus in the Gospels*, 314–15.

27 This is particularly to be seen in Luke 9:51: "When the days drew near for him to be taken up, he set his face to go to Jerusalem." On this passage see Fitzmyer, *Luke*, 1:827–28; Green, *Luke*, 402–4; Marshall, *Luke*, 405; and Tannehill, *Luke*, 168–69.

Jesus as God's Outgoing Love

It is still tempting to defuse the passion of Jesus by means of atonement theory: God is just and cannot simply forgive the infinite debt of sin that humans owe. Sin requires a punishment of the offensive human race, a punishment that balances God's books. The theandric Jesus is punished as a human, making his punishment just; and he is punished as God, making his punishment adequately large. The scales are balanced. Everything rises back into place. The great hierarchy of being is intact.

C. S. Song has recently called such customary atonement thinking into question. The ministry of Jesus is not about the restoration of the status of a vindictive, abstractly just God. It is about the outgoing love of the God he calls "Abba." When even early on in his story Jesus turns not away from but *to* sinners, and "mixes with them," he is already "intent to 'incarnate,' to 'make flesh,' this [Abba] God of his in his life and work."[28] His journey to the cross is his journey of mixing with the lost. Sin is not heaped on him as punishment, forcing God to turn away so as not to look upon what would only defile the Holy One. Rather God goes with him to the cross. Even if it were to be accepted, Song says, that on the cross the sins of the whole world are piled on Jesus, there is no reason for the love of his heavenly Abba to leave him there alone. The love of Abba is a love that on the contrary "must be working with full force" especially here.

> [Instead] of turning away from Jesus on the cross, should not Abba-God be "running to Jesus, putting arms round him, kissing him"? . . . Jesus, whose body is to be broken and whose blood is to be shed, is not just a sign. He is more than a sign. The metaphor of God's passing over at the sign of the lamb's blood does not apply to Jesus. God did not pass over Jesus on the cross; God was with him. God did not leave Jesus behind; God . . . remained with him even on the cross.[29]

28. Song, *Jesus, the Crucified People*, 77.

29. Ibid., 77–213.

If God is with us when Jesus touches the man lowered through the roof on a bed, touches him through and through (Luke 5:17–26), then God is surely with us when the body of Jesus is broken and his blood is shed, when death, sin, and the devil touch *him* through and through.

Song does not dispute the notion that Jesus was crucified "in the place of" sinners. He freely agrees that "God proves his love for us in that while we were still sinners Christ died *huper* us" (Rom 5:8), that "the blood of the covenant" was "shed *huper* many" (Mark 14:24). But this preposition *huper* does not in Song's work connote "for" in the sense of "instead of." Rather it affirms "on the side of," "in solidarity with." "[Jesus] certainly was a strong spokesperson in behalf of the marginalized people. But finally he was found in their company, on their side and in solidarity with them."[30]

> Jesus, in short, is the crucified people! Jesus means crucified people. To say Jesus is to say suffering people. . . . By people I mean those women, men, and children whose company Jesus enjoyed, with whom Jesus liked to eat and drink, to whom, Jesus declared, God's reign belongs.[31]

Immanuel touches and is touched by crucified people. There is no longer any debasement so low that the Exalted One must push it away to keep itself clean, to keep itself exalted. It is precisely the Crucified whose name is exalted above every name.

To understand Jesus Christ one must understand him as the place where forsaken death and holy life concur. Thus it is not only on Good Friday that the significance of Jesus takes place. Furthermore the full weight of Good Friday is by no means felt until the following Sunday. The *mysterium tremendum* and not only the *fascinans* of "Holy Week" is above all an event happening on and about Easter morning. When

---

30. Ibid., 216. Song continues: "By 'people' I do not mean people in general. . . . In fact I do not know what people in general means. It is an abstraction; but people are not abstraction. It is not a common noun; people with flesh and blood are a proper noun, a noun with a particular name and a special identity. . . . By people I mean those men, women, and children, in Jesus' day, today, and in the days to come, economically exploited, politically oppressed, culturally and religiously alienated, sexually, racially, or class-wise discriminated against."

31. Ibid.

the women make their way to the tomb, when the men travel along the Emmaus Road and then sit to break bread with the stranger they happen to meet, when a week later Thomas is invited to close the hands and side of the one who stands before him behind closed doors, the one who is encountered is yet the Crucified One. He has not gotten better. He has not been resuscitated. His stripes are not healed. His body yet carries the cross. Its curse cuts through him, body and soul. He remains the lamb slain. His life ended when he breathed out his last prayer. Minutes, hours, and days are not added to his span. He remains what he was on Good Friday, defined by the final punctuation mark of the bloody end of that bloody day. The death and damnation he touched and that touched him are yet all over his cut and broken body. And it is *this* that is exalted. It is this name that is raised above every name. It is this ignominy that is to the glory of God the Father. It is this resurrection that is the hallowing of the flesh.[32]

It is because the resurrected Jesus has not gotten better that he is the savior. Were his resurrection his healing, were he in his appearance before Thomas a human being without wounds, were the sin that he became blotted out, were his name that is now above every name no longer the debased name, then he would be the savior only of those healed, unscathed, and sinless, only of those who have gotten better; the debased, the sinner, the wounded would be left to rot. But this is not what happens. The history that Jesus *is* reaches its defining end when he breathes his last. It is that forsaken history which is raised, which is

---

32. "His resurrection qualifies the one who has been crucified as the Christ, and his suffering and death as a saving event for us and for many. The resurrection 'does not evacuate the cross' (I Cor. 1:17), but fills it with eschatology and saving significance. From this it follows systematically that all further interpretations of the saving significance of Christ's death on the cross 'for us' must start from his resurrection. Furthermore, when it is said at length that only his death has a saving significance for us, that means that his death on the cross expresses the significance of his resurrection for us and not, vice versa, that his resurrection expresses the significance of his cross. The resurrection from the dead qualifies the person of the crucified Christ and with it the saving significance of his death on the cross for us, 'the dead.' Thus the saving significance of his cross manifests his resurrection. It is not his resurrection that shows that his death on the cross took place for us, but on the contrary, his death on the cross 'for us' that makes relevant his resurrection 'before us.'" Moltmann, *The Crucified God*, 182–83.

transfigured, which is transformed bodily by the Spirit of God. The binary opposition between good and evil—the opposition known so well by Adam—prevails through Good Friday and conquers Jesus there. This is the opposition of health versus disease, life versus death, "without sin" versus sin, exaltation versus debasement, master versus servant, first versus last, God versus flesh. In the concurrence of Good Friday and Easter Sunday, that binary opposition bursts open like the belly of a dragon slain from within.

The "Dunamis" of the Trinity

This is finally what the christological and trinitarian thinking of the early church yields. The Creeds of Nicea and Chalcedon emerge from the adamant conviction that only that is saved which God assumes; that God must become what we are (without ceasing to be what God is), if we are to become what God is (without ceasing to be what we are).[33] Salvation is in this theological milieu *theosis*. Salvation is sanctification. Salvation is the binding of God's creatures to the God who comes unconditionally to them and binds all that God is to all that they are.[34] The salvation of the crucified Jesus—the binding of God to the crucified Jesus in his resurrection from the dead—is the salvation of all those who are in fellowship with him, for he, "the Word become flesh," is already in fellowship with them.[35] Flesh is here made holy because God touches it and it touches God.

33. See among many places J. N. D. Kelly, *Early Christian Doctrines*, 223–51; 310–43. Athanasius is illustrative, as is Gregory of Nyssa. See Athanasius, *Orations Against the Arians*; Gregory of Nyssa, *Against Eunomius*, 179 (5.4). It is, however, Gregory of Nazianzus who coins the phrase "what has not been assumed, has not been healed." Meredith, *Cappadocians*, 44.

34. It is indeed true that the extent to which this entails the entry of God into the sin of the human race is not adequately clarified in the early church. However, when God is understood as in Orthodoxy, of course, to be essentially immortal, the affirmation of God's involvement in human mortality is already near the affirmation of God's involvement in human sin.

35. "In Jesus Christ there is no isolation of [human being] from God or of God from [human being]. Rather, in [God] we encounter the history, the dialogue, in which God and [human being] meet together, the reality of the covenant *mutually* contracted, preserved, and fulfilled by them. Jesus Christ is in His one Person, as true

This is a difficult thought to think, and not only for us. It was difficult for the early church to think as well. Thinking it moved the church over the early centuries of its history to the affirmation of the doctrine of the Trinity. That is, it is because of what it was compelled to say of God's work in Christ, of God's assumption of the flesh, that the church came by the end of the fourth century to say that God is Father, Son, and Holy Spirit. It was not only due to changing social and political conditions and the earlier absence of the peculiar self-interest of Constantine that it took the church so many centuries to come out as decisively trinitary.[36] The emergence of trinitary thinking was in particular due to the difficulty of saying and thinking that the history of Jesus—the history that the gospel tells—is the event of the God who in coming close remains other. The Son is sent by the Father. The Son is absolutely no less God than the Father who sends him; that is, the Son is *homoousion to patri*: this is the eccentric thought and phrase at the destabilized center of the controversy surrounding the Council of Nicea and of all trinitary discourse.

Thus in the creed of this council God's unity is not monolithic. God is one as a complexity, as an outgoing, an othering, a movement the extremes of which are woven together without ceasing to be extremes, that is, without the neutrality of integrity and identity. The doctrine that takes shape in the fourth century is not an account of two or three gods

God, [*human being's*] loyal partner, and as true [*human being*], *God's*. He is the Lord humbled for communion with [human being] and likewise the Servant exalted to communion with God. He is the Word spoken from the loftiest, most luminous transcendence and likewise the Word heard in the deepest, darkest immanence." Barth, *Humanity of God*, 46–47.

36. Of course, there had been from the beginning passages of Scripture, liturgies, baptismal creeds, rules of faith, and the affirmations of particular theologians that had had at least a trinitary flavor. However, phrases were slow in coming that said with some clarity that God is none other than Father, Son, and Holy Spirit. It was not until 325, at the Council of Nicea, that the church, despite enormous controversy, declared that what makes the Son God is identical with what makes the Father God: that the Son is *homoousion to patri*. And it was not until 381, at the Council of Constantinople, that the church, again despite controversy, declared that the Holy Spirit is fully God, that the Spirit is "to be worshiped and glorified together with the Father and the Son." That the word *homoousios* is not used of the Spirit in the Constantinopolitan Creed indicates how difficult it was half a century after Nicea to affirm the full deity of that person.

who share space, one of whom is morphed into human anatomy and physiology, one of whom flits about human beings fairylike, whispering eternal secrets.[37] Nor is it an account of a monad who awakens a dormant memory of the divine in finite beings by the attractive power of its own utterly perfect goodness, truth, and beauty. It is an account of the entry of the Holy into what is not and cannot be holy—an entry that unmakes that old order that would keep the Holy out—and opens a path of holiness for those hitherto even hopelessly far gone. And yet in all this, the Holy One remains holy, other. There is no diminution of the Wholly Other in the sending of the Son.)

Nor is there any distraction from this christological tension when pneumatology moves into the heart of trinitary discourse after the Council of Nicea. The decentering movement of the Other is a hallowing of the world only if at once there are, first, an outgoing fellowship of God with the lost and, second, an outgoing fellowship of the lost with God. The doctrine of the Son speaks to the first side and the doctrine of the Spirit speaks to the second side of this duplexity. Thus (the Cappadocians' constant theme is that the Son is the one *through* whom the Father works reconciliation with the world, and the Spirit is the one *in* whom the Father's work through the Son occurs) Thus it is the Spirit who "glorifies the Father and the Son"; by whom "whatever is good, coming from God . . . through the Son, is completed"; who unites us to God; who sanctifies; who "perfects grace"; that is, without whom there is no faith in the Son.[38] In other words, the Holy Spirit is to be understood to be God because without the Spirit the work of God in

---

37. Cf. Schnackenburg, *Jesus in the Gospels*, 292.

38. Gregory of Nyssa, *Against Eunomius*, 84, 130, 132 (1.36; 2.14, 15); idem, *On the Holy Spirit*, 319–24; idem, *On the Holy Trinity*, 329; idem, *On "Not Three Gods,"* 334, 338. Cf. Gregory of Nazianzus, *Theological Orations*, 201, 211–12 (5.12, 5.29): "It is the Spirit in whom we worship, and in whom we pray . . . Look at these facts: Christ is born; the Spirit is the forerunner. He is baptized; the Spirit bears witness. He is tempted; the Spirit leads him up. He works miracles; the Spirit accompanies them. He ascends; the Spirit takes his place. [The Spirit is] sanctifying, not sanctified; . . . the creator-spirit, who by baptism and by resurrection creates anew; . . . that guides, talks, sends forth, separates . . . ; that reveals, illumines, quickens, or rather that is the very light and life; that makes temples, that deifies . . . ; that does all things that God does . . ."

Christ stops short. The Spirit carries those for whom Christ died into the hallowing work of Christ. *God* is *with us* in Christ. By the Spirit *we* are *with God* in Christ. For the Cappadocians it is impossible to approach or acknowledge the Father and the Son except by the Spirit. Yet when the Father and Son are acknowledged by the work of the Spirit, one participates in the trinitary movement—in the Spirit, through the Son, to the Father.[39]

That means that theosis, deification, sanctification, salvation, is a participation in what is essentially other; it is a movement from one's own center as a creature to the moving eccentricity of the Trinity: in the Spirit, through the Son, to the Father. The Cappadocians' understanding of the interpenetration, the perichoresis, of the trinitary persons is not as speculative as it is devotional.[40] The Father is in the Son and the Spirit, the Son is in the Father and the Spirit, the Spirit is in the Father and the Son; no trinitary person is separable from the other two. This is simply the way it happens. One knows the Father through the Son in the Holy Spirit. One knows Father, Son, and Spirit perichoretically. And so, to say, as Gregory of Nazianzus says, that "unity, having from all eternity arrived by motion at duality, found its rest in trinity"[41] is to speak out of a theotic relation to that Trinity. Furthermore, trinitary/theotic "rest" is one that stirs with life. Thus for Gregory of Nyssa knowing this God is a "never-ending search for God and aspiration to likeness with him. . . . Such a stretching-out must from the nature of the case be in principle insatiable."[42] The theosis that the Spirit works, then, is a movement that transgresses the integrity of the creature precisely as the creature

---

39. "Basil . . . writes, '[S]ince we show that we are not capable of glorifying God on our own, only *in* the Spirit is this made possible.' Whereas the Father is made visible in the Son, the Son can be recognized only *in* the Holy Spirit. The Spirit is the enabler of worship; only by the Spirit can we say 'Jesus is Lord!' (1 Cor. 12:3)." LaCugna, *God For Us*, 120; see also Kelly, *Early Christian Doctrines*, 258–63.

40. Meredith, *Cappadocians*, 32, 107–8; cf. Gregory of Nyssa, *Against Eunomius*, 228 (10.4).

41. Gregory of Nazianzus, *Theological Orations*, 161 (3.2).

42. Meredith, *The Cappadocians*, 77; cf. 81 for Gregory's account of the wound of love.

participates in the Trinity, that is, in the Spirit, through the Son, to the Father, an unfathomable abyss.[43]

It is perhaps the christological notion of the enhypostaton that best clarifies the disintegrative movement of the Trinity. According to this idea, the hypostatic union of the human and divine natures of Christ happens in such a way that all that Jesus Christ is as the child of Mary is yielded and thus becomes transparent to all that he is as Immanuel. Without the loss of his human nature or his human will, without the loss of his human heart or soul or mind or strength, without the loss of his human ignorance or weakness or vulnerability, that is, without the loss of his "flesh," Jesus becomes that human life which is the concrete movement of God into the world. His human being is thus decentered, hallowed, sanctified, set utterly aside to God. Simultaneously, however, his *deity* is decentered, abased, emptied, incarnated. Here human being is opened to God and God is opened to human being. The word *enhypostaton* says that all that is human in Jesus takes place "in" the outgoing second person (*hypostasis*) of the Trinity. It is crucially important to understand that this hypostasis is not the substitute of some extra-hypostatic nature, some abstract divine reality out of which Father, Son, and Spirit are expressed. The divine nature occurs nowhere else than as the trinitary hypostases, the trinitary persons. To say that the hypostasis of the Son assumes "the flesh" is really to say that *God* enters into that fallibility. The closure, the quarantine, that is suggested by the idea of the Supreme Being who cannot be affected is transgressed by the doctrine of the enhypostaton; for in order for human being to enter radically into the outgoing person of the Son, God must be open.[44] This is the implication of the Creeds of Nicea and Chalcedon, the implication of

43. Gregory of Nazianzus, *Theological Orations*, 189–91 (4.17–20); Gregory of Nyssa, *Against Eunomius*, 69, 97, 99, 103, 146, 198 (1.26, 42; 2.3; 3.5; 7.4); idem, *On "Not Three Gods*," 332.

44. "The hypostasis is not a product of nature: it is that in which nature exists, the very principle of its existence. Such a conception of hypostasis can be applied to Christology, since it implies the existence of a fully human existence, without any limitation, 'enhypostatized' in the Word, who is a divine hypostasis. This conception assumes that God, as personal being, is not totally bound to [God's] own nature; the hypostatic existence is flexible, 'open'. . . ." Meyendorff, *Christ in Eastern Christian Thought*, 77.

the incarnation. God and the flesh touch.[45] Thus the human hypostasis of Jesus is hallowed and the hypostasis of every human being whom the Spirit unites with him is hallowed. The incarnation as a sanctifying participation is an event that opens God to human being and human being to God.

> The notion of participation implies not only openness in the divine being but also a dynamic, open and teleological concept of [human being]. Since Gregory of Nyssa, the destiny of [human being] is viewed, in Greek patristic thought, as an ascent in the knowledge of God through communion into divine life. [The human being], therefore, is not conceived as an autonomous and closed entity: [the human's] very life is in God . . . , while sin consists precisely in a self-affirmation of [human being] in an illusory independence.[46]

45. This is more than implicit in the official documents that accompany the Definition of Chalcedon in 451. Cyril of Alexandria, who was the theological guide of that council, wrote this of Jesus Christ: "We do not say that the Logos became flesh by having his nature changed, nor for that matter that he was transformed into a complete human being composed out of soul and body. On the contrary, we say that in an unspeakable and incomprehensible way, the Logos united to himself, in his hypostasis, flesh enlivened by a rational soul, and in this way became a human being and has been designated 'Son of Man.' . . . Since . . . the body that had become his own underwent suffering, he is . . . said to have suffered these things for our sakes, for the impassible One was within the suffering body. Moreover, we reason in exactly the same way in the case of his dying. God's Logos is by nature immortal and incorruptible and Life and Life-giver, but since, as Paul says, 'by the grace of God' his very own body 'tasted death on behalf of every person' [Heb. 2:9], he himself is said to have suffered this death which came about on our account." Cyril of Alexandria, "Second Letter to Nestorius," 132–34.

46. Meyendorff, *Christ in Eastern Christian Thought*, 211; see also 210: "What is involved in this particular issue . . . is the whole Greek patristic notion of 'participation in divine life,' of deification, as the real content of soteriology, which the Christologies of Athanasius and Cyril meant to preserve. The hypostatic . . . union of divinity and humanity in Christ . . . presupposes an interpenetration of divine and human life. This interpenetration, however, . . . excludes confusion or total absorption of the human by the divine. . . . [The human being] is truly [human] when [she] participates in divine life and realizes in [herself] the image and likeness of God, and this participation in no way diminishes [her] authentically human existence, human energy and will. Now this notion of participation presupposes that God is in not

The doctrine of the Trinity is thus a very different doctrine from the monotheistic hierarchical ontology that moves to the front and center of the speculation and imagination of the "Christian West."[47] However, the doctrine of the Trinity was emerging precisely as theologians were "plundering the Egyptians" and unfolding the church's doctrines and arranging their arguments on the "Egyptians'" hierarchies. Further, the doctrine of the Trinity emerges precisely as the transgression both of the integrity of the integral God those hierarchies are constructed to honor and of the human beings who hope to climb them.[48] It is as if the doctrine of the Trinity were from the beginning a critique of supremacy, even if a critique that remains parasitic upon the very object of its critique.

When the doctrine moves into the heart of modern theological and philosophical discourse with Hegel, it again flies in the face of hierarchical metaphysical thinking. If Hegel's profoundly influential proposal

---

only an immutable and imparticipable essence but also a living and acting person. By assuming humanity hypostatically, the Logos 'becomes' what [the Logos] was not before and even 'suffers in the flesh.' This 'openness' of a hypostatic or personal God to the creature implies that the creature, and especially [the human being], is a *reality*, even in respect to God, since, in a sense, it 'modifies' God's personal existence."

47. Eusebius, who praises Emperor Constantine's likeness to the divine monarch in his famous "Oration on the Thirtieth Anniversary of Constantine's Reign," resisted signing off on the Creed of Nicea. He was much more comfortable with a monotheistic God than the sociality of a moving Trinity. For example: "Having been entrusted with an empire, the image of the heavenly kingdom, he looks to that ideal form, and directs his earthly rule to the divine model and thus provides an example of divine monarchic sovereignty. The King of the universe grants this to human nature alone of all other beings on earth. For the law of imperial power has been defined by the establishment of one sole authority to which all beings are subject. Monarchy by far surpasses all other constitutions and forms of administration; for its opposite, the rule of the many, with equality of privilege for all, is, rather, anarchy and chaos. Therefore, there is one God, not two or three or even more; for, in a word, polytheism is atheism." Eusebius of Caesarea, "Oration on the Thirtieth Anniversary of Constantine's Reign," 51 (III); see also 48 (I) and passim; and see Kelly, *Early Christian Doctrines*, 231, 235–36.

48. The word *hierarchy* is coined by Pseudo-Dionysius. But even here there is ambiguity. Whatever is said is unsaid apophatically by Dionysius. Yet there is no question that he thinks of the order of things as ascending and that he thinks in terms of higher and higher. See Pseudo-Dionysius, *The Divine Names*, 66–67 (II.11); see also Rorem, "Foreword," in *Psuedo-Dionysius: The Complete Works*, 1.

does not break free from the grip of modern foundational thinking and Enlightenment "ultimate reality," it does at least raise serious questions about it. In Hegel, God as Trinity is explicitly an othering movement; God goes out as God's own other and spends all of cosmic history overcoming this opposition.[49] In the end, for Hegel, A = A once more, though infinitely more richly than in timelessly abstract mathematics. In other words, for Hegel otherness is finally surrendered to sameness: there is a return of the otherness expended in the creation/incarnation, an absolute return that balances the books and turns a profit, even if the costs are excruciatingly high. Yet, on the other hand, inasmuch as this return suggests the thought of an other than God to which God goes, the stage is set by Hegel for a consideration of the doctrine that is more unsettling to the modern exacerbation of Western constructionism.

It is Karl Barth who makes the move that Hegel could not make. Although early on inclined to find the kingdom of God hidden in the private human soul, Barth learned from the social injustice of the modern industrial age, from the insane nationalistic violence of World War I, and from theologians spanning from Luther and Calvin to Kierkegaard and Dostoevsky to St. Paul that there is nothing implicitly divine in this world.[50] However, the idea of God's radical difference is even less for Barth than it is for the early church an abstraction about the aseity of God. God, according to Barth, is *known* to be radically other precisely because God is *revealed* that way.[51]

For Barth, God's revelation (*die Offenbarung*[52]) is insuperably God's own act. There is no revealer (*der Offenbarer*[53]) other than God. There is no recognition of revelation except by the God who works that

---

49. See, e.g., Hegel, *Phenomenology of Spirit*, 17–19.

50. "If I have a system," Barth wrote in the preface to the famous second edition of his *Epistle to the Romans*, "it is limited to a recognition of what Kierkegaard called the 'infinite qualitative distinction' between time and eternity." Barth, *Romans*, 10. For a discussion of the relation of the *Römerbrief* to Barth's later work see McCormack, *Karl Barth's Critically Realistic Dialectical Theology*, 14–23 and passim.

51. Barth, *CD* I/1, 315–16.

52. From the adjective *offen*, meaning "open." *Die Offenbarung* means "openness" in a very strong sense.

53. That is, "the one who opens."

recognition (*das Offenbarsein*[54]). Therefore, revelation is never reducible to a possession of those to whom it comes;[55] it is never able to be cut loose from the God who *freely* gives it. As such it is purely occurrent. It is present, but present in such a way that it never becomes "a past fact of history," a manipulable and dissectible thing.[56] Thus even as God comes closest, comes most concretely, comes "here and now," that coming is no less open to God's freedom. Yet this is good news, for it is the otherness of God's revelation that is liberating. Of course, were revelation simply to stand opposite us, quarantined as a closed integrity, it would be utterly irrelevant and inconsequential. Further, were it to come to reside in us as something proper to us, as our property, we would perhaps be well funded, but we would be prisoners of our own propriety, our own sameness, our own identity. However, revelation is an openness in which by its own sufficiency we participate. The openness of revelation enters into us, by grace through faith, and *we* are opened.[57] And since knowing God is nothing other than participation in God's revelation, one freely knows God to *be* free, occurrent, active, alive.[58] In other words, the event of revelation is for Barth an event in which God truly enters into what God is not and does so in such a way that God is there as an other. God opens, God is openness, God is open here and now.

All of this is the way Barth says "Jesus Christ." "We should still not have learned to say 'God' correctly," he writes, "if we thought it enough simply to say 'God.'"[59] In other words, the three-letter word "God" is not for Barth a generic term for any object of exceptionally intense reverence. Rather, "God" here is that which happens as one is drawn in a very particular way into the very particular history of Jesus. It is in this sense that because all that *is known* of God and, therefore, all that *can be known* of God is what is known of God in the history of Jesus, that

---

54. This word is most often translated as "revealedness" or "being revealed." Its point is that revelation is completed, fulfilled.

55. Barth, *CD* II/1, 225.

56. Ibid., 262.

57. Barth, *CD* II/2, 94–95.

58. And so, "with regard to the being of God, the word 'event' or 'act' is *final*, and cannot be surpassed or compromised." Barth, *CD* II/1, 263; cf. 305–7.

59. Barth, *CD* II/2, 5.

what is known there is what one must say God *is*. Further, the God in this place is "One which in virtue of its innermost being, willing and nature does not stand outside all relationships, but stands in a definite relationship *ad extra* to another."[60] That is, everything that this God *is* goes out as Jesus Christ. There is no hidden divine essence that is untouched by this outgoing. God specifically as God is entry into what is essentially other than God. The movement of God into the world cuts all the way through God, "as a spontaneous *opus internum ad extra* of the trinitarian God."[61]

> God is not *in abstracto* Father, Son and Holy Ghost, the triune God. [God] is so with a definite purpose and reference; in virtue of the love and freedom in which in the bosom of [God's] triune being [God] has foreordained [God's own self] from and to all eternity.[62]

What cuts all the way through God according to Barth is "the specific relationship which [God] has established with [human being] in Jesus Christ,"[63] viz., the election of human being "to participation in [God's] own glory."[64] In Jesus Christ, God suffers with suffering human being, God is rejected with rejected human being; in entering into human life as it is plunging into total destruction, God has "tasted damnation, death and hell."[65] In this extreme manner God chooses human

60. Ibid., 6.

61. Ibid., 25.

62. Ibid., 79.

63. Ibid., 78.

64. Ibid., 94.

65. The context in which that phrase appears does not file down the edge of that phrase: "In giving [God's own self] to this act [God] ordained the surrender of something, i.e., of [God's] own impassibility in face of the whole world which because it is not willed by [God] can only be the world of evil. In [God's own self] God cannot be affected either by the possibility or by the reality of that will which opposes [God]. . . . But when God of [God's] own will raised up [human being] to be a covenant-member with [God], when from all eternity [God] elected to be one with [human being] in Jesus Christ, [God] did it with a being which was not merely affected by evil but actually mastered by it. . . . God does not merely give [God's own self] up to the risk and menace, but [God] exposes [God's own self] to the actual onslaught and grasp of evil. . . . [God as God] tasted damnation, death and hell which ought to have been

being—and chooses it for "participation in the life of God."[66] Indeed this is what the history of Jesus of Nazareth tells. Human being is defined here as that distinctively creaturely existence that is utterly "for God."[67] "To be [human] is to be with God."[68] In other words, for Barth human being is that which with Jesus Christ moves to God, which in gratitude is a being toward God.

> It is not enclosed within the circle of its intrinsic possibilities, but opened towards that other and new reality of God its Creator which has broken through to it in [God's] Word, and in that Word as this promise has come to dwell within it. . . . To be summoned is to be called out of oneself and beyond oneself. Because it is God who speaks here, what is said has the right and power to enable the creature to transcend itself. . . . As God comes to it in [God's] Word, it is a being open towards God and self-opening, transcending itself in a Godward direction.[69]

The othering movement of God—the giving that holds the Father and Son apart and together; the love that denies that they are either two phases of the same self-identical Supreme Being or two self-identical deities; the hallowing of the flesh that not only drives Jesus into the wilderness and onto the hill outside the city of the great King, but also raises him from the dead and transfigures his crucified body—this is the Holy Spirit. It is this same Holy Spirit that gathers a community together in the hallowed flesh that is Jesus Christ raised, a community that has Jesus Christ as its being.[70]

---

the portion of fallen [human being] . . . [God] elected our rejection. [God] made it [God's] own." Ibid., 163–64; cf. Barth, *CD* IV/2, 225, 357.

66. Barth, *CD* II/2, 413. Barth calls this participation in God "gratitude": "Gratitude is the response to a kindness which cannot itself be repeated or returned, which therefore can only be recognised and confirmed as such by an answer that corresponds to it and reflects it. Gratitude is the establishment of this correspondence."

67. Barth, *CD* III/2, 70.

68. Ibid., 139.

69. Ibid., 165–66, 168.

70. "What the Holy Spirit positively wills and effects—that to which [the Spirit] awakens and calls—is always a human existence that deserves to be called a life to the

[The Holy Spirit] does not put the Christian at a point or in a position. [The Holy Spirit] sets [her] on the way, on the march. And it is a forced march, in a movement which never ceases and in which there can be no halting. [The Holy Spirit] does not put anything in [her] hands. . . . [The Holy Spirit] makes [her] a seeker . . . [Christians are] like a sacrifice which, whether it be small or great, costly or less costly, can only be given unreservedly, can only be presented, can only pass from their own determination to that of the One who demands and receives it, can only cease to belong to those who offer it. The sanctification of [human being], and the *vita christiana* as its result, is that the claim for this claimless self-sacrifice finds a place and authority and power in a human existence. We share in the exaltation of the royal [human being] Jesus as we may and must yield to this claim.[71]

Life in the Spirit, through the Son, to the Father

There is little in the doctrine of the Trinity that resonates with hierarchical Western metaphysics, with onto-theology, with the ontology of the Supreme Being. There is a radical relationality to the doctrine that will not let simple identities be, but that invites them in no uncertain terms to deny themselves. Of course, the doctrine of the Trinity can fall into a kind of variation of the metaphysics and logic of identity. Champions

---

extent that it is lived in the light of the royal [human being] Jesus, in an attentiveness and movement to [this human being], because the Christian who receives and has the Holy Spirit recognises and acknowledges that this [human being] died for [her] and has risen again for [her], that [this human being] lives for [her], that [this human being] is the Owner and Bearer, the Representative and [Sovereign] of this life, and that in [this human being's] exaltation [she] too is exalted and set in a living fellowship with God, that in [this human being] [she] is a new creature (2 Cor. 5:17). The Spirit wills and effects that in accordance with [her] being in this One [she] should cleave to [this human being], that [she] should be [this human being's] disciple, scholar, fellow, companion, follower and servant. [The Spirit] leads [her] to this One, and keeps [her] there, and calls and causes those who are led by the Spirit to this One, and are kept there, and go forward with [this One]." Barth, *CD* IV/2, 375.

71. Ibid., 376–77.

of the *filioque* have often enough pulled that off. Further, the notion of an immanent Trinity quarantined from an economic Trinity that is seen only imperfectly to represent it cleverly finds its own place for an identity undefiled by the world.[72] Yet the doctrine of the Trinity itself has arisen and still arises out of wonder and gratitude in the face of the sanctification of the unholy, the hopeless, a sanctification in which the Holy and the unholy touch. The God who is Wholly Other opens to God's creatures and they miraculously open to God.

This double transgression of integrity is not the end of the story, however. Were this simply a reciprocal, balanced meeting of polar opposites, then a new center of identity might be teased out of it, a kind of Hegelian *Aufhebung*. However, there is no reciprocity here, no law of investment and return. The direction is outward. It is a concurrence of giving, of oblation. Furthermore, the sanctification of God's creatures that occurs as the Spirit gathers them into the glorified history of Jesus is no return to the warm amniotic fluid of Eden, no ascent to the upper echelons of sanctity, no passage out of this present evil age. To be hallowed, to be separated to God, is to be separated to the God who in love has already gone and is already on the way precisely to what one has been liberated out of. Thus to be separated to God, to be holy, is to be separated with God to those whom God loves, the unholy.

It is particularly here that the work of John Wesley is helpful. Wesley was, of course, no speculative theologian. His was a "practical divinity." His written work on the doctrine of the Trinity makes no claim to have solved any trinitary puzzles. He leaves speculation to others and asks for tolerance in regard to the fine points of trinitary debate.[73] Yet at the same time he is an exceptionally trinitary thinker. His thought and life are constantly moving to the Father. Holiness is about that move. He contextualizes all that he has to say about holiness in the incarnate Son,

72. This is not to advocate a kind of skeptical and disappointed acceptance of a merely economic Trinity. To deny the immanent Trinity is not humility, but both a failure of nerve and a failure of doxology. It is because of what one has been gathered into in the economic Trinity that one's voice must rise to the immanent Trinity. However, such a theology of worship is not a new quarantine of God. Rather the economic Trinity is the hand of the immanent Trinity as it touches this untouchable world. Cf. Rahner, *Trinity*.

73. Wesley, "On the Trinity," in *WJW*, 2:383–84 (§§13–15).

our prophet, priest, and king, the "out-beaming" from the Father.[74] And

74. Wesley, "The Great Assize," in *WJW*, 1:359 (II.1); idem, *A Plain Account*, in *WJWJ*, 11:417. Wesley is convinced that the whole point of life is Christ. The point is not to achieve conformity to some universal norm of behavior or well-being. It is not to escape the fires of hell and flee to the easy comfort of heaven. It is not to return to the warm womb of Eden. It is Christ. Of course, Wesley is confident that in Christ one encounters the very law of God; the pattern of a happy spiritual life; the way from hell to heaven; the restoration of human being in the image of God. And yet, the primacy of Christ in Wesley is such that these matters are defined in him and not him in them. This can be seen well in his sermon of 1782, "God's Love to Fallen Man," in *WJW*, 2:422–35. The sermon seems on the surface to be concerned with a speculative question: "since the omniscient creator, foreknowing everything, must have known from all eternity that the first humans would fall into sin, why create them?" Wesley's answer is a strong and somewhat surprising one: that the coming of Christ to lost sinners brings more than could ever have been achieved by the most uncorrupted in the most ideal of circumstances. In the garden across all time—free from sin, living in unbroken fellowship with God and each other, torn by no strife, no pain, no disease, no guilt, no regret—Adam and Eve would never have risen to what descends in the crucified one to those who are otherwise dead to God. It is because of the fall that Christ has come. "For if Adam had not fallen Christ had not died" (425 [I.1]). And what Christ brings is well beyond even the highest imaginable human achievements. There comes in the coming of Christ immeasurably more holiness and happiness, greater faith in and love for the Father, Son, and Holy Spirit, "an unspeakable increase" in our love for our neighbors (425–26, 428 [I.1–2, 5]). "In Christ! Let me entreat every serious person once more to fix [her] attention here. All that has been said, all that can be said on these subjects centres in this point. The fall of Adam produced the death of Christ! Hear, O heavens, and give ear, O earth!" (433 [II.13]). Wesley's argument in this sermon seems so obviously burdened by fallacies that one might be inclined to give it to a first year logic student to dissect and critique. But then again Wesley was himself a logic teacher and perhaps knew what he was saying even when on his deathbed he called out, "where is my sermon on The Love of God? Take it and spread it abroad; give it to everyone" (422). At any rate, logically flawed or not, what Wesley says in this sermon bears witness to the openness of God's creative act, the openness of human being, the openness of the Father's love, the openness of the incarnation, the openness of the work of the Spirit. God created not a static perfection, but that which was not what it was to be, that whose definition stretched out into the future. This future is given by the love of God the Father, out of whom the gift of the Son comes; by the love of God the Son, the act of divine self-giving, self-oblation, self-sacrifice; by the love of the Holy Spirit, the Spirit who reveals and applies the giving Father and the given Son, the Spirit who raises the dead, opens their eyes, renews their souls, brings them out of darkness and into God's own light (426–27 [I.3]). God here is understood precisely to be *for us* from the foundations of the world. Human being is understood precisely to be *for God* from the foundations

we come to the Son only by the Spirit who draws us.[75] Thus though one does not find anything like a well-developed doctrine of the Trinity in Wesley's works, one does find a consistently trinitary rhythm. The holy life, life renewed in the image of God, is life in the Spirit, through the Son, to the Father.

This hallowed life in Wesley is radically decentered with the freedom of joy and prayer and thanksgiving to the One it is not, but to whom and for whom it was created. A sanctified human life is in Wesley an open place to be filled by the holy God, the God who is love.[76] It is Wesley's concern with the outgoing trinitary love of God that intensifies in his work the particular decentering of the love of neighbor. Jesus is a love that no one of us can ever hope to equal. Yet, moment by moment, entry into our prophet, priest, and king brings us into a neighbor-love that leaves nothing intact.[77]

That is, Wesley would agree with Luther that "a Christian lives not in [herself], but in Christ and in [her] neighbor. . . . [She] lives in Christ through faith, in [her] neighbor through love."[78] However, Wesley would take a shorter breath between the two directions of this ecstasy. He is quicker than Luther to affirm that living outside oneself in Christ *is always* immediately a living outside oneself in one's neighbor.[79] There is for Wesley no faith in God that is not also love for those whom God

---

of the world. Neither is a closed integrity. The line that might otherwise keep them quarantined from one another is transgressed by the love that happens precisely as Jesus Christ—the hallowing of the flesh.

75. Wesley, "The Great Privilege of Those That Are Born of God," in *WJW*, 1:434–35, 442 (I.8–10, III.2); idem, "The Unity of the Divine Being," in *WJW*, 4:70–71 (§§22–23).

76. Wesley, *A Plain Account*, in *WJWJ*, 11:440–41. "For what is the most perfect creature in heaven or earth in thy presence, but a void capable of being filled with thee and by thee; as the air which is void and dark, is capable of being filled with the light of the sun, who withdraws it every day to restore it the next, there being nothing in the air that either appropriates this light or resists it? O give me the same facility of receiving and restoring thy grace and good works! I say, *thine*; for I acknowledge the root from which they spring is in thee, and not in me" (441).

77. Ibid., 417–18, 444.

78. Luther, *On Christian Liberty*, 62.

79. Cf. Luther, *Commentary on St. Paul's Epistle to the Galatians*, 137.

loves. In that sense it is not unfair to say that for Wesley salvation is by grace alone through faith and love alone.[80]

It is thus a complex single movement for Wesley for a Christian to move to Christ and to her neighbor.

> "Beloved, what manner of love is this," wherewith God hath loved us! So as to give his *only Son!* In glory equal with the Father; in majesty coeternal! What manner of love is this wherewith the only-begotten Son of God hath loved us! So as to "empty himself," as far as possible, of his eternal Godhead! As to divest himself of that glory which he had with the Father before the world began! As to "take upon him the form of a servant, being found in fashion as a man"! And then to humble himself still farther, "being obedient unto death, yea, the death of the cross"! If God *so* loved us, how ought we to love one another![81]

The love of God that empties itself and moves into what God is not, into God's other, is precisely the love to which *we* are called. For Wesley life is to be separated, hallowed, to the God that is already on the move in Christ to the marginalized, the poor, the dying, the sinner. Thus to be separated to God is to be separated with God to one's neighbor. It is not to get, to rise to greatness, to succeed. It is to be emptied in love for the other, "loving our neighbor . . . as ourselves, as our own souls."[82] That is, the love of God that transgresses one's integrity "in a Godward direction" transgresses it again as one's identity is surrendered in and to one's neighbor.[83] It is in this above all that we are most like God in

---

80. Wesley, "Upon our Lord's Sermon on the Mount, V," in *WJW*, 1:559–60 (III.9).

81. Wesley, "God's Love to Fallen Man," in *WJW*, 2:428 (I.5).

82. Wesley, *A Plain Account*, in *WJWJ* 11:416; cf. 371–72. In other words, for Wesley God works to save the lost. The efficacy of God's work is the stirring of the human being, the energizing of the human being, by the energy of God. Idem, "On Working Out Our Own Salvation," in *WJW*, 3:203 (I.3); see also 208 (III.7): "God worketh in you; therefore you *must* work: you must be 'workers together with [God].'" And the work that one does by this movement of the Spirit into one's life is the work of love.

83. Thus when Wesley imagines God's restoration of creation at the eschaton, he imagines perfect fellowship with the Trinity and with all of God's creatures: "Hence will arise an unmixed state of holiness and happiness far superior to that which Adam

the holy life—not because we have come to something in ourselves that might be taken as a kind of representation of God, but instead because by the very energy of God we move beyond ourselves as God has in Christ and in the Spirit. No metaphysical hierarchy can get its hands around this free love.

enjoyed in paradise. . . . As there will be no more death, and no more pain or sickness preparatory thereto; as there will be no more grieving for or parting with friends; so there will be no more sorrow or crying. Nay, but there will be a greater deliverance than all this; for there will be no more sin. And to crown all, there will be a deep, an intimate, an uninterrupted union with God; a constant communion with the Father, and his Son Jesus Christ, through the Spirit; a continual enjoyment of the Three-One God, and of all the creatures in [God]." Wesley, "The New Creation," in *WJW*, 2:510 (§18).

2

After Crucifixion
Unhanding Metaphysics in the Liturgy of the Eucharist[1]

I

THOSE SEERS WHO KEEP their notebooks booted and their eyes fixed on global trends tell us that the center of gravity of what they call "Christianity" is shifting, socioeconomically and geographically. If one could quickly scan the faces of the members of local churches half a century from now, they say, the features that would most recur would be dark, young, female, and ground by poverty. Were you to make your way to that future (and you may well, if you are both young *and* privileged), to a country across which those little churches will have been abundantly strewn, and you were to come face to face with one of their faithful, odds are that her tired eyes would rise to meet yours in her native Nigeria or Brazil. Further, projections are that churches of pure European descent will continue generally to decline in number. Populations to the north of the Rio Grande will remain strongly "Christian," but largely because of what will have accompanied *newer* immigrants, both the "documented" and the "undocumented," as they

1. A paper delivered at the Center of Theology and Philosophy's Conference, "Belief and Metaphysics," Seminario Mayor Diocesano de Granada, Granada, Spain, September 15–18, 2006.

carve out living space alongside the grandchildren of the immigrants of another era.[2]

And what will have accompanied these newer arrivals? Even if we imagine that they are especially savory salt of the earth, it is too easy without further ado to call it "belief." Certainly, as a devout woman with a history among ecclesial people holds her baby close and clings to the rough hand of her man as they cross the Pacific or the Atlantic or the Imperial Desert, powerful memories and hopes carry her. Do these not count as "beliefs"? Perhaps, perhaps not. At the very least, what draws her is other than certain psychic acts to be graphed someplace on one or another version of Plato's Divided Line, or electrochemical events located some centimeters behind her anterior cranium. The memories and hopes journeying with her north from, say, Brazil are not her private property, as if they could be counted among her assets on a credit application. One would speak more faithfully of them were one to say that *she* is *in them* rather than that *they* are *in her*. If one wished to meet them, one may need to travel with her to where *she* met them, these memories and hopes, viz. into a very particular[3] and concrete social body of work that has aligned (even if unevenly) all her thoughts, practices, and language, one in which she has come to live and move and have whatever goods she carries on her back. And so, if under the glaring, bare bulb of cross-examination, we were to determine that her "beliefs" were anything but clear, that she could hardly articulate them, it may only be that we have pressed ourselves upon her too hard, that we have been too swift to make determinations, that in our aggression we have not opened ourselves to her, that we have not loved her.

Were we to love her, we would not too quickly leave her side. We might even go with her to prayer, to those venues of action and passion

---

2. Jenkins, *Next Christendom*, 2–3, 90–105.

3. The word *particular* seems to trace its ancestry to a root meaning "to grant, allot." See Claiborne, *Roots of English*, 193. In any case I use *particular* in this essay not as equivalent to a metaphysical entity, say, an Aristotelian "substance," nor to "the solitary individual" that is too quickly associated with Kierkegaard, nor even simply to a kind of mathematical "singularity," but rather as "that one," perhaps a face in a crowd or, as here, a concrete social body, one that comes as an unanticipated gift, one that is lost when laid hold of, e.g. categorically, and possessed, say with "the eyes that fix you in a formulated phrase" (Eliot, "Love Song of J. Alfred Prufrock").

that still bear her even so far from home, that have been at work in, with, and under her as long as she has been drawn to the gathering of ecclesial bodies. We may call this—this bodily bearing and working and drawing and gathering, this prayer—"the liturgy of the Eucharist," whether or not the people who have raised her would know what to make of those words.[4] It is the liturgy of the Eucharist that has been at work in her to will and to work a certain "belief" (Phil 2:12), that has inscribed belief across her body, as one might with one's finger inscribe an elusive message across the dust of the ground (Gen 2:7; 18:27; John 8:6–8).

Such "belief" is in her prayer no statistician's phenomenon, to be circumscribed by assertions having predictive value. Indeed, remembering and hoping with the assembly of the faithful from whom so many steps have separated her, she may in the heat of the moment join her voice to theirs in prayer that this time in this lonely desert, too, will have been honest and true to the liturgy into which she was born, that this time, too, will have been an outcry evoked from her throat, opened by a breath that blows without consulting your forecasts or mine (Gen 2:7, Ps 104:1, John 3:8).[5]

Moreover, the liturgical event that still holds them together does not float in empty space. It, too, is situated. It defers explicitly to the life and death of a very particular human being, whom its words of hope remember in a very strong sense of the word. That is, she and they gather in the story of a suffering, dying, then dead and damned dark-skinned carpenter whose end is in this story wrapped into a neat, if bloody, package at the close of a decrepitly old week (John 19:30) and then liberatively undone on the first day of a week of new beginning (John 20:1). The outcry of the faithful, they may even explicitly recall, is *his* outcry—articulated in two tensive ways: (1) "My God, my God, why have you forsaken me?" (Mark 15:34) and (2) "Father, into your hands I commend my spirit" (Luke 23:46). They pray his prayer—his prayer that opens a way through the stone wall of his tomb—that a way will be opened for them, too, and for all, that in his abased and exalted

4. An ecclesiastical leader's saying at a press conference that a church is "non-liturgical" or "non-sacramental" doesn't make it so.

5. See Wolff, *Anthropology of the Old Testament*, 10–25.

body *all* things will have one day shown new (2 Cor 5:17). They pray that the logic of this new life—the logic of crucifixion/resurrection—will be given them, that they will have the mind of this carpenter (Phil 2:5), that they will be graced with *metanoia*. There are even moments when they pray that they might join him in his sufferings, die as he died, and thereby bear witness to his resurrection (cf. Phil 3:8–15). This is the passion of martyrdom. When it arises (and to some degree it arises with every liturgical gesture), it is an incalculable act resting on nothing more solidly weight-bearing than a parable, an icon, a prayer.)

II

Certainly, the people who gather are flesh—muscles and blood and skin and bones, people with a past. When they are stirred to move together down any (even uncharted) path, their steps leave a residue, in reference to which the curious might calculate, might make bankable forecasts. Indeed, there are fewer and fewer bodies of discourse and action that must strain to find a place for these people, for what we all too casually call "church." The staffs of professional sociologists and politicians turn their attention to it with ease. Philosophers, too, of whatever stripe, attend to it, to its structures and its doctrines, and with little disquiet wrap their minds around it, finding about it nothing anomalous. That it might have a particularity that would elude all appropriation, we are tempted to say, is unthinkable. Even those not quickly felled by temptation might be only so bold as to speak or write of that which, though one might strive in vain to lay hold of and appropriate it, nonetheless makes in the striving a difference—a difference conjoined with or disjointed from identity. More than that, a truly radically elusive particularity could only unmake, only tear down, we think. Such elusion would simply abandon the determination of good and evil, would hold nothing in its hand, would step into a future to be determined without our help; such elusion is "nihilism," we say (cf. Gen 3:4–10 and Phil 2:5–11). It would turn every accomplishment into rubbish, into excrement (cf. Phil 3:8). It would send one forth without[,] a prayer (cf. Matt 26:36). (The woman who holds her baby close, while her man stands watch in the blackness of an Imperial Desert night, is above all a prayer.)

In the face of that kind of disaster, it is understandable that we would in our anxiety yearn for a panoptic vision which would take in and hold all that we have discerned and might ever discern, a ground for proper action and passion, a foothold off of which we might push to make our way into an otherwise paralyzingly uncertain future in the face of an otherwise inhospitably untamed natural world. Besides, we are people who wonder, we have a longing for rational unity, and we are driven by an aesthetic desire for a vision both coherent and adequate to the broad range of our experience or an erotic urge for far-reaching intellectual satisfaction. We are people who desire a grand, integrating vision. Surely no one could fault the pious for engaging in just this enterprise, specifying in some detail *God's* relation to all the goods (*ousia*) their inquiries have surveyed, goods that come into their hands as their inquiries grow more and more ambitious (cf. Luke 15:12). Of course, the pious would not wish too quickly to nail God to any vision. They perhaps remember that God will not stay nailed down. They would want to give God the power to move about freely. Nor would they wish to give God only limited free range—as one might a June bug tied by the leg to a long thread. And so, the pious might even dare to say that God is in league with that goodness or truth or beauty and in combat against that evil or falsehood or ugliness they have by rigorous and pious effort come to some degree to determine—*but* they would say this perhaps with downcast eyes, humbly, uncertainly, or skeptically or with a knowing, hushed caveat that God stands not only in analogical agreement with, but concomitantly in analogical opposition to—even in judgment against—their determinations. That a displaced young woman, holding a little child, would have no place in their ordered whole could not be definitive, they think.

In this way—perhaps against one's best intentions—one has stumbled into the imposing tradition of the Greeks, those masters of health and unity, of balance and justice, of virtue and well-being, of ethics and ontology. The Greeks understood as well as any ever have that a people must keep the lines well drawn that mark the difference between "we are" and "we are not." The literature of the Greeks is rich with a paideic vision, cosmic in scope, for the integrity of the body, the soul, and the city-state. The Odysseus of Homer's *Odyssey*, the Socrates of Plato's *Apology*, and the walled *polis* of Plato's *Republic*—each rises tall, silhouetted against the ethereal sky of a sublimely conceived cosmos, threateningly mature, overtly or covertly beautiful, strong, virile, courageous, daring, wise, complex, well armed, just: whole. To be well adjusted is here to be hale, an inherent harmony properly exercised in controlled agony at one or another battlefield or *palaistra* or *agora*, centered, stalking steadily like a pelican on defensible ground.[6] That there are the ill adjusted among us simply means, they held, that *therapeia*[7] is to be performed, a *therapeia* in fact that serves not only the patient, but even more the divine that radiates from the temple at the heart both of the city and of the heroic citizen.[8] Indeed, we human beings, they held, are here at the center of the cosmos to rise by struggle to become "like the divine, so far as we can."[9] The more we are like the divine, the more we are ourselves, and vice versa. Thus, *therapeia* is in the strictest sense of the word a healing act. Who could blame anyone, especially the pious, for praying for such healing? Indeed, who could blame them for conceiving of prayer as such as a salutary act, the deed in itself (whether it is heard or not) as therapy, as a medicine of the soul?

For the headier Greeks, the grandest *therapeia* is what they called *philosophia*, a pursuit of wisdom that—far from fearing or petitioning the gods, for example for some undue ephemeral benefaction—aspires and conforms to the surpassing divine goodness, truth, and beauty that the gods, too, serve.[10] Though it is certainly idealized, a kind of monolatrous prayer plays still in the background history of *philosophia*. And yet the gods, idealized though they, too, may be, are honored and trusted to do well the tasks that they have been assigned (without the distraction of our entreaties). And we are to do well the tasks that we have been assigned, to fit no less into this beautiful cosmos that is our native soil and theirs. The end of philosophical *therapeia* is adjustment to the eternally concentric *archai* that order the many, an adjustment that centers the

6. Plato, *Symposium* 221b.

7. See Liddell et al., eds., *Greek-English Lexicon*, 792–93.

8. See Plato, *Timaeus* 90c.

9. See Plato, *Theatetus* 176b; *Republic* 613a–b; *Phaedrus* 248a, 249c; and *Timaeus* 47c.

10. See Plato, *Laws* 716c–717a; Jaeger, *Paideia*, 2:285–88.

attendant's otherwise disparate faculties and makes him whole. What is truly one, truly whole, is simply self-identical, untouched by what is other than itself: A ≠ ~A! It simply *is*. "Integrity" = "identity," "identity" ✓ = "being." I *am* insofar as I participate in the integrity that most truly *is*. It is not accidental that the devotion of the Greeks to integrity led them into that discipline that sets out to clarify the foundational meaning of "being." An inquiry into the significance of "being" is thus no idle pastime; it is a quest for *healing*.[11]

Early Greek thinkers were in fact in more than one sense "physicians." They were above all concerned with what they named *physis*, with thinking it and thus serving it. It would be fitting, if anachronistic, to describe at least some of them also as "metaphysicians," but not in the much later sense that discounts *physis*. The prefix *meta-* would not in their case mean "beyond," but rather "in pursuit of." *Physis*, which is typically translated into English as "nature," comes from the same root as the English "be."[12] It signifies "what is," what rises by force out of the darkness to make a stand.[13] Beholding *physis* filled Greek thinkers with awe and wonder. There could be nothing higher, deeper, richer, stronger, or purer. Indeed, the Greeks would have found odd any suggestion that there might be something beyond it. In this morning of Western civilization, *physis* embraced everything without exception, including the earth's rational animals and their gods. Homer and Hesiod, Parmenides and Heraclitus, Plato and Aristotle all agreed:[14] there is by definition only one whole. It is the task of competent thinkers to show

11. Members of the church who take on this divinely humane intellectual task are set to work. In their aspiration to the Goodness, Truth, and Beauty to whom *they* pray, they must specify—more diligently than did Plato or the Stoics—the way *their* God is to be conceived ontologically. God, they may say—without forsaking Plato or the Stoics—is (a word that may be used only in passing) "the Supreme Being," "the ground of being," "the cause of being," "being itself"—perhaps even "beyond being" (a less ambiguously ontological assertion than it may seem). It is to this God *who is* that they then pray and in so doing look to obtain integrity themselves.

12. Claiborne, *The Roots of English*, 9. A "physician" in this sense would be one who served the cause of one's "being," swearing, e.g., to do no harm.

13. I admit that I am thinking of Heidegger's most self-consciously "German" account of *physis* here. See, e.g., Heidegger, *Introduction to Metaphysics*, 14–19, 147–48, 167–72, 188–92, and passim.

14. As would their heirs, Hegel, Whitehead, and Heidegger, by the way.

how and why and in that way to adjust to it—to imitate it, insofar as they can—and in turn to lead especially their kind to adjust to it as well.[15] The intelligibility of the cosmos implies, they maintained, that "what is" constitutes a definite totality.[16] *Physis* is one, a beautifully spherical inherence.[17] Here everything *is*. There simply cannot be an outside. If we thought that we had identified an outside, it would by the very act of identification be *inside*; and an outside with no place inside is literally unthinkable (cf. Luke 9:58). (She shivers in the cold midnight of the Imperial Desert or faints in the heat of its afternoon. She hides from the INS and even more from the "Minutemen" who would cast her out, with her baby and her man. "Pai Nosso, que estás nos Céus, santificado seja o Teu nome. Venha o Teu reino, seja feita a Tua vontade, assim na Terra como no Céu. O pão nosso de cada dia nos dá hoje. Perdoa-nos as nossas dívidas, assim como nós perdoamos aos nossos devedores. E não nos deixes cair em tentação o mas livra-nos do mal. Amém.")

III

But might there be another—uncanny, irrevocably prayerful—way of thinking, a way, say, not out to apprehend, overpower, deport, or naturalize the alien, but rather to defer to her? Might one be of a different mind than that of the founding geniuses of Western civilization, one that opens to what it is not and cannot be? Might there be another way of thinking that would let the outside in without assimilating it? Now, such thinking—if it were possible—would undo the thinker. It would open wounds through him out into the ground that had hitherto so well supported him, wounds possibly undoing integrity, well-being, wholeness, *physis* itself. The thinker who would think what cannot be thought would undergo a kind of passion.[18]

It was that tradition which does not shrink back from, but rather celebrates, passion that first gave trouble to Greek thinking, viz. that tradition that not only acknowledges, but adores, a Creator "who

15. See Plato, *Theatetus* 149a–152c, and *Apology* 29e–30b.

16. Integrity also means definiteness.

17. Dupré, *Passage to Modernity*, 21; Parmenides, Fragment 8.

18. Kierkegaard [Johannes Climacus], *Philosophical Fragments*, 37.

remain[s] outside the cosmos,"[19] who is free in relation to *physis*, to "nature."[20] Perhaps Israel (and the church that remembered Israel) was less quick to grasp after an integral totality, because its people remembered what it was like to pray, frightened in the Imperial Desert of Egypt, and heard the declaration "I am the [Sovereign] your God" only as the command "you shall love the alien as yourself" still rang in their ears (Lev 19:33–34).

And yet the church has not always remembered Israel well. The church's intellectuals gradually, if unevenly, came to appropriate the synthetic presence of mind of the Gentiles of the northern Mediterranean basin. Theirs was a long and difficult journey: from Jerusalem to Athens and to Rome.[21] Along the way they faced "some severe crises."[22] And how could crises not come? Both older and newer metaphysics had much to be said in their favor, of course. However, the church's geniuses could only go so far toward synthesizing even the most purely idealized essences they and others had distilled from such decidedly opposing histories.[23] Ideas never completely shake off the social bodies whose stories had given them life. Before the Edict of Milan more often than not both the members of the church and those of proper Roman society were struck and shaken by the difference that held them apart from each other, for example when from either side of an open space, immeasurable in Roman feet, they turned their faces toward each other, a few in the bloody dust of the coliseum floor, many in the wooden or marble coliseum seats above.

Unlike the divine of the physicians and metaphysicians of the Greeks (and their heirs), the Creator-God of the Testaments of the

19. Dupré, *Passage to Modernity*, 3; cf. 22, 29, and 126–27.

20. "An all-inclusive concept of *kosmos* such as the Greeks knew did and could not exist in Israel. The whole of creation manifested Yahweh's power and presence, but it never attained the kind of self-sufficient unity that the Greek *kosmos* possessed. Moreover, the later [teaching of the church] . . . of a world created 'from nothing' [*ex nihilo*] and hence devoid of intrinsic necessity would have conflicted with the divine character of Greek nature." (Dupré, *Passage to Modernity*, 29–30.) It is worth noting that Dupré does not celebrate this apparent impasse (see his "Introduction," e.g. 7).

21. Do not think that I am in league with Tertullian on this point.

22. Dupré, *Passage to Modernity*, 31.

23. Of course, they oppose each other in very different ways.

church was declared in its baptismal credo first to be "the Father" of the "one Lord Jesus Christ" (and only then the "maker of heaven and earth, of all that is, visible and invisible.") And the "one Lord Jesus Christ . . . through whom all things were made" is no universal, no centered identity, no bloodless, faceless integrity, but the one "who was crucified under Pontius Pilate." Even when one finds in the texts of the young church what might be called "cosmic symbolism," the cosmos is subsumed under the "one Lord Jesus Christ," not the other way around. Indeed, the church's Holy Scriptures affirm that the whole cosmos was created in, through, by, and for this abased/exalted one. Though freely and without anxiety welcomed into a roomy sanctuary, universality blinks before the broken body of the "one Lord Jesus Christ," lifted up for all to see.[24]

Yet the church's metaphysicians again and again struggled to find ways of thinking at once both the God at work in the Gospels' narratives and the "nature" that has no outside—and to do so without forgetting the difference between the things of this world and the things of God. Certainly, they recited the Creed of Constantinople with gusto, forsaking all to follow the incarnate heavenly Logos. Certainly, they knew in their bones that God is sharply different from this world. They sang doxologies to that God. And yet . . . it was so very hard to resist the temptation to gather all their thoughts on the way to a profitable vision of a more magnificent, integrated *physis*, one finally with everything inside.

What is impressive is the way this temptation was resisted time and time again in the work of the church's doctors. Thus, though Francis of Assisi was certainly unlikely and exceptional, he was not even among intellectuals without foreshadowing. Yet it is perhaps telling that the revolt he heralded arose above all as he gave himself in naked prayer to the *particular, human* Jesus. That there might be revolution in *this* signals among *these* people the extent to which authorities (even ecclesiastical authorities) tend to pass by particularity—even *that* particularity—in order to get at the stable, integrating principles of which any particular-

24. "Moreover, if God had definitively revealed [God] in the 'man of sorrows,' how could one continue to regard the splendor of the universe as the image of a God who had appeared 'in the form of a slave'?" (Dupré, *Passage to Modernity*, 31.)

ity is by default taken to be an instance—and this, all the while rending a crusty, brown loaf of bread, bread the color of the skin of a tired young mother crossing the Imperial Desert, and lifting a cup of deep red wine, wine the color of her thick blood starving for food, water, and air.

She, sojourner that she is, finds no comfort in nature's appropriation of God. She is not drawn to its physicians and the well-being they hawk. It is out into the open that she calls and steps. A God at home in the presence of "what is" lacks the freedom to turn to "what is not" simultaneously, to call her Godward *and* into an open future. That is, the weak, the least, the stranger, the alien finds in *physis* only more of the same hopelessness that has always told her to get back in her place. That liturgy of the Eucharist that fills her memory, on the other hand, invites her to voice her deeds, her body to the living God; it lays out before her a path to a holy eschaton[25] that is coming for her and her little baby, a future free to place in radical crisis, say, an empire's judgment concerning her value for its growth potential.

Still, the liturgy of the Eucharist smiles hospitably upon any who would make it their own in order to consume it. It only asks that in the eating and drinking a reversal take place. Adam is at this wedding banquet to defer to Christ. The bread and the wine of the Eucharist are gifts to be given, of course; but *we* who eat and drink are to be consumed by *them*, to be written into their story. The Eucharist is hospitable by definition. It invites any and all who labor and are heavy laden to come in and yield themselves, their gathered thoughts and deeds. All that is asked is that those "that are" in eating might be "reduced to nothing" and find fellowship with the elect from among "the things that are not" (1 Cor

25. Note the ancestors of the word *eschaton* (the third numbered item in its language family): "Definition: Out . . . . Derivatives include *strange*, and *extreme*. 1. Variant *eks. a. ex1, ex-, from Latin *ex, ex-*, out of, away from; b. ecto-, ex-, exo-, exoteric, exotic; electuary, lekvar, synecdoche, from Greek *ex, ek*, out of, from. 2. Suffixed (comparative) variant form *eks-tero-. a. estrange, exterior, external, extra-, strange, from Latin *exter*, outward (feminine ablative *exterā, extrā*, on the outside); b. further suffixed (superlative) form *eks-t(e)r-ēmo-. extreme, from Latin *extrēmus*, outermost (*-mo-, superlative suffix). 3. Suffixed form *eghs-ko-. eschatology from Greek *eskhatos*, outermost, last. 4. Celtic *eks-, out (of), in compound *eks-dī-sedo- (see sed-). 5. samizdat, from Russian *iz*, from, out of, from Balto-Slavic *iz." (*The American Heritage Dictionary of the English Language*, 4th ed., "Appendix I: Indo-European Roots," s.v. "eghs.")

1:28). In this they will find fellowship with that particular dark-skinned woodworker who during Holy Week was hanged on a wooden cross in solidarity with "the things that are not." But they will find also that they will have been driven to this end by the same life's breath that drove him to the cross and awakened to new life by the same gift that awakened him from the dead. Or so the liturgy of the Eucharist promises.[26]

The promise is that in a living, ecstatic sacrifice of worship a particular child held by his particular mother will have opened toward an eschatologically holy Trinity that in one life history places all claims to ownership under a crisis that crucifies/resurrects every worldly good (and evil), however tightly grasped. Indeed, to say "Trinity" is to say the "outside" of the "eschaton." The Trinity occurs as the unspeakably exalted Father and the unspeakably abased Son are held apart and together by the unspeakably quick Spirit. Thus, the man who stands watch in the night of the Imperial Desert prays (perhaps only because of his habitual proximity to her [cf. 1 Cor 7:13–14]) to the Father through the Son in the Spirit—even if he would hardly admit that such words come and go with his heavy breath. He leans against a rock still warm from the day's hot sun, and is drawn by the body of the friend of outcasts, who in their memory and hope is lifted up still (John 12:32). In that prayer in the darkness of the Imperial Desert he is sent from the Father through the Son in the Spirit into the world that is bent on taking him out, along with his little family. To him and to his woman and his baby a Mystery gently and lovingly calls out: "The Peace of God is coming and it is coming for you!"

The liturgy of the Eucharist is nothing but prayer. It is an eating and a working, but an eating not about getting full and a working not about getting paid. In the liturgy of the Eucharist, the people eat a very particular performance of the will of the Father. Crucifixion/resurrection is the food that makes all their meals nourishing (cf. John 4:34). As their throats open to this food and drink, far from centering on itself, their work (*leitourgia*) overflows as a petition that all they do will have been gifted with gratitude and joy (*eucharistia, charis, chara*). To eat and drink the performance of the will of the Father is to pray that we

26. A promise that, far from being a bribe, is taken in only *with* the bread and the wine of the liturgy and the baptism in whose wake they work.

would be <u>inscribed into the particular story of Jesus</u>. It is indeed to hunt and gather, to build and sculpt, to speak and think—all week long. It is to breakfast, dine, and sup. But as written into *this* story, a week's meals and work become free acts of abandon. One carries them to that altar at which a gathering of people is taken into the history that is totalized to death on Good Friday and set loose to life on Easter Sunday. We might call this history that is simultaneously crucifixion and resurrection "a living sacrifice."[27]

Thus, every proud discourse, experience, and belief is invited at the ecclesial assembly again and again to be given away. What these people weave all week long makes a fabric, but one that in their prayers unravels outward to a world made new, an outside, an *eschaton* that liberates what was and is, in the future of the particular body of redemption and novelty named "Jesus Christ." The *telos* of work is here no longer the "goal" of Greek teleology.[28] The circle is completed only when an eschaton breaks in to complete it, that is, as an outside refusing either to be appropriated or expelled. The liturgy declares that there will have been "perfection," "fulfillment," "satisfaction," "abundance," "maturity," "sanctification." Even now, it is said, there is a donation of that eschatological *teleios*. Yet it will have happened only because it will have *come*; it is not and will not be achieved. Furthermore, it is a *holy* circle that is *one* precisely as many partake ecstatically in that elusive Holy Trinity that will forevermore occur gratuitously, as a kind of disruptive "other-ing." This circle is *enhypostatically* one, as is the body of Jesus Christ—which is to say that it is the love that does not dissolve difference into some uninterrupted unity.

The liturgy of the Eucharist is gift. It is given with the particularity of the name Jesus, a name with a baptismal history, a name washed in the coming of the Reign of that Holy Father who opens among and to

27. In the call to such a sacrifice one might especially turn a questioning eye to the body's reason, its mind. "I appeal to you therefore, brothers and sisters, by the mercies of God, to present your bodies as a living sacrifice, holy and acceptable to God, which is your [*rational*] worship. Do not be conformed to this world, but be transformed by the renewing of your *mind* . . ." (Rom 12:1–2a).

28. Cf. *American Heritage Dictionary of the English Language*, 4th ed., "Appendix I: Indo-European Roots," s.v. kwel-1: "Greek telos, 'completion of the cycle,' consummation, perfection, end, result."

the little ones of this world and speaks there in the wing-beat of the dove: "this is my beloved child in whom I am well pleased." Is it a healing act, this corporate work? Yes, but not as the institution of a closed integrity, a "wholeness." It is healing only as a sacrifice, a "making holy," that stands out prayerfully into the faithfulness of the holy one who comes to dwell in the work of these people—without ceasing to be holy. It is a healing act in the same way that the evocation of Abram from his Chaldean home, never to return, was a healing act, viz. as a journey of promise (Gen 12:1). It is a healing act in the same way that the march of Moses into Egypt from the backside of the desert was a healing act, viz. buoyed by the shout of the unimaginably free God: "Let my people go!" (Exod 5:1; cf. 3:14). It is a healing act in the same way that the raising of Lazarus was a healing act, viz. as a call issuing out of the coming Reign of God to "come forth" (John 11:43). It is a healing act in the same way that the resurrection of Jesus was a healing act, viz. as the emptying of a tomb by egress of a body still wounded—gloriously open and inviting (Luke 24:39; John 20:27). It is that healing act that breaks through "what is" from a future never to be cordoned off by a fence.

IV

Let us say that the poor, young Brazilian mother and her little family make their way across the Imperial Desert. Let us say that they find kindness among strangers and a place to sleep and eat in South Central Los Angeles. One Sunday morning she makes her way with her man and her baby to a little church there. Let us say that she and they sit just across the aisle from a theologian with a professional interest in the metaphysics of well-being, a politically sensitive and curious man in town to attend a vigil at South Central L.A. Farm. Let us say that he is the kind of man who is troubled when the common good is not served or when in the shadows the powerful rob the powerless of their due. He is there, because he has the power to be there, even if he also genuinely wishes to join people from this neighborhood in worship. Let us say that he and the little Brazilian family rise at the same moment, fall together into the same line, walk one after the other toward the front of the church, and together kneel side by side at the same altar rail to receive the same bread and drink the same wine of the Eucharist. When that bread and then that wine touch their tongues, with what have they been fed? How are they now to live, to respond, to pray—she with nothing having exchange value in this world, he with a head full of academic capital?

It seems simplistic, if not cruel, to say that they are both to give up everything with the one whose flesh and blood they have just been given—but that is in part what is to be said. And yet she knows well already how to go about making that move. She has given up everything already on the long journey to this little church. Her task now is by the gifting of the Spirit again to enter into solidarity with the abased Jesus, who on the cross has entered preveniently into solidarity with her— and she is in him to receive once more the boldness and audacity of that resurrection which no death can threaten, that resurrection which carried her to this very neighborhood. She, among "the things that are not," is elected in this enacted memory of crucifixion/resurrection to perform every day of the coming week the hope against which no fence or stone wall can prevail. Each week she is called to this task—and it is a task that will never be put behind her: to let go of what she has done and to move boldly into a new day, assured that the Reign of the Father of Jesus is coming—and it is coming for her and her baby and her man (Phil 3:12–14).

One with a head full of academic capital has the same task, though he may well spend the rest of his days only beginning what waking nightmares have taught her too well, what she would never wish that he or anyone else might go through. Nonetheless, he is in this liturgy called to remember the crucifixion of Christ, his baptism into it, the resurrection of Christ, and the call that he walk in newness of life, the life that is a gift (Rom 6:3–4). How is he to do that? More to the point, how is what he holds dear, how is his world view, the metaphysical wholeness of mind he has worked so hard to build, his vision of health and integrity for everyone and everything, how is his intellectual property to fare, when his hand brushes against hers ("pardon me"), as he kneels beside her in prayer to eat and drink the body and blood of Jesus? As with every work, here it will not stand. Jesus lifted up on the cross calls the conception of *physis*, integrity, and well-being to be drawn to him as well, to die with him. Certainly, the promise is that they are to be raised with him as well. And yet, the mind that has joined Christ on the cross cannot any longer presume, for example, truly to have determined what is good and what is evil, what is and what is not, what is inside and what is outside. And though *physis* is a brilliant vision and metaphysics is honorable work, when ideas have been gathered into a coherent whole, they are to be given away—given away in praise to the Holy Trinity, given away to our neighbors (Mark 10:17–39).

There is no way to say definitively and in detail what this will mean for the work of such a theologian. Perhaps it will mean that the hard work of well-grounded kataphasis will open to the groundlessness of apophasis, an epiktatic unsaying that performed in this ecclesial work force is never to have been concluded. Perhaps it will mean that supplementing the language of comprehensive thought there may be a "Spirit-language" in which all that had been well placed comes to be displaced in glorious adoration of a Redeemer who lives. Perhaps it will mean a movement of neighbor-love in which our tight metaphysical thinking loosens, even against itself becomes roomy, before the faces especially of the destitute—those who never have a room in any system. Perhaps it will mean that he will come to learn to let go of the structures to which he is both tempted and trained to cling tightly, those structures that determine who is in and who is out. This is not to say that all structures are simply to be eliminated. It is not clear what that could even mean. It is certainly not to say that the theologian is to have an "experience" of "belief" and then "express" that experience in a "more egalitarian vision." However, when work is done among people whose bodies have been catechized by the story of Jesus, perhaps the thinker's constructs are to be broken, to be cut open, to be breeched, as was the body of Christ, when it was lifted up, when it was given to *his* neighbor, the thief dying beside it, when it was most blatantly Emmanuel among the poor—having prayed the "nevertheless" of Gethsemane.

Breaking, cutting, and breeching are perhaps to be *thought* and *said* as well by the professional theologian with a metaphysical interest—viz. against himself. He need not quit his day job at the university. Yet perhaps the *way* he works there is to undergo a decentering *metanoia*. Perhaps he is yet to teach, but teach *people*, to teach people to

think and *speak* in the concrete and particular body of Christ, viz. praying the "nevertheless" of Gethsemane, as a *way* of learning to let go of
the structures to which he is both tempted and trained to cling tightly.
Perhaps, that is, he is to do *the impossible*, to teach *grace*, the breaking
in of the agape[29] gift that will not yield to become anybody's property
(Acts 8:17–23). Thus, perhaps, it will become much less important for
him to be a person of integrity with an integral world view, than to be
disrupted, to be interrupted, by the joy of that grace; perhaps it will become much less important to know, than to be known (1 Cor 8:3; 13:12;
Gal 4:9). Perhaps he will work, as she works, with the prayer on his lips
that is silently on hers:[30] "O eternal Trinity! / Eternal Trinity! / O fire and
deep well of charity! . . . / Just as you gave us yourself, / wholly God and
wholly [human], / so you left us all of yourself as food / so that while we
are pilgrims in this life / we might not collapse in our weariness / but be
strengthened by you, heavenly food. . . . / What drove you? / Nothing
but your charity, / mad with love as you are!"[31]

29. This word may be read in Greek or English.

30. "Is this Brazilian woman an actual, living, flesh-and-blood person, a woman
with a name and address? I mean, do you know this woman, have you met her, have
you talked with her? Because if she is and you have—*how dare you tell her story?!*
What gives you the right to steal her narrative voice?! What gives you the right to
objectify her?! Frankly I find it offensive that you would presume to represent her
here, to commodify her, to force her into this work and force us to become voyeurs of
your exploitation!" "Your questions are the best questions that could be asked of this
little essay. There is no answer that could presume to resolve them. And yet they call
for an answer, just as she does. 'Do I know this young Brazilian mother?' I believe I
do. 'Have I met her, say, on the streets of L.A.?' I bet I have. 'Do I know her name?' I
think I do. 'Have I held her baby?' I feel his weight even now. 'Have I shaken the hand
of "her man"?' Many times, I believe. 'Are then my words hers?' I could never presume
to answer that most unsettling of questions with a 'yes'; and yet I pray that, by the time
this essay has done its work, they will have at least stopped being 'mine.' 'Do I claim to
speak for her?' No. I make no claim, certainly not that one. 'Is this all, then, fictive? Is
she a symbol of something?' If she is a 'symbol,' she is a nonrepresentational one, an
iconic one, or at least this is my prayer ('Lord, hear my prayer!'). And, if she is 'fictive,'
she exceeds fiction, the way every saint, Catherine of Siena, for example, exceeds not
only her story, but also all the stories of the saints."

31. Catherine of Siena, Prayer 10, in *The Prayers of Catherine of Siena*, 78–79.

3

The Resurrection of the Body
The Liturgy of Martyrdom and the Hallowing of the Flesh[1]

I. What Might Engage Us in the Face of a Woman Who Stretches Out Her Hand?

WE MIGHT IMAGINE A fluid motion, an arm extending, fingers reaching to lay hold of a cup or a lover or the shoulder of a teetering child or a torn fragment of bread or the hand of an absent friend. Where do we go to learn what it means, this gesture? What are we to say? That it is the expression of a prior idea formed by and forever secondary to the private soul that occupies and pilots this body? Or that whatever might be declared of this "extending hand" is a sentence imposed by an objective judge upon an otherwise meaningless and isolated datum? Or should we rather think in grander metaphysical terms of a ground that supports and is exemplified in this event, some ultimate reality with or without purpose, some matter or form or creativity or energy or will to power? Or should we perhaps give ourselves to a more originary ontology, one that will open a clearing for the contending and expanding relations that appear when receptive thinking lets this event be? Or are

1. A paper delivered to the thirty-ninth annual meeting of the Wesleyan Theological Society, Roberts Wesleyan University, Rochester, NY, March 4–6, 2004. An earlier version of the present essay was first published in *Wesleyan Theological Journal* 40 (2005) 172–207.

we not at least to understand this extending hand in the light of the motives that lie behind it or of the consequences that lie before it or of the character from which it flows? Or does all of this distract us from the most pressing of questions? Is it that in straining to interpret the world in various ways we have lost the real point, viz., to change it?

These questions do not lie outside the theologian's purview. But they are not the ones first asked. The work at hand is not a kind of psychology, epistemology, metaphysics, ontology, or ethics. If the theologian takes up such questions at all, it is done freely, from the outside, with passion, perhaps with desire, but without need. They have been denatured in the crucifixion and resurrection of the body of the Christ in whom she now lives and moves and thinks and speaks. Thus if these questions are to be found in her office, they have come there on loan—to do a job for which they were not trained.

II. What Might Engage Us in the Face of a Woman Who Stretches Out Her Hand?

It was not first in the sixteenth century that the church asked about the relation between grace and works. New Testament texts already give one pause to consider the matter. At the close of the Sermon on the Mount, after Jesus has laid out what seem to be impossibly difficult dicta for the lives of those who would follow him, he announces that "not everyone who says to me, 'Lord, Lord,' will enter the [reign and rule] of heaven, but only the one who does the will of my Father in heaven" (Matt 7:21). The Letter of James is even more direct: "What good is it, my brothers and sisters, if you say you have faith but do not have works? Can faith save you? If a brother or sister is naked and lacks daily food, and one of you says to them, 'Go in peace; keep warm and eat your fill,' and yet you do not supply their bodily needs, what is the good of that? So faith by itself, if it has not works, is dead" (Jas 2:14–17). And yet Pauline texts seem to be of a different mind: "To one who without works trusts him who justifies the ungodly, such faith is reckoned as righteousness" (Rom 4:5). "If it is by grace, it is no longer on the basis of works, otherwise grace would no longer be grace" (Rom 11:6). "We know that a person is justified not by the works of the law but through faith in Jesus Christ"

(Gal 2:16). "For by grace you have been saved through faith, and this is not your own doing; it is the gift of God—not the result of works, so that no one may boast" (Eph 2:8–9).

The fifth-century collision of Augustine and Pelagius opened new questions concerning the righteousness of which these and other texts speak. The debate that ensued culminated in the Council of Orange (529 CE). While coming short of an unqualified acceptance of all that Augustine maintained, Orange does loudly condemn Pelagius. It declares that the whole human being—"both body and soul"—and the whole human race have been corrupted by sin (canons 1, 2, and 15); that without exception any movement of prayer, will, desire, or assent in the direction of God is the work of the Spirit's prevenient grace (canons 3–8, 14, and 23);[2] that any holy work at any stage of one's life is the gift of God for which no one can take credit (canons 9–11, 16–18, 20, 22, and 25); that salvation itself does not grow from what *is* ("nature"), but is the coming of the free mercy of God (canons 19, 21, and 24).[3]

It is unclear how much of an impact Orange had upon subsequent theology or even the extent to which it was known. The positions it takes do, however, indicate something of the trajectory of medieval doctrine.[4]

2. Canon 6 is particularly strong: "If anyone says that God has mercy upon us when, apart from [God's] grace, we believe, will, desire, strive, labor, pray, watch, study, seek, ask, or knock, but does not confess that it is by the infusion and inspiration of the Holy Spirit within us that we have the faith, the will, or the strength to do all these things as we ought; or if anyone makes the assistance of grace depend on the humility or obedience of [the human being] and does not agree that it is a gift of grace itself that we are obedient and humble, [she] contradicts the Apostle who says, 'What hast thou that thou hast not received?' (I Cor. 15:10)." The "Council of Orange," in Leith, ed., *Creeds of the Churches*, 39.

3. The conclusion of Orange begins with these words: "The sin of the first [human being] has so impaired and weakened free will that no one thereafter can either love God as [she] ought or believe in God or do good for God's sake, unless the grace of divine mercy has preceded [her]. We therefore believe that the glorious faith which was given to Abel the righteous, and Noah, and Abraham, and Isaac, and Jacob, and to all the saints of old, and which the Apostle Paul commends in extolling them (Heb. 11), was not given through natural goodness as it was before Adam, but was bestowed by the grace of God. And we know and also believe that even after coming to our Lord this grace is not to be found in the free will of all who desire to be baptized, but is bestowed by the kindness of Christ . . ." Ibid., 43–44.

4. Pelikan, *Christian Tradition*, 1:329–30; 2:81.

Even late medieval nominalists, so often laid into by their Protestant progeny, wanted above all to affirm the priority of God's good favor. It is, however, with Martin Luther that the tensions that play between grace, faith, and works come most radically to light.

Luther gives a vivid account in the year before his death of what he regarded as the moment of the radical transformation of his life, of the irruption into his soul of God's liberating grace thirty years earlier.[5] He had before understood God to be an angry autocrat that demands that the lonely sinner rise by her own power to meet the conditions by which her soul, otherwise damned to hell, might be granted a heavenly salvation. He found that no matter how hard he tried, these were conditions that he was unable to meet. Hatred rose in him, he tells us, and cut two ways—toward himself and toward God. In the midst of mutilating anxiety, Luther, by his own account, came suddenly to a revolutionary belief that salvation is not the result of good deeds or good intentions, that is, good works, but is the gift of the Spirit who moves through one's soul in the shape of a very personal and radical trust in *God's* faithfulness.[6] Although certainly what he maintains does not abandon human embodiment,[7] Luther makes very clear that the question of grace, faith,

5. That a story which is staged in an individual's inner life has been received with such affection and excitement for so long indicates how much Luther's offspring have longed for privacy—and that long after the passing of Luther's world, a world in which Luther's story was not and could never be private.

6. Luther puts it this way: "I could not believe that [God] was placated by my satisfaction. I did not love, yes, I hated the righteous God who punishes sinners . . . Nevertheless, I beat importunately upon Paul at that place . . . At last by the mercy of God, meditating day and night, I gave heed to the context of the words [of Rom 1:17], namely, 'In it the righteousness of God is revealed, as it is written, "He who through faith is righteous shall live."' There I began to understand that the righteousness of God is that by which the righteous lives by a gift of God, namely by faith. And this is the meaning: the righteousness of God is revealed by the gospel, namely, the passive righteousness with which merciful God justifies us by faith, as it is written, '[The one] who through faith is righteous shall live.' Here I felt that I was altogether born again and had entered paradise itself through open gates. . . . And I extolled my sweetest word with a love as great as the hatred with which I had before hated the word 'righteousness of God.' Thus that place in Paul was for me truly the gate to paradise." Luther, "Preface to the Complete Edition of Luther's Latin Writings," 11–12.

7. For example: "[F]lesh, according to Paul, as also according to Christ in John 3 [:6f.], means everything that is born from the flesh, i.e. the entire self, body and soul, including our reason and all our senses. . . . The term 'spirit' applies to a person who,

and works is to be situated in one's own soul. Further, however alien Christ, as God's righteousness, continues to be, by grace I come to be his and he comes to be mine.[8] It is not enough that Jesus died. Jesus must have died *pro me*.[9] No work, no desire, no will can bring this about. It must come freely, from an insuperably free Spirit.

Even apart from their function in the legal restraint of the destructive personal and social forces of sin and the manifestation on the way to salvation of our powerlessness before the righteous wrath of God, works have a place of honor in Luther's theology.[10] However, even here they are secondary. Grace alone saves through the dawning of a faith that from the beginning is distinguished from works. Works flow gracefully from a believing heart. And as much as they are acts of utterly other-regarding love, their battleground—no less than the battleground of faith—is where God has touched *my* soul.

It is in the context of this history—from Augustine through the Reformers—that the theology of John Wesley is commonly considered. It is not just because Wesley was born into and nurtured by the century of "the self" *par excellence* that his theology seems so oriented to the "I." The history of the doctrine of salvation in which he is so versed seems anchored there as well. But something else opens in Wesley that breathes a different air.[11]

---

in thought and fact, lives and labours in the service of the spirit and of the life to come." Luther, "Preface to the Epistle of St. Paul to the Romans," 25.

8. "Therefore through the first [alien] righteousness arises the voice of the bridegroom [Christ] who says to the soul, 'I am yours,' but through the second [proper righteousness] comes the voice of the bride [the believer] who answers, 'I am yours.'" Luther, "Two Kinds of Righteousness," 89.

9. "I believe that it has now become clear that it is not enough or in any sense Christian to preach the works, life, and words of Christ as historical facts, as if knowledge of these would suffice for the conduct of life. . . . Rather ought Christ to be preached to the end that faith in him may be established that he may not only be Christ, but be Christ for you and me, and that what is said of him and is denoted in his name may be effectual in us." Luther, *On Christian Liberty*, 30.

10. For example: "Our faith in Christ does not free us from works but from false opinions concerning works, that is, from the foolish presumption that justification is acquired by works." Ibid., 65; see 33–74 for an extended discussion of the role of works in "Christian liberty."

11. And it can be argued as well that this, too, is no novelty, that such a space, such

Wesley's theology is slippery; it tends not to stay put where we would expect it to. Even where we would predict that Wesley would least tolerate interruption—for example, when he is working out the way by which the particular human being comes to salvation—aporias rise up. Wesley engages them, of course; but he does so by thinking in unexpected and multiple directions, as if his logic were not uniform, hierarchical, and linear, but a complex root system growing through rich, if rocky soil.[12]

Thus according to his account, from the beginning every particular human being is in herself utterly ruined by the fall, dead to God, a child of the devil, able only to sin, that is, to reject God's grace.[13] She is laid hold of by the Spirit of God, who awakens her: impossibly and through a painful struggle, she is opened to her own desperate position and of God's sovereign love for her; that is, she is brought to the Christ, hanging powerlessly on the cross on Good Friday, redeemed on Easter Sunday morning. She is carried here, and in this space she is carried farther; through confession, repentance, and faith she moves out into the capaciousness of holiness, renewed in the image of God. Wesley, the great advocate of human responsibility, Wesley, the Arminian,[14] finds that the coming of salvation is wrapped in a mystery that no intent theological gaze can master even by the most complex idea.[15] In a sermon on Philippians 2:12–13 ("Work out your own salvation with fear and trembling; for it is God that worketh in you, both to will and to do of [God's] good pleasure"), Wesley writes this:

air, such breathing were already all over traditional soteriology, but unperceived by thinkers paralyzed under the heavy weight of modern foundationalism.

12. See, e.g., Wesley's procedure in "The Scripture Way of Salvation," in *WJW*, 2:155–69.

13. Wesley, "Original Sin," in *WJW*, 2:172–85.

14. It is important to remember that when Wesley calls himself an Arminian he is affirming both his discontinuity from and continuity with Calvinism. Though he denies such characteristically Calvinist notions as unconditional election, he affirms the sovereignty of God's grace in all human righteousness, particularly that of the event of faith. See Wesley, "What Is an Arminian?," in *WJW*, 10:358–61.

15. "It is hard to find words in the language of [human beings] to explain 'the deep things of God.' Indeed there are none that will adequately express what the children of God experience." Wesley, "The Witness of the Spirit, I," in *WJW*, 1:274 (I.7); cf. 276 (I.12).

The meaning of these words . . . removes all imagination of merit from [the human being], and gives God the whole glory of [God's] own work. Otherwise we might have had some room for boasting, as if it were our own desert, some goodness in us, or some good thing done by us, which first moved God to work. . . . The expression ["worketh"] is capable of two interpretations, both of which are unquestionably true. First, "to will" may include the whole of inward, "to do" the whole of outward religion. And if it be thus understood, it implies that it is God that worketh both inward and outward holiness. Secondly, "to will" may imply every good desire, "to do" whatever results therefrom. And then the sentence means, God breathes into us every good desire, and brings every good effect.[16]

There is tension here. Wesley really means that God is sovereign in all that salvation entails, even when it must be said that human beings are active participants in that salvation.[17] Unlike Luther, who can speak of faith, hope, and love as the Spirit's flowing through the human being as through a "pipe," Wesley thinks of them much more as the Spirit's engagement of the actions and passions of the human being.[18] And yet every righteous event in every human life is graced, is God's work; it has no impermeable boundary around itself and certainly no center in itself.[19] The deed I perform is concomitantly and more significantly *God's* deed. Grace opens the human in a gratitude that cannot find in

16. Wesley, "On Working Out Our Own Salvation," in *WJW*, 3:202–3 (I.1–2).

17. And it does seem that the Protestant discussion both of monergism and of synergism does not help one understand Wesley at this point. Whether the Orthodox use of the term *synergism* is helpful is yet to be decided. In any case Wesley does not play a "zero-sum game," he is not thinking of the work of God and of our work as making up two fractions the sum of which is the total work of salvation. Were it possible to quantify the work of salvation (and it is not), it would all be God's.

18. For a twentieth-century account, not unlike Wesley's, of the relation between human action and divine grace, an account that is worked out in contrast to Luther's position, see Barth, *CD* IV/2, 752–83.

19. These two sides—the human and the divine—are particularly affirmed in Wesley's sermons, "Witness of the Spirit, I and II," in *WJW*, 1:267–98.

the human being itself a ground for boasting.[20] The in-spiration of the Spirit is an invitation to an ex-spiration of thanksgiving without which the soul would suffocate.[21]

Furthermore, from its beginning, this way of salvation entails bodily life, the life in which one is acted upon and performs acts of response. Grace is always the immediate work of the Spirit of God. However, it comes to bodies entangled in a bodily world, a world not only of subtle thoughts and softly spoken words, but also of backs and hands and bellies, of the beaten and the exhausted and the hungry. Therefore, the Spirit comes to us calling us not out of embodiment, but to it. The *immediacy* of grace, that is, comes through certain very worldly *means*. And as if to deny our lust to know good and evil, Wesley says that God uses means with no inherent spiritual status. They are means of grace only because they are specifically ordained by God as such, they are *made* to be the site of grace, that is, from the outside.[22] We in turn are called to "wait" for God here.[23]

20. Thus it is passive and active at once, a deed received.

21. "Now one who is so born of God . . . , who continually receives into [her] soul the breath of life from God, the gracious influence of [God's] Spirit, and continually renders it back; one who thus believes and loves, who by faith perceives the continual actings of God upon [her] spirit, and by a kind of spiritual re-action returns the grace [she] receives in unceasing love, and praise, and prayer; not only 'doth not commit sin' while [she] thus 'keepeth [herself],' but so long as this 'seed remaineth in [her] [she] cannot sin,' because [she] is a child of God. . . . [We] learn . . . [that] the life of God in the soul of a believer . . . necessarily implies the continual inspiration of God's Holy Spirit: God's breathing into the soul, and the soul's breathing back what it receives from God; a continual action of God upon the soul, the re-action of the soul upon God; an unceasing presence of God, the loving, pardoning God, manifested to the heart, and perceived by faith; and an unceasing return of love, praise, and prayer, offering up all the thoughts of our hearts, all the words of our tongues, all the works of our hands, all our body, soul, and spirit, to be an holy sacrifice, acceptable unto God in Christ Jesus." Wesley, "The Great Privilege of Those Who Are Born of God," in *WJW*, 1:435–36, 442 (II.1, III.2). Theodore Runyon notes that "the Oxford English Dictionary traces its definition of *reaction* ('the influence which a thing, acted upon or affected by another, exercises in return upon the agent, or in turn upon something else') to this use in Wesley." Runyon, *The New Creation*, 237 n. 26.

22. "There is no *power* in this [that God uses as a means of grace]. It is in itself a poor, dead, empty thing: separate from God, it is a dry leaf, a shadow." Wesley, "The Means of Grace," in *WJW*, 1:396 (V.4); see Runyon, *The New Creation*, 62–64.

23. "We know this salvation is the gift and the work of God. But how . . . may I

Wesley's 1781 sermon, "On Zeal," situates the means of grace among a complex of practices that he sharply contrasts with those of the politics of perverse religious power that in recent centuries had torn Europe apart.[24] He knows quite well that it is a short step from excitement to aggression and from aggression to violence. And so, he knows that it is crucial to clarify the distinctive character of the zeal he understands the gospel to be about. In doing so, Wesley portrays the holy life as a life that is pierced more and more by God's love and in response is more and more given away to others.

Thus, a pattern emerges in Wesley's account of Christian zeal. Holy, humble, meek, patient zeal occurs in the specific form of the church, "the entire, connected system of Christianity."[25] The church in turn—*qua* church—gives itself to certain works of piety and mercy, hoping not in its own effectiveness but in God's love, ordering itself wisely, that is, in accord with what God calls good. And in everything the church loves: "Christian zeal is all love. It is nothing else. The love of God and [human being] fills up its whole nature. . . . True Christian zeal is no other than *the flame of love*."[26] The church occurs, because the energy of a graced life cuts outward to God and to those whom God has always already loved. Indeed, the church is nothing but the societal energy of graced life, that mutually provocative gathering of the gifted, of those who are to be given away:

> The several parts of [the church] rise one above another,
> from the lowest point, "the assembling ourselves together,"
> to the highest, love enthroned in the heart. . . . [God] saw
> "it was not good for [human beings] to be alone," even
> in this sense, but that the whole body of [God's] children

---

attain thereto? If you say, 'Believe, and thou shalt be saved,' [one] answers, 'True; but how shall I believe?' You reply, 'Wait upon God.' 'Well. But how am I to wait?' . . . According to this, according to the decision of Holy Writ, all who desire the grace of God are to wait for it in the means which he hath ordained; in using, not in laying them aside." Ibid., 383 (II.7), 384 (III.1).

24. Wesley claims that since the Reformation, forty million people have died as a result of perverted religious zeal. Wesley, "On Zeal," in *WJW*, 3:310 (§1).

25. Ibid., 312 (II.1–3), 314 (II.6).

26. Ibid., 312 (I.2–3).

should be "knit together, and strengthened, by that which every joint supplieth."[27]

That is, Wesley's account of the patterns of zeal does not drop a private individual onto a field where lonely spiritual exercises are to be performed. Even when his rhetoric is the most personal, it never calls for privacy. As love grows in intensity in "that one" (as Kierkegaard might say), it is the church—where "that one" acts and is acted upon—that is zealous. And so, when Wesley places zeal for the church at the lowest level of his taxonomy, he is not relativizing the church's significance.[28]

It is because Wesley holds that different kinds and different degrees of intensity are called for in response to God's grace that God has formed the means of grace into a certain pattern.[29] Those committed to the church are first to give themselves to works of piety, to open to God's Spirit through prayer, Scripture reading, and the Eucharist. These are the means of grace Wesley mentions specifically in his 1746 sermon on the subject, and they are obviously important to him.[30] However, Wesley

27. Ibid., 314 (II.6), 318 (III.7); see Maddox, *Responsible Grace*, 202.

28. Though he does not speak explicitly of care for the church as such as a means of grace, insofar as there is no faithful act, however subtle, that is not ecclesial, it is fair to use the term here, too.

29. It is because there is a kind of system of priority to what God has ordained that it can be said that we are to be more intensely given to certain actions than others. That is, it is simply *better* to be zealous for some matters than for others; and it is better, because God "sees" it to be better, is more "pleased" with it: "Hence also we learn . . . that [true zeal] is always exercised . . . 'in that which is good,' so it is always *proportioned* to that good, to the degree of goodness that is in its object" (Wesley, "On Zeal," 314 [II.6]). Further: "There is a . . . property of Christian zeal. . . . This we learn from the very words of the Apostle: 'It is good to be zealously affected' (not to have transient touches of zeal, but a steady, rooted disposition) 'in a good thing'—in that which is good; for the proper object of zeal is good in general, that is, everything that is good, really such, in the sight of God." Wesley continues, with questions that suggest that "good" for him implies an order to things: "But what is good in the sight of God? What is that religion wherewith God is always well pleased? How do the parts of this rise one above another? And what is the comparative value of them?" (312–13 [II.4–5]).

30. On prayer, "searching the scriptures," and the Eucharist, see Wesley, "The Means of Grace," 378–80 (III.1–6); 386–89 (III.7–10); and 389–90 (III.11–12), 393–94 (V.1), respectively. Wesley adds fasting to this list at times. See idem, "The Scripture Way of Salvation," 166 (III.9).

maintains that it is, in fact, for "works of mercy"[31] that one is to have a higher degree of zeal. He says:

> Thus should [she] show [her] zeal for works of piety; but much more for *works of mercy*; seeing "God will have mercy and not sacrifice"—that is, rather than sacrifice. Whenever, therefore, one interferes with the other, works of mercy are to be preferred. Even reading, hearing, prayer, are to be omitted, or to be postponed, "at charity's almighty call"—when we are called to relieve the distress of our neighbour, whether in body or soul."[32]

The ecclesial works that rise in intensity through works of piety to works of mercy are to have their open end in grace and what *grace* works.[33] It is because no work is holy unless it stands out into the coming of God's love that promoting "holy tempers" in oneself and in others is to be given the highest priority.[34] There is no righteous deed—whether aiming at one's own piety or the welfare of others—that pushes off from the hard inner ground of the actor. No work of piety, no spiritual excitement, no deep inner sense of the divine, no "religious experience,"[35]

31. These "works of mercy" for Wesley include "[works] such as feeding the hungry, clothing the naked, entertaining the stranger, visiting those that are in prison, or sick, or variously afflicted; such as the endeavouring to instruct the ignorant, to awaken the stupid sinner, to quicken the lukewarm, to confirm the wavering, to comfort the feebleminded, to succour the tempted, or contribute in any manner to the saving of souls from death." Wesley, "The Scripture Way of Salvation," 166 (III.10).

32. Wesley, "On Zeal," 314 (II.9).

33. Ibid., 313–14 (II.5–7).

34. Ibid., 314–15 (II.10): "But as zealous as we are for all good works, we should be still more zealous for *holy tempers*; for planting and promoting both in our souls, and in all we have any intercourse with, lowliness of mind, meekness, gentleness, long-suffering, contentedness, resignation unto the will of God, deadness to the world and the things of the world, as the only means of being truly alive to God." In the light of the role played in Wesley by these tempers and by the "affections," one might think of a similar role played by "passion" in Søren Kierkeegaard. See in particular what Kierkegaard has his pseudonym, Johannes Climacus, say in *Concluding Unscientific Postscript to* Philosophical Fragments, 1:583–84, 610–11.

35. The exceptionally problematic phrase placed here within scare quotes is used in part to call it into question. It could be argued and perhaps should be argued that it is a phrase that can no longer be used without qualification in any Wesleyan discourse

but also no act of compassion is to be left to itself.[36] The sinner saved by grace is gifted by the breath of God's love, a love a-gape concretely to the outside, an open play within the holy life of God. It is precisely because God is love and the call is to be caught up into that love that any work is to be done. The momentum of this call is not finally toward one's own inner life, but outward into God and with God in every direction that God moves. And so, the child of God—gratefully entangled in the church—is poured out to her neighbor and for this reason can only be saddened if the circumstances of life obstruct the concrete, tangible praxis that embodied love desires.[37]

Zeal for God's love excludes the destructive politics of hatred.[38] It has no program, no opinions to push. It has one "foundation": "Jesus

---

that has taken account of the dreadful history of modernity.

36. That none of Wesley's four levels of zeal is a ladder to be kicked down after one climbs up it is clarified by this passage: "In an exterior circle are all the *works of mercy*, whether to the souls or bodies of [human beings]. By these we exercise all holy tempers; by these we continually improve them, so that all these are real *means of grace*, although this is not commonly adverted to. Next to these are those that are usually termed *works of piety*: reading and hearing the Word, public, family, private prayer, receiving the Lord's Supper, fasting or abstinence. Lastly, that [God's] followers may the more effectually provoke one another to love, holy tempers, and good works, our blessed Lord has united them together in one—the *church*, dispersed all over the earth; a little emblem of which, of the church universal, we have in every particular Christian congregation." Wesley, "On Zeal," 313–14 (II.5).

37. Wesley's whole *via salutis* is a double if not a triple movement—simultaneously into the depths of one's heart, soul, mind, and strength and out into the holy God and into those whom God loves. Thus even in the miracle of the repentance that is to accompany justifying faith, one is to *wait actively* upon God. Election to salvation is by grace through faith, for Wesley; however, even this faith is not confined to the privacy of one's inner life. Faith emerges first in an atmosphere of overt action. Thus "fruits meet for repentance" (e.g., the cessation of evil deeds and performance of good deeds) are to occur. In theory the occasion for them may not be given, as in the case of the thief on the cross. However, even then the direction of repentance and faith is always external. Further, overt repentance is not only to occur in the moment one first becomes a child of God. There is also a repentance that is to occur subsequently in the spiritual dynamic that Wesley calls "full salvation" or "entire sanctification." See Wesley, "Scripture Way of Salvation," 162–67 (III.1–13). Here it is quite clear that the centered self is ruptured by embodied grace.

38. Wesley, "On Zeal," 308–11; 315–18 (§§1–4; III.1–6).

Christ and him crucified."³⁹ "Holding fast this one principle, 'The life I now live, I live by faith in the Son of God who loved *me*, and gave himself for *me*'; proportion your zeal to the value of its object." Therefore, "be most zealous of all for *love*, the queen of all graces, the highest perfection in earth or heaven, the very image of the invisible God, as in [us] below, so in angels above. For 'God is love; and [she] that dwelleth in love, dwelleth in God and God in [her].'"⁴⁰ This is a very different politics, a politics of those whose privacy has been transgressed by God's grace and opened to the outside, a politics of active waiting for the freedom of God's love in the means of grace—works of piety, works of mercy, and what finally is the energy of all the rest: works of love.⁴¹

The sociality at play in Wesley's soteriology rises to particular prominence in a brief preface he wrote to a collection of poems and hymns in 1739.⁴² He was worried that a few lines written at an earlier time, when he was under the influence of certain "mystics," might lead readers astray. In an attempt to avoid the erroneous view that salvation is by works, they had opted for a salvation by "virtuous habits and

39. One wonders if "foundation" functions as an appropriate metaphor when one is speaking of the one who is crucified in mid-air.

40. Wesley, "On Zeal," 320–21 (III.12).

41. Wesley lays out his taxonomy particularly succinctly in ibid., 313–14 (II.5): "In a Christian believer *love* sits upon the throne, which is erected in the inmost soul; namely, the love of God and [human being], which fills the whole heart, and reigns without a rival. In a circle near the throne are all *holy tempers*: long-suffering, gentleness, meekness, goodness, fidelity, temperance—and if any other is comprised in 'the mind which was in Christ Jesus.' In an exterior circle are all the *works of mercy*, whether to [human] souls or bodies. By these we exercise all holy tempers; by these we continually improve them, so that all these are real *means of grace*, although this is not commonly adverted to. Next to these are those that are usually termed *works of piety*: reading and hearing the Word, public, family, private prayer, receiving the Lord's Supper, fasting or abstinence. Lastly, that his followers may the more effectually provoke one another to love, holy tempers, and good works, our blessed Lord has united them together in one—the *church*, dispersed all over the earth; a little emblem of which, of the church universal, we have in every particular Christian congregation." More specifically of zeal for holy tempers, Wesley says: "But as zealous as we are for good works, we should be still more zealous for *holy tempers* . . . as the only means of being truly alive to God" (314–15 [II.10]).

42. Wesley, "Preface to the *Hymns and Sacred Poems*," in *WJW*, 14:319–22; see Runyon, *New Creation*, 112.

tempers."[43] Wesley declares that this is no less an error: "the ground of our acceptance is placed [by these mystics] in ourselves. . . . [And yet] neither our own inward nor outward righteousness is the ground of our justification, but the effect of it." The "cause" of our salvation, he says, is "the righteousness and the death of Christ." The condition for receiving that salvation is faith.[44]

Wesley is similarly troubled by the *route* they attempt to take to God. They propose withdrawal from human society "in order to purify the soul." Wesley is adamant:

> [A]ccording to the judgment of our Lord, and the writ-
> ings of his Apostles, it is only when we are knit together
> that we "have nourishment from [God], and increase with
> the increase of God." . . . When [Jesus' disciples] were
> strengthened a little, not by solitude, but by abiding with
> him and one another, he commanded them to "wait," not
> separate, but "being assembled together," for "the promise
> of the Father."[45]

Thus the complete opposite of the teaching of solitude is the teaching of the gospel. "'Holy solitaries' is a phrase no more consistent with the gospel than holy adulterers. The gospel of Christ knows of no religion, but social; no holiness but social holiness."[46]

There is a more extended parallel to this brief preface in Wesley's 1748 sermon on Matthew 5:13–16. His claim there is no less strong: "I shall endeavor to show that Christianity is essentially a social religion, and that to turn it into a solitary religion is to destroy it."[47] His explicit

---

43. Wesley's critique of this view must give one pause as one considers the importance of the notions of tempers and affections in his doctrine of holiness.

44. Wesley, "Preface to the *Hymns and Sacred Poems*," 319 (§2). Note the externality of grace here!

45. Ibid., 320 (§3).

46. Ibid., 321 (§5). And it is for this reason, Wesley says, that we are to work: "And in truth, whosoever loveth [her sisters], not in word only, but as Christ loved [her], cannot but be 'zealous of good works.' [She] feels in [her] soul a burning, restless desire of spending and being spent for them."

47. Wesley, "Upon our Lord's Sermon on the Mount, IV," in *WJW*, 1:533 (I.1).

concern in this sermon is with "externals."[48] That is, "social religion" is that devotion to God that will not stay put in one's private soul, but must always and everywhere move to the outside, to those others whom God loves. And thus the holy life is lived ecclesially and missionally.[49] Of course, Wesley knows that outgoing can also be perverted. However, the holiness he finds all over the life of Christ is a holiness that "puts forth branches." This is a "*sacrifice of our . . . bodies*, which [God] peculiarly claims; which the Apostle 'beseeches us, by the mercies of God, to present unto him, a living sacrifice, holy, acceptable to God.'"[50] In this way one bears witness to Christ.[51]

The complex of ideas laid out by Wesley concerning works—that they are called forth by grace, that they are an active waiting upon grace, that they are works of gratitude and faithfulness and mercy and love, that they take place through the righteousness and death of Christ, that they are social, that they are sacrificial, that they are acts of the body, that they are ecclesial—invite one eucharistically to contextualize those works in a way only softly suggested in his writings. There is no question that the Eucharist is important to Wesley. His sermon "On the Duty of Constant Communion" stresses the importance of entering into this sacrament not only with great frequency, but with constancy, living uninterruptedly from and to the eating and drinking of Christ's body and blood.[52] And there is no question that he himself made his way to the celebration several times a week throughout his life and that the

---

48. Wesley's use of the word "outward" in this sermon is delightfully excessive: he speaks of "outward action" (ibid., 532 [§3]), "outward religion" (532; 541–42, 543 [3; III.1, 3]), "outward things" (541, 543–46 [III.1, 4–6]), "outward obedience" (542 [III.1]), "outward services" (542 [III.1]), "outward works" (543–45 [III.3–4, 6]), "outward commandments" (544 [III.4–5]). This externality—cutting from God's irruption into the "soul"—is precisely being agape, loved and loving.

49. Even though there are indeed to be times of quiet personal meditation, they, too, are to be contextualized within "living and conversing" with others, one's brothers and sisters and one's enemies. Ibid., 533–35 (I.1–4).

50. Ibid., 542 (III.1); emphasis added.

51. Ibid., 541 (II.6). It is perhaps from these views in particular that a Wesleyan articulation of martyrdom might be laid out.

52. Wesley, "On the Duty of Constant Communion," in *WJW*, 3:430 (I.6) and 431 (II.1).

"evangelical revival" in England over which he presided was also a eucharistic revival.[53] However, Wesley's treatment of the Eucharist seldom if ever strays far from the place he has given it among the works of piety. And yet there is a eucharistic *logic* in his theology of works. It is a logic that cuts two ways: out into the life of God, praying in the Spirit through the Son to the Father, and out into the world this God loves, laboring from the Father through the Son in the Spirit. This logic dislodges Wesley's theology from the enclosure of the private self, the individual soul, the "I," and sends it into the space opened by God's love for this world.

In his *Outward Sign and Inward Grace*, Rob Staples has explored the significance of the sacraments for Wesleyan thought and life. He lays out in his chapter on the Eucharist the kinship of Wesley's theology to Calvin's, particularly in their similar understandings of "the real presence" of Christ in that event. Like Calvin, Wesley rejected the Lutheran notion that with his ascension Christ's body came to saturate the whole of creation. Like Calvin, Wesley affirmed that the body of Christ has its place forevermore at the right hand of God the Father in the mystery of heaven.[54] In eucharistic celebration it is the Spirit that unites the celebrant with Christ. This is a trinitary "spiritual presence." One meets the exalted Son in the Spirit, and through the Son worships the Father. This is a "real presence," Staples says, though not one that is fixed geographically, perhaps on a table in a big room. Unlike Calvin, however, Wesley thinks of the real presence of Jesus Christ, Staples says, not primarily as the coming of "power," but as a "divinity" that in that event is bestowed.[55]

> Wesley's view of the real presence is what Borgen calls "dynamic" in that it is related to God's action. "Where God acts, there [God] is." It is "real" presence because it is "living presence." Thus the objective presence of Christ in the supper "cannot be thought of as the static presence of

---

53. See Cummings, "John Wesley and Eucharistic Ecclesiology," 150–51; Maddox, *Responsible Grace*, 202–3; Stoeffler, "Tradition and Renewal in the Ecclesiology of John Wesley," 316; and Runyon, *New Creation*, 128–29, 136–40.

54. Staples, *Outward Sign and Inward Grace*, 221, 226.

55. Ibid., 227.

an object, but rather as that of a living and acting person *working* through the means."[56]

Therefore, Staples calls the Eucharist in Wesley's account the "sacrament of sanctification," the sacrament of the hallowing of life, of a partaking of the divine nature. In it one lives, giving thanks to the holy Trinity;[57] one lives out of the memory of the life history of Jesus;[58] one lives in fellowship with the church;[59] one lives from the coming reign and rule of God;[60] and one lives a martyr's life, with Christ sacrificing all that falls into one's hands to the Father and to those whom the Father loves.[61]

If it can be said that Wesley's theology as a whole is a theology of sanctification, it is also to be said that Wesley's theology as a whole is a theology of the liturgy of the Eucharist. In it there is a spirited call for a prayer and a thanksgiving and a joy that do not cease, an anamnetic journey out into the infinite space of the exalted history of the tortured Jesus, an entanglement in the whole ecclesial network of the body of Christ, a hope in the coming of the holy mystery of God, and the most unrestricted presentation of the body as a living sacrifice out into the agape love of God. Yet to affirm this is to go beyond the explicit account Wesley himself gives of the Eucharist. It is to think of the Eucharist as a *pattern of work*, a faithful entry into God's faithfulness to us in the crucifixion and bodily resurrection of Jesus Christ. It is to think of eucharistic *liturgy* as a gifted entry into the immemorially ancient coming of the Spirit. And yet thinking Eucharist in this way is by no means a violation of Wesley's theology, but is rather a kind of anthology of what Wesley has already given us.

56. Ibid., 227.
57. Ibid., 229–32.
58. Ibid., 232–36.
59. Ibid., 240–43.
60. Ibid., 243–49.
61. Ibid., 236–40.

III. What Might Engage Us in the Face of a Woman Who Stretches Out Her Hand?

There is perhaps nothing more characteristic of the thinking of the present than its *élan* to domesticate human life by means of a logistics of eras. The phrase "the postmodern age" is no less a power-move than is the more blatant "Renaissance" caricature "Middle Ages."[62] When it is not easily dismissed as pathological, what seems ill founded or dis-oriented, excessively heavenly minded or earthy, unbounded or identity-transgressing, fanatical or traditionalist is turned into some instance of a parenthetical phase through which the human race is going. In this way the masters of knowledge can at least put it in its place. Indeed, the era card can be played to trump any suit. And oddly, once this card is played, disregard can wear the clothes of admiration or confraternity. One may even insert oneself imaginatively into a set of parentheses, wearing some designer label with admiring pride: "modern," "postmodern," "progressive," "Wesleyan," "evangelical." An idiosyncratic eighteenth-century theologian, say, or a twenty-first-century philosopher need not be looked in the face. She may well become just one more image, like a cast member in a sitcom that glistens on a television screen.

And indeed, as Jean-Luc Marion reminds us, we are in a day of images, in a television show, twenty-four hours a day, seven days a week. We sit and we watch, as voyeurs.

> A "viewer" [*Voyeur*]: thus is defined the one who, under the most neutral names of "spectator" or "consumer," undergoes, governs, and defines the image [*l'image*]. . . . The viewer watches for the sole pleasure of seeing: thanks to technology, [she] is finally able to succumb without limit or restriction to the fascination of the *libido vivendi*, which was always denounced by the fathers: a pleasure [*jouissance*] of seeing, of seeing all, especially what I do not have the right or strength to see; the pleasure also of seeing without being seen—that is, of mastering by the view [*vue*]

62. The word *Renaissance* is, of course, also a caricature, in this case a self-promoting one.

> what does not return to me without exposing me to the
> gaze of another.[63]

I expect, and the image must meet my expectation, satisfy my *eros*. I fix my gaze on the image, demanding that it return to me what I desire. I recline before it in "respectful veneration,"[64] and it becomes my idol. My response is to conform to that upon which I am fixated, however much it is my own gaze that is reflected by it. "I must constitute myself as an image," Marion writes, "no longer first an image of me, but rather an image of the idol expected by the viewers—an idol of a desire, thus of a voyeuristic gaze."[65]

Not only the brilliant statue of Athena standing forth from her temple on the Acropolis, not only a glistening television star rising and setting upon a liquid crystal display, but also an idea, for example, the idea of "God," may shine before us, like an image upon a mirror that reflects the searchlight of our own gaze.

> When a philosophical thought expresses a concept of what
> it then names "God," this concept functions exactly as an
> idol. It gives itself to be seen, but thus all the better con-
> ceals itself as the mirror where thought, invisibly, has its
> forward point fixed, so that the *invisable*[66] finds itself, with
> an aim suspended by the fixed concept, disqualified and
> abandoned; thought freezes, and the idolatrous concept
> of "God" appears, where, more than God, thought judges
> itself.[67]

The intentionality of consciousness thus makes an ontological move. My vision pierces space and time until it is fixed upon the idol

63. Marion, *Crossing of the Visible*, 50; idem, *La Croisée du Visible*, 91–92; cf. idem, "Blind Man of Silioe," 61.

64. Marion, *Crossing of the Visible*, 60; cf. idem, "Blind Man of Siloe," 65–66.

65. Marion, *Crossing of the Visible*, 52–53; cf. idem, "Blind Man of Siloe," 62.

66. "Term coined by Marion, the *invisable* indicates that which cannot be aimed at or taken into view (from the verb *viser*, to aim at)." Marion, *God Without Being*, 201 (translator's note). More specifically, God is the one at which we cannot aim, the one whom we cannot make the object of our intentionality, our consciousness of . . . It is this invisability that the conceptual idol denies.

67. Ibid., 16

and from the idol it comes home.[68] In the idol I find that for which I am looking. It conforms to my desire and I can now conform to it; and all else is seen in its light. It is as if I reached out to an object and in reaching embraced everything else, the whole network of being.[69]

The *icon*, on the other hand, signifies differently. For Marion one must still think of an intentional gaze, but of one differently convened. It is the icon that *faces* and it is I who am *gazed upon*.

> The icon does not result from a vision but provokes one. . . . Whereas the idol results from the gaze that aims at it, the icon summons sight in letting the visible . . . be saturated little by little with the invisible. The invisible seems, it appears in a semblance (*eikō/eoika*) which, however, never reduces the invisible to the slackened wave of the visible. . . . In this sense, the formula that Saint Paul applies to Christ, *eikōn tou theou tou aoratou*, icon of the invisible God (Col. 1:15), must serve as our norm; it even must be generalized to every icon, as, indeed, John of Damascus explicitly ventures: *pasa eikōn ekphantorikē tou kruphiou kai deiktikē* [every icon manifests and indicates the secret].[70]

68. "The gaze precedes the idol because an aim precedes and gives rise to that at which it aims. The first intention aims at the divine and the gaze strains itself to the divine, to see it by taking it up into the field of the gazeable. The more powerfully the aim is deployed, the longer it sustains itself, the richer, more extensive, and more sumptuous will appear the idol on which it will stop its gaze. To stop the gaze: we could do no better than to say, to stop a gaze, allow it to rest (itself) in/on an idol, when it can no longer pass beyond. In this stop, the gaze ceases to overshoot and transpierce itself, hence it ceases to transpierce visible things, in order to pause in the splendor of one of them." Marion, *God Without Being*, 11.

69. Ibid., 2–3; 217–18 n. 67. Marion is thinking here of the metaphysical idea of God. However, his work is a post-Heideggerian critique of Heidegger. It moves from a critique of the notion of God as *causa sui* through a critique of Heidegger's ontology to an affirmation of one whom no metaphysical gaze can grasp (see 33–37 and passim).

70. Ibid., 17, 202 n. 18.

The icon of the invisible God faces the one with receptive eyes. The icon, the face, is no abstraction, no graspable idea.[71] It is concrete and specific, as specific as is the face of Jesus, a face that does not exclude, but expansively opens to every concrete and specific face. God peers through his face—and because it is *his* face, because he is the one for others, it is to be said that God peers through every face.[72]

But the icon is not an "in itself," a circumscribed identity. "Christ Jesus only comes to earth to glorify the Father and in no way to draw attention to his own glory. . . . The paradox of iconic monstration of the invisible in the visible would allow only the reception of Christ, without the crucifixion for blasphemy."[73] The icon, of course, is there to be seen, with the eyes or with consciousness. However, in the icon it is what is *not* seen and *cannot* be seen that comes to vision. The icon "teaches the gaze, . . . summons the gaze to surpass itself by never freezing on a visible, since the visible only presents itself here in view of the invisible."[74] The *idol* is caught in a loop, going out to return, like Odysseus. Through the *icon* a call irrupts, a call from the unknown, a call that beckons one out into the unknown, into uncharted territory—like the promise that unsettled Abram and took him away from home, never to return.

It is in the icon that the invisibility of God transcends metaphysical presence—*ousia*, being—and, as is declared in the ecumenical creeds, entails rather a *hupostasis*, a *persona*, a "person."[75] We may think of paint on a plane of wood, a painting perhaps of a woman who faces us as she stretches out her hand. Not fixed by the aim of the artist or the art critic, the incarnate face of the Son of God gazes at us in the icon, a face that does not shine from afar on a visual screen. Aesthetics is subjected to crisis. The coming of the iconic gaze is an apocalyptic event, an irruption into the whole realm of being and measure; it is "the pure grace of

---

71. Marion's dependence upon Levinas is evident here.

72. "If [the human being], by [her] gaze, renders the idol possible, in reverent contemplation of the icon, on the contrary, the gaze of the invisible, in person, aims at [the human being]. The icon regards us—it *concerns* us . . ." Marion, *God Without Being*, 19; cf. 21, 23–24.

73. Marion, *Crossing of the Visible*, 57–58; cf. idem, "Blind Man of Siloe," 64.

74. Marion, *God Without Being*, 18.

75. Ibid.

an advent" not held fast within a network of being. The gaze of the face in fact disrupts ontology and provokes a "read[ing] in the visible the intention of the invisible."[76] Thus even a concept might become an icon, if it gives up the pretension of apprehending the divine, if it ceases its intention to measure "God," if it yields to the envisagement that moves toward the thinker in, through, by, and for the face of the Christ—only, that is, if the eyes that hold the concept are opened, "as one opens a body with a knife."[77]

Marion acknowledges that our natural mode of operation is one that is immersed in the waters of being. Human life happens naturally as *Dasein*, as the "place" where the forces of being battle. We find our-selves in fact thankful to being for having granted us all that we are and all that those about us are—as beings. A boundary line is in this way thrown out, encircling every past, present, and future, every here and there. Every region in which the beings of the world are acknowledged is an openness given by being and for being. We fix our consciousness on an entity, but it is elusive being that gives that entity to be fixed, so that in it being is given but not owned.[78] That something different, something not given by being, might break into this realm is impossible by definition. Only a freedom that "does not have to be" might do so.[79] That we fixate on and close to the impossibility of such a "crossing of be-ing," that we do not give ourselves to it with joy, is a sign of the distance of what might come and of our refusal of that distance.

Of course, the mere suggestion of "what crosses being" throws us into confusion. We demand to know what such a thing might *be*. However, no answer will be heard as long as our question demands resolution on our own terms. Nevertheless, if we were to be so bold as to suggest a language of openness to the coming of "the other than being," Marion says, we might venture the word *agapē*.[80] God, we might say, "is"

76. Ibid., 21. "The invisible summons us, 'face to face, person to person' (1 Cor. 13:12), . . . our face as the visible mirror of the invisible. . . . It transforms us in its glory by allowing this glory to shine on our face as its mirror—but a mirror consumed by that very glory, transfigured with invisibility . . ." (22).

77. Ibid., 24.

78. Ibid., 108.

79. Ibid., 138.

80. Ibid., 108–9.

agapē, the love that is free to call into being what is not and reduce to nothing what is.[81]

Marion draws attention to one New Testament passage in particular that articulates the honored Greek word for being, *ousia*. It is the story of the prodigal son, the son who has asked for and received from his loving father what he is one day to inherit, "his" *ousia*. Having received and then squandered this "substance," he returns to his father without demand and finds with surprise that there is no end to the old man's freedom to give, much to the chagrin of the prodigal's older brother, who sees his own inheritance (his own *ousia*) ripped from his hands only to be wasted on his unworthy brother. The father sees differently.

> The father does not see the *ousia* as the sons see it. In it the latter read, according to desire, the object of a possession without concession which abandons every trace of a paternal gift. The father sees in it the gift ceaselessly re-given at a new cost (eventually in forgiveness). Or rather, the father does not see the *ousia*, and indeed the term appears only in the speech of the sons; the father does not allow his gaze to freeze on a transitory term, an idol. . . . The father is not fixed on the *ousia* because with his gaze he transpierces all that is not inscribed in the rigor of a gift, giving, received, given: goods, common by definition and circulation, are presented as the indifferent stakes of those who, through them, give themselves to each other, in a circulation that is more essential than what it exchanges.[82]

81. Ibid., 87–88.

82. Ibid., 99. The passage continues: "The *ousia* is valuable to [the father] only as the currency in an exchange of which it can mark, at the very best, but a moment, an exchange whose solemnity of infinite generosity most often is masked by the title of property. . . . All that is mine is also yours; in other words: nothing becomes *ousia* (as request for possession without gift) amid 'that which' is woven by the invisible tissue of aims that are themselves exchanged in the glances that they cast and return to each other without loss, end, or weariness; as a sign of the gifts, the 'that which' has neither the occasion nor the temptation to make a possession of itself, *ousia* separated, delimited, and given to the possession of a solitary individual. *Ousia* is dispossessed of itself in the infinite exchange of possessives (yours, mine), so poorly named by grammar, since here they indicate only perfect dispossession. *Ousia* appears as such only to the gaze that abandons the admirable exchange of aims enough to freeze on one point

The Father is free in relation to being. The Father in fact requires no ground upon which to balance. What might have been grasped and held and owned is released in a movement of giving that invites a giving response. The gift of the Father itself gifts. To be its recipient is to have been set free to give, to give what one might have claimed as property, as proper to oneself, as one's *ousia*. Thus it must be said that "God [is] love." Saying this, however, is no mean feat. It calls for the gift of one's whole heart and soul and mind and strength; it calls for entry into an event that shakes off the abstraction of every ideology. Such an event is the cross of Christ. Such an entry into it is the church.

If theology is the giving text of the God who [is] love, if it is to be understood as the deed in which the radically free God comes to word in the work of a cruciform people, it therefore occurs as a gift, a gift of joy "played in distance, which unites as well as separates the [one] writing and the Word at hand—the Christ."[83] That is, the word that speaks of the free God speaks from and to the gift in which this God denatures every author from her own authority, her own goods, her own *ousia*. Theology plays in gratitude.

> Theology always writes starting from an other than itself. It diverts the author from [herself] . . . ; it causes [her] to write outside of [herself], even against [herself], since [she] must write not of what [she] is, on what [she] knows, in view of what [she] wants, but in, for, and by that which [she] receives and in no case masters. . . . For theology consists precisely in saying that for which only another can answer—the Other above all, the Christ who himself does not speak in his own name, but in the name of his Father. Indeed, theological discourse offers its strange jubilation only to the strict extent that it permits and, dangerously, demands of its [worker] that [she] speak beyond [her] means, precisely because [she] does not speak of [herself]. Hence the danger of a speech that, in a sense, speaks

that, thus fixed, is forged into an idol" (100).

83. Ibid., 1.

against the one who lends [herself] to it. One must obtain forgiveness for every essay in theology. In all senses.[84]

To bear witness to the inapprehensibility of God, Marion uses the critical trope "G⊘d," bringing the cross of St. Andrew into play as a reminder both of the temptation to idolatry that lurks in every three-letter word, and also of the hope of God's being-surpassing love in the cross and resurrection of Christ.[85]

Such an impossible exercise as theology has a performative site: the body of Christ. Speech here is an act of entry into a history of disintegration. The Christ is poured out to the one he calls "Father," and his Father is poured out to him. Jesus is the Christ as he sacrifices his *ousia* to the one who loves—who loves across the vast distance that separates and binds Father and Son—and Jesus' sacrifice is acknowledged and exalted and filled by his Father's holy love.

> The Servant of Yahweh literally allows himself to be disfigured (shedding [*perdre*] the visible splendor of his own visage) in order to do the will of God (which will appear only in his actions). The Servant sacrifices his visage—he allows the effacement of his "image": "the multitudes were astonished at the sight of him: his form, disfigured, lost all human likeness; his appearance so changed he no longer looked like a man" (Isaiah 52:14; cf. Psalms 22:7). By completely effacing the glory of his own image, to the point of obscuring even his humanity, the Servant allows nothing other than his actions to be seen:[86] these result from obedience to the will of God and thus allow it to become manifest. . . . In fact, it is precisely at the moment that he loses his human appearance [*figure*] that Christ becomes the figure of the divine will: in him, it is no longer his hu-

84. Ibid., 1–2.

85. Ibid., 46–52. The cross of Saint Andrew is shaped differently than the cross of Christ, "because it is believed that Saint Andrew, at his own request, was crucified on this form of cross, counting himself not worthy to die on the same kind of cross as his Lord. It is said that, while dying slowly on it, he continued to preach to those around him." Stafford, *Christian Symbolism*, 69.

86. One might add "and his being acted upon." See Frei, *Theology and Narrative*, 36–37.

man appearance [*figure*] that is imagined [*se figure*]; and shedding appearance, he gives shape [*donne figure*] to a holiness that would have remained invisible without the shrine [*écrin*] (not screen [*écran*]) of his body. When, on the face, it undoes the glory of every image, the body remains what, in obedience to the will of another, shows this other all the more . . . .[87]

Theology is gifted to speak here. And the site of the theology that is as such kenotically self-effacing, "focused on God's holiness," is the eucharistic work of the self-effacing people of this Christ. Theology is done as a liturgical movement. Liturgy is certainly a perceptible display, overflowing with sights and sounds and smells and tastes and textures. And yet in these actions and passions a working class presumes to be given to do all that they do in the person of Christ, to perform the very crucified body of Christ. "Christ speaks in the readings, makes himself seen, touched, eaten, and breathed in his eucharistic body."[88] Here these people pray; that is, gifted, they give themselves to be gazed upon by another, to pour out what they are, "so that in this way might appear the splendor that the eyes can neither hope for nor bear, but a splendor that love—shed abroad in our hearts [Rom. 5:5]—makes it possible to endure."[89]

It is in the prayerful work of these people that the witness to the Christ remains forever unfinished. The open place of the body of Christ is unsurpassable. There is an interminable deferral moving in every theological act. Everything is given specifically in this body, this church: "space: the nations; time: the days." And yet ecclesial movement is not progress; it is open liturgy in an open range "accomplished definitively at Easter," and still "pregnant with a future." It is more than enough for such a bodily witness to turn in its work to the incarnate Word of God, again and again, like a rich young ruler, forever selling his goods, his *ousiai*, giving to the poor, and following the incarnate *hupostasis* of God. "We are infinitely free in theology: we find all already given, gained,

87. Marion, *Crossing of the Visible*, 61–62; cf. idem, "Blind Man of Siloe," 66–67.

88. Marion, *Crossing of the Visible*, 64; cf. idem, "Blind Man of Siloe," 68.

89. Marion, *Crossing of the Visible*, 65; cf. idem, "Blind Man of Siloe," 69.

available. It only remains to be understood, to say, and to celebrate. So much freedom frightens us, deservedly."[90]

Theology occurs on the road to Emmaus. *Our* eyes, too, are unable to recognize the Christ, even when we have sacred texts before us, even when he is walking beside us. It is only in the insuperably new breaking of the eucharistic bread "that the referent in person redoubles, completes, and disqualifies the hermeneutic that we can carry out from this side of the text, through another hermeneutic that, so to speak, bypasses its text from beyond and passes on this side."[91] Indeed, no text can contain him. "He remains outside the text"; he "transgresses the text to interpret it to us, . . . less explaining the text than explaining himself with it, . . . through it . . . ."[92] It is not enough to know, not even to know the sacred Scriptures. All knowing is to be given to that work in which the body of Christ is broken and his blood shed. The attempt to speak of God elsewhere has averted its gaze from the gaze of the infinitely capacious God who comes in Christ. But the theology at work in the broken body of Christ is gifted by the Sovereign and Giver of Life. There is no "meaning" outside of this event to which it is to yield.[93] Of course, this is not to fixate on a metaphysics of the body of Christ as a delineated present reality, as a *res*, a thing. Nor is it to affirm that the collective consciousness of the gathered people is a presence of the body of Christ.[94] It is, however, to affirm that here in this liturgy "the consecrated host imposes, or rather permits, . . . the irreducible exteriority of the present that Christ makes us of himself in this thing that to him becomes sacramental body."[95] In the eating and drinking of this body and blood, one does not assimilate Christ to oneself; one is rather consumed by him and enters into his body, the called—alive with the life of his body, moving with its motion, working with its work.[96] To

90. Marion, *God Without Being*, 158.

91. Ibid., 147; cf. Marion, "They Recognized Him; and He Became Invisible to Them," 149–52.

92. Marion, *God Without Being*, 148.

93. Ibid., 152.

94. Ibid., 163–69.

95. Ibid., 169.

96. Ibid., 179.

do so is to bear witness that the crucified "Jesus [is] Lord": no ordinary declaration, certainly. Indeed, the one who bears this witness in truth has been gifted by an agape love and so is at play in a new creation in which even death is no competitor with new life. To bear this witness is thus already to be a martyr, like Stephen.[97]

IV. What Might Engage Us in the Face of a Woman Who Stretches Out Her Hand?

Bearing witness to Christ is no solitary's display of disembodied abstractions. Bearing witness to Christ is a scarifying script upon the body, a thinking and writing in a fellowship exposed to assault in the postures of prayer. As such, theology is a narrative tempo of an epiktatic martyr-journey into the spacious word become flesh, a deed of worship that is as tangible as bread, as social as the kiss of peace. Alexander Schmemann works this out unrelentingly:

> [Worship is] the public act of the church, in which there is nothing private at all, nor can there be, since this would destroy the very nature of the church. The purpose of worship is to constitute the church, precisely to bring what is "private" into the new life, to transform it into what belongs to the church, i.e., shared with all in Christ. In addition its purpose is always to express the church as the unity of that body whose head is Christ. And finally, its purpose is that we should always "with one mouth and one heart" serve God, since it was only such worship which God commanded the church to offer.[98]

The speaking of God, Schmemann tells us, is nothing if cut off from this public move. To declare the inseparability of the *lex credendi* from the *lex orandi*—the rhythmic deed of belief from the rhythmic deed of prayer—is not to make theology an exercise for the pious heart; it is to place it in the particular pilgrimage of a particular people: what

---

97. Ibid., 197.

98. Schmemann, *Introduction to Liturgical Theology*, 24.

these people do, how these people work. The speaking of God is thus nothing, if excised from its ecclesial tissue.[99]

Indeed, the church itself *is* this liturgy, this work of these people (this *laos-ergon*); it is thus "the *work* of Christ."[100] As such the church is where these people rise to the hope that plays from the creation of the world. This is not simply to repeat the platitude that the church is no building. Of course, buildings are not churches and churches are not buildings.[101] However, neither is the church some Populist Party notion of "the people," some collection of individuals, say, with their own economic interests. The church rather is the *work* of the people, the people of God.

> [Originally the Greek word *leitourgia*] meant an action by which a group of people become something corporately which they had not been as a mere collection of individuals—a whole greater than the sum of its parts. It meant also a function or "ministry" of a [human being] or of a group on behalf of and in the interest of the whole community. Thus the *leitourgia* of ancient Israel was the corporate work of a chosen few to prepare the world for the coming of the messiah. And in this very act of preparation they became what they were called to be, the Israel of God, the chosen instrument of [God's] purpose.[102]

The church, then, is to be understood in terms of the call that collects persons together as this particular people freely and laboriously embodying the passion narrative of the Christ.

> Christ did not establish a society for the observance of worship, a "cultic society," but rather the church as the way of salvation, as the new life of re-created [human being]. This does not mean that worship is secondary to the church. On the contrary, it is inseparable from the church

99. Schmemann, *Eucharist*, 13.

100. Ibid., 77.

101. Schmemann, *Introduction to Liturgical Theology*, 118–21; idem, *For the Life of the World*, 20.

102. Schmemann, *For the Life of the World*, 25.

and without it there is no church. But this is because its purpose is to express, form, or realize the church—to be the source of that grace which always makes the church the church, the people of God, the Body of Christ, "a chosen race and a royal priesthood" (1 Peter 2:9). In fact, . . . [the church] embodies in worship her participation in God's [reign and rule], gives us a glimpse of the mystery of the age to come, expresses her love to the Lord who lives with her, and her communion with the Holy Spirit.[103]

In the work of this people time is gathered together and renewed. All week the people move from and to the celebration that occurs with Easter Sunday. Christ is raised not on the Sabbath, not on the last day of the week—but on a new day that exceeds the old order of a seven-day cycle. Resurrection joy irrupts as the dawning of an unprecedented first day—a first day that will not stand in competition with the old order, but penetrates it, saturates it, and folds it into the new. Thus, this new first day in its relation to the old is also the eighth day.[104] And this is the day of the celebration of the Eucharist, the day in which a peculiar working class enters into the apocalyptic coming of God.

But then this is the whole point: though the Eucharist is celebrated on a *statu die*, though it has its own day and thus reveals a connection with and is set in the framework of time, still this day is not simply "one out of many." . . . [T]his connection of the Eucharist with time emphasizes the eschatological nature of the Eucharist, the manifestation in it of the Lord's Day, the New Aeon. The Eucharist is the Sacrament of the Church. It is the *parousia*, the presence of the Risen and Glorified Lord in the midst of "His own," those who in Him constitute the Church and are already "not of this world" but partakers of the new life of

---

103. Schmemann, *Introduction to Liturgical Theology*, 24.

104. Ibid., 75–80. "The eighth day is the day beyond the cycle outlined by the week and punctuated by the Sabbath—this is the first day of the New Aeon, the figure of the time of the Messiah. . . . This eighth day (coming after and standing outside the week) is also, therefore, the first day, the beginning of the world which has been saved and restored" (77–78).

the New Aeon. The day of the Eucharist is the day of the "actualization" or manifestation in time of the Day of the Lord as the Kingdom of Christ.[105]

The day of the Eucharist is the day of faith, the day that throws together (that is, as *sym-bol*) the unseen and the seen (Heb 11:1).

Therefore if the symbol presupposes faith, faith of necessity requires the symbol. For, unlike "convictions," philosophical "points of view," etc., faith certainly is contact and a thirst for contact, embodiment and a thirst for embodiment: it is the manifestation, the presence, the operation of one reality within another. . . . In it—unlike in a simple "illustration," simple sign, and even in the sacrament in its scholastic-rationalistic "reduction"—the empirical (or "visible") and the spiritual (or "invisible") are united not *logically* (this "stands for" that), nor *analogically* (this "illustrates" that), nor yet by *cause and effect* (this is the "means" or "generator" of that), but *epiphanically*. One reality *manifests* (*epiphaino*) and *communicates* the other, but—and this is immensely important—only to the degree to which the symbol itself is a participant in the spiritual reality and is able or called upon to embody it.[106]

God's future reign and rule are the redemption of time. Therefore, as we enter that coming apocalyptic event in the celebration of the Eucharist, the works of days and hands enter into it too. This is no ethereal shadow play. It is as actual as is the crop that is threatened in every growing season by drought, flood, disease, pestilence, and fire. But it is also as actual as "the *hupostasis* of things hoped for" (Heb 11:1). In the Eucharist our praxis enters God's peace and is sent back into the world alive with the freedom of God's coming glory. "We can therefore say that the symbol [of the Eucharist] reveals the world, [human being], and all creation as the 'matter' of a single, all-embracing sacrament."[107]

---

105. Ibid., 79–80.

106. Schmemann, *Eucharist*, 39.

107. Ibid., 40.

It is thus in the liturgy of the Eucharist that we come to what we are created for: to gather the fruit of the earth and to offer it in adoration to its creator.

> "[The human being] is what [she] eats." With this state-
> ment the German materialist philosopher Feuerbach
> thought he had put an end to all "idealistic" speculations
> about human nature. In fact, however, he was expressing,
> without knowing it, the most religious[108] idea . . . For long
> before Feuerbach the same definition of [human being] is
> given by the Bible. In the biblical story of creation [human
> being] is presented, first of all, as a hungry being, and the
> whole world as [her] food. . . . [The human being] must eat
> in order to live; [she] must take the world into [her] body
> and transform it into [herself], into flesh and blood. [She]
> is indeed that which [she] eats, and the whole world is pre-
> sented as one all-embracing banquet table for [humans].
> And this image of the banquet remains, throughout the
> whole Bible, the central image of life. It is the image of
> life at its creation and also the image of life at its end and
> fulfillment: "that you eat and drink at my table [under my
> reign and rule]."[109]

The church has no sacred function, standing in opposition to the profane.[110] That line of separation is transgressed in Christ's resurrection. The eucharistic liturgy is a gathering of people who *in gathering* bring the "world" with them. Admittedly, in one sense they do leave the world in this journey. The assembly on Sunday is in order to *ascend* to the God who *transcends* all of creation. However, that heavenly "place" to which these people move is more precisely a time, the future full-

---

108. It is curious that Schmemann uses the word "religious" here. Just a few pages later he declares: "Nowhere in the New Testament, in fact, is Christianity presented as a cult or as a religion. Religion is needed where there is a wall of separation between God and [human being]. But Christ who is both God and [human] has broken down the wall between [humans] and God. He has inaugurated a new life, not a new religion." Schmemann, *For the Life of the World*, 19–20.

109. Ibid., 11.

110. Ibid., 16.

ness of time, in which all that will have occurred is glorified in God's embrace. "But [heaven] is not an 'other' world, different from the one God has created and given to us. It is the same world, *already* perfected in Christ, but *not yet* in us."[111] The world as it stands is taken to the world as it is redeemed. The two meet in the glorified Son of God—the deified human temple of God—the pivot upon which the whole liturgical procession turns.[112]

Schmemann's account of the first/eighth day particularizes the time of the world in one day, a day that exceeds and embraces all days. Thus eucharistic liturgy begins when the celebrants get out of bed in their homes.[113] It continues as they trace out a line of movement in their journey to the place of assembly.[114] Their journey eddies as the assembly enters together into the site of Christ's exaltation in heaven at the right hand of the Father.[115] There is no fixation here on what is laid out on a plate or contained in a cup. It is the whole liturgy, embracing as it does the works of every day, that is the eating and drinking of the body and blood of Christ: food, life. "The purpose of the eucharist lies not in the change of the bread and wine, but in our partaking of Christ, who has become our food, our life, the manifestation of the church as the body of Christ."[116]

It is because liturgy is the work of the redemption of the whole of time, of every week and day, that departure from the assembly does not bring the Eucharist to an end. One leaves heaven precisely to enter back into the world.[117] Thus Schmemann's book *For the Life of the World* is

111. Ibid., 42.

112. It is also to be noted, however, that every liturgical move is enlivened by the Spirit to whom the prayer of epiclesis cries out in appeal. There is no liturgy—no journey, no assembly, no entrance—without the Spirit. There is indeed no epiclesis without the prevenience of the Spirit. "The liturgy is served on earth, and this means in the time and space of 'this world.' But if it is served on earth, *it is accomplished in heaven, in the new time of the new creation*, in the time of the Holy Spirit." Schmemann, *The Eucharist*, 218; see also 213, 222.

113. Schmemann, *For the Life of the World*, 27.

114. Schmemann, *Eucharist*, 11.

115. Ibid., 49–50.

116. Ibid., 226.

117. Ibid., 244–45.

a liturgical study guide for Christian mission.[118] The church is sent to embody Christ in time. It does so not by marketing a solution to some speculative question. It offers rather a gift, a gift that can never become someone's private property.[119]

> Christianity was the revelation of the gift of joy, and thus, the gift of genuine *feast*. Every Saturday night at the resurrection vigil we sing, "for, through the cross, joy came into the whole world." This joy is pure joy because it does not depend on anything in this world, and is not the reward of anything in us. It is totally and absolutely a *gift*, the "*charis,*" the grace. And being pure gift, this joy has a transforming power, *the only really transforming power in this world.* It is the "seal" of the Holy Spirit on the life of the church—on its faith, hope, and love.[120]

That is, what the church is sent to offer is Christ, the food of the world. It offers that food not as a product to be owned, but as a life and freedom into which to enter. It is in this sense that the church's mission occurs within the pure gift of the living God—a gift that brings not satiety, but joy. The church goes where life is threatened, taken, undone, and offers itself as the bread of heaven, that is, as Christ is offered. The church is sent to work as God works in Christ. The church is this work.

---

118. Such a mission, Schmemann says, occurs between the times: "We are always *between* morning and evening, *between* Sunday and Sunday, *between* Easter and Easter, *between* the two comings of Christ. The experience of time as *end* gives an absolute importance to whatever we do *now*, makes it final, decisive. The experience of time as *beginning* fills all our time with joy, for it adds to it the 'coefficient' of eternity. . . . 'There is no new thing under the sun.' Yet every day, every minute resounds now with the victorious affirmation: 'Behold, I make all things new. I am the alpha and omega, the beginning and the end . . .' (Rev. 21:5–6)." Schmemann, *For the Life of the World,* 64–65.

119. Ibid., 47.

120. Ibid., 55. Italics in original.

V. What Might Engage Us in the Face of a Woman Who Stretches Out Her Hand?

The church as eucharistic liturgy—as the concrete, temporal movement of a people out into the infinite space opened by the Spirit's resurrection of the crucified one—is work: the ecclesial work of hands and backs, of mothers and day laborers, that is, of bodies. The church is the gathered labor of eating, of life—the dance out into the mystery of the crucified Jesus exalted to the right hand of God the Father, the dance out into the world redeemed in the history of that poor child of Mary. It is a double movement of abandonment of everything that one might otherwise have claimed to have devoured: a hunger and thirst for the God of Holy Week and thus a hunger and thirst for those embraced by that history; a hunger and thirst for the trinitary line of descent and ascent, of ascent and descent, that cuts through the body of Christ and the world his history takes in. It is the agape love of God that makes this cut—that is this cut. The world into which it irrupts is without it a world of closure, injustice, atomization, suffering, death—of disappearance, execution, and torture.

William Cavanaugh's haunting *Torture and Eucharist* speaks to this liturgical movement directly. His case study is Chile in the broken time of the virulent Pinochet regime. General Augusto Pinochet—a self-proclaimed "Christian"—came to power with the declaration that he would right the wrongs of the godless government he had overthrown, that of Salvador Allende, Chile's democratically elected, Marxist president.[121] A nation-state with an atheist order was under Pinochet to be cleansed and transformed into a "Christian" nation-state, in which the church was to have a place, though one cordoned off from the body politic.

The means by which Pinochet carried out this "cleansing" included random late-night arrests ("disappearances"), secret execution, and torture—all on a massive scale, performed with a rigorously programmatic stealth. Life in Chile became a nightmare.[122] Its victims included those

---

121. In Pinoceht's own words: "I am a committed Christian and I pray every day. We must combat communism." Cavanaugh, *Torture and Eucharist*, 72–73.

122. "The following account from a victim . . . is typical. 'I was arrested at about midnight on the 26th of December, 1975. Around 8 civilians arrived at my house, all armed with machine guns and small arms; after searching the house . . . they

who had overtly sympathized with Allende, but in larger numbers those with loose, even negligible, ties to his rule: "members of leftist parties banned by the military Unity coalition, . . . union organizers, church activists, or people involved in grassroots organizations, which often operated under the aegis of the church, . . . those involved in public protests, . . . [and finally] people who were associated with, or could possibly be associated with, any of the above classes of people."[123] Although it might seem that the purpose of torture in particular was to obtain information useful to Pinochet, this was not in fact the case. Interrogation and pain worked together as a single tool of humiliation and control.[124] Questions were asked, but as an act of aggression, of invasive control, of meaning-theft: to force "victims . . . to speak the words of the regime, to replace their own reality with that of the state, to double the voice of the state."[125] And this rape had as its object not only those strapped to the rack; less directly, others living constantly under the uncertain threat of violence were to be drawn silently into the anxious recitation of the language and imagination of the state. The bodies of the people were

---

handcuffed me together with my wife, put tape over our eyes and dark glasses over that. The whole operation was carried out without them identifying themselves at any moment, nor did they show any arrest warrant. We were put into a private car, that is, one without any distinctive marks, and taken to the Villa Grimaldi. They took us out of the car and immediately I was taken to the torture chamber. There they made me undress and with my hands and feet tied to the metal frame of the lower part of a bunkbed they began to apply electric current to me. This is the "grill." During the rest of the night they had me, applying electricity over my whole body, accompanied by blows with sticks, because of which I came out with several fractured ribs. While they applied electricity they threw water on my whole body. It was already dawn when I was taken off the grill and thrown, with my feet and hands chained, on the patio of the Villa. During the day on several opportunities I was again taken to "interrogation," where I was beaten by various men with kicks, fists, and sticks. . . . Until the 31st of December I was taken to "interrogation" every day and every night.' Behind this account stand thousands of similar stories, shocking in their brutality, yet numbing in their bureaucratic precision and repetitiveness." Ibid., 25–26.

123. Ibid., 27.

124. There were "many cases in which a prisoner who had resisted giving a piece of information through the most brutal treatment finally gives in, only to be told by the torturer, 'We already knew.' . . . It is the form of the answer, or the fact of answering, that is of prime importance." Ibid., 28, 30.

125. Ibid., 30.

oppressively disciplined, their work made the work of the nation-state, their reality made its reality.

Pinochet's torture, Cavanaugh says, instituted an unholy rite.

> Torture may be considered a kind of perverse liturgy, for in torture the body of the victim is the ritual site where the state's power is manifested in its most awesome form. Torture is liturgy—or, perhaps better said, "anti-liturgy"—because it involves bodies and bodily movements in an enacted drama which both makes real the power of the state and constitutes an act of worship of that mysterious power.[126]

Torture humiliates; it reduces its victim to "filth." Under a horrific technology of pain, no one fails to strip herself of what is demanded—to "inform," to "confess," to "betray."[127] Friends, family, everyone will be named under unrelenting, isolating violence. And the word heard in response is "you have cut yourself off from your world, you are now utterly alone, putty in our hands." The state thus exercises control, a control that worms its way into everything the tortured might otherwise have been. The victim of torture is alone, a solitary in-dividual, surrounded and upheld by what has become an *almighty* state.[128] "Torture breaks down collective links and makes of its victims isolated monads. Victims then reproduce the same dynamic in society itself, with the net result that all social bodies which would rival the state are disintegrated and disappeared. . . . The key to this project is individualization."[129] By torture—especially in the context of secret arrests in which the state actively "disappears" bodies—social networks are cut into isolated points where once there were intersections. And behold, *the individual is created.* The body is destroyed: it has no word to speak, only barely

126. Ibid.

127. That these are not the words for the speech that a torturer wrests from a victim is clear when the nature of torture is understood. Ibid., 37–38.

128. Quoting a Chilean victim of torture, Cavanaugh writes: "They would say: 'You're dirt.' 'Since we "disappeared" you, you're nothing. Anyway nobody remembers you.' 'You don't exist.' . . . 'We are everything for you.' 'We are justice.' 'We are God.'" Ibid., 33.

129. Ibid., 34.

articulated moans in the mathematical point of what might have been the space of a prison cell, in the abstract instant of what might have been time.[130] The individualization of Chile's citizens was effective, moving with isolating anxiety from the tortured to those to whom she was once related, like rings radiating from the point at which a stone falls into a black lake. Torture is anti-liturgy.

The church hierarchy, at first relieved that an atheist government had been ousted by a "Christian" one, was quickly shocked before the means by which it came to operate; but it could find among its theological resources no way effectively to respond. Cavanaugh maintains that it had already surrendered the body to the nation-state and had left to its own care only a depoliticized "soul." The church was to awaken from this nightmare only by finding once more what it had lost: *the body of Christ.*

Cavanaugh's ecclesiology emerges as the church rises out from under the heel of Pinochet's boot. The theology that had informed ecclesiastical operations in Chile—drawing deeply from the work of Jacques Maritain—was a theology that looked first to the deep inner core of the self and in so doing came subtly to abandon the body. Maritain's theology is neither unreasonable nor strategically apolitical. In fact, Maritain did his work with an eye to social action. That it produced something utterly antisocial, by Cavanaugh's account, is its particular tragedy.[131] Cavanaugh maintains that, though Maritain is no explicit advocate of individualism (indeed he explicitly condemns it), he does distinguish sharply between "the things of Caesar and the things of Christ" in such a way that a depoliticized individualism emerges.[132]

Maritain's distinction between "the spiritual" and "the temporal" is not exactly a dualism, for those who are devoted to the things of Christ also live in and thereby affect the realm over which Caesar rules. A good

130. "Sheila Cassidy, an English doctor who was tortured in Chile, writes of her stay at the Villa Grimaldi, 'It was as though I was suspended over a pit: the past had no relevance and I could see no future. I lived only for the minute that was and in the fear of further pain.'" Ibid., 37.

131. Cavanaugh's account of Maritain's influence on Chilean thought is so well documented that one need not seriously question it. See especially ch. 4 of *Torture and Eucharist*, 151–202.

132. Ibid., 156.

Christian, then, will bring to bear upon this world the righteousness
she has learned in the church, leavening the world, transforming it.
Therefore, a transformative Christian patriotism becomes possible, for
example, in the form of a Christian nationalism, an external loyalty to
one's nation imbued with the spirit of Christ.[133] It is through this indirect means that the church is to make an impact on the state in which it
is placed. The church ministers to the souls of the faithful. The faithful
minister to the state—that is, once they've heard the benediction and
have gone to homes not themselves woven into ecclesial worship.[134]

> [Maritain] sets up the problem such that there is a mono-
> lithic "culture" structured by the state and coterminous
> with the temporal sphere, confronted by a purely spiritual
> "religion" which is the responsibility of the church. Meant
> to be free by essence from entrapment in "culture," yet un-
> able by natural law simply to reject "culture," the church
> is bound to work on "culture" spiritually, to penetrate it,
> transform it, and redirect it toward God.[135]

It is "the individual" with a Christian heart, not the church, who is to be
politically active.

133. Chilean bishops trying hard to speak out against Pinochet's harsh measures
wrote of their loyalty to and love for their country. In the context of the affirmation
that "Jesus was a patriot," they declared that had he been born in Chile, Jesus would
have been "one hundred percent Chilean, in love with our countryside and our history, with our way of being and living, an authentic son of our people and our land."
Ibid., 98.

134. Of course, on rare occasions, the church is to get directly involved in politics;
but "only to remove some obstacle to the spiritual salvation of the individual soul or
the freedom of the church which mystically binds those souls together. . . . However,
for Maritain . . . Christian truth is not directly applicable to concrete problems in the
political sphere." Ibid., 159, 169.

135. Ibid., 165. Maritain's words, as cited by Cavanaugh: "on the plane of the
spiritual, I appear before [others] *as a Christian as such*, and to this extent I engage
Christ's church; . . . on the plane of the temporal, I do not act *as a Christian as such*,
but I should act *as Christian*, engaging only myself, not the church, but engaging my
whole self . . . who by my faith, my baptism, and my confirmation, and insignificant
as I may be, have the vocation of infusing into the world, wherever I am, a Christian
sap" (167).

Maritain understood that the political activity invited by the modern state is often undeniably violent. The task of the individual Christian who has been formed by the church is tragically to enter even into that violence, but to do so with a purity of Christian intention.

> It is clear that force and, generally speaking, what I have called the carnal means of war are not intrinsically bad, because they can be just. . . . The worst anguish for the Christian is precisely to know that there can be justice in employing horrible means. . . . We cannot touch the flesh of the human being without staining our fingers. To stain our fingers [however] is not to stain our hearts.[136]

Of course, those raised on a theology informed by Maritain knew that torture is "wrong," that those who subject other human beings to such violence have thrust themselves deeply into darkness. However, they also "knew" that even the most apparently evil deed—for example, the violence of war—could be justified when placed in the context of the pursuit of a greater good. Thus even those with hands stained red by the blood of their victims were given a theology that permitted them to claim to have unstained hearts. They had entered into darkness that their children and grandchildren might live in the light.

As well-meaning as is the kind of theology given voice by Maritain, its consequences have been so crushing that a radical alternative is demanded. No therapeutic program of soul salvation, however intense and prolonged, can any longer be taken as a doctrine of sanctification that is good news for the victims of torture. What is called for is the body of Christ. A church that has sold its body to the modern nation-state for the sake of the salvation of souls must remember that it is the body that is resurrected from the dead on Easter morning—and it is the body that is gifted by the Spirit at Pentecost.

To understand the church *as body* is to understand the church as a politics, a politics in contradistinction to the politics of torture.[137]

136. Ibid., 170.

137. "First, there are individual, physical bodies, which are never 'just physical,' but are always already invested in certain social performances or practices. Second, there are social bodies, which are more than just groups of individual bodies; rather,

"Torture creates fearful and isolated bodies, bodies docile to the purposes of the regime; the Eucharist effects the body of Christ, a body marked by resistance to worldly power. Torture creates victims; Eucharist creates witnesses, *martyrs*."[138] The church has already fallen when its people think of the body of Christ not as what they themselves enter, but as what they *watch* in the spectacle of the transformation of bread and wine into supernatural things.[139] The eucharistic liturgy is a people gathered into the coming reign and rule of God. It is an entry into the future peace of God. In it one moves in fellowship not simply with those with whom one shares a national or ethnic or civil "identity." One's fellowship is with the categorically irreconcilable, many of whom God will have gathered into the mystery of God's own reconciliation in their poor brother's crucifixion and resurrection.[140] God's peace is the coming peace of all of embodied life. (The Eucharist is not having one's roots ripped out of the earth; it is having one's roots thrust deeply into an earth made new.) Therefore, those who eat the food of heaven are filled with the life that comes to this world, and no loss in this present evil age has the last word. It is the fellowship of the crucified who together are raised to glory. For this reason early Christians readied themselves for martyrdom by the liturgy of the Eucharist.[141]

Here we see clearly that Christian performance of the Eucharist depends on taking quite seriously the designation of the church as the body of Christ; the church's

they are 'bodies' in the sense that they—like individual human bodies—involve the coordination of many different members into certain coherent shared activities or performances." Ibid., 17.

138. Ibid., 206.

139. Ibid., 213.

140. Ibid., 224.

141. Ibid., 224–25. For a stunning account of the continuity between the Eucharist and martyrdom in the early church, see Young, *In Procession before the World*. For example: "[E]arly Christian communities trained for their own, quasi-eucharistic sacrifice of martyrdom and expected it; they did this by imitating examples from life or from literary works; they scrutinized their own behavior for conformity to traditional expectations; they envisioned themselves to be fighting in a cosmic battle upon which hinged the salvation of the world and their own participation in the heavenly court and temple" (2).

performance of self-sacrifice is in fact the "proof" of the presence of Christ in the bread and wine. In order for the church at the Eucharistic table to offer what Christ offered, the church must offer its own self in sacrifice, because the community of Christians is nothing less than Christ's *corpus verum*. . . . One of the peculiarities of the Eucharistic feast is that we become the body of Christ by consuming it. Unlike ordinary food, the body does not become assimilated into our bodies, but vice versa. . . . The fact that the church is literally changed into Christ is not a cause for triumphalism, however, precisely because our assimilation to the body of Christ means that we then become food for the world, to be broken, given away, and consumed. . . . Martyrs offer their lives in the knowledge that their refusal to return violence for violence is an identification with Christ's risen body and an anticipation of the heavenly banquet.[142]

It is the Eucharist, the church's entering into and becoming the broken body of Christ, that keeps it from being "disappeared." The Eucharist disciplines it, teaches its body what the body is to be about, how it is to bear witness to God's gift. The church is the action and passion of "performing the body of Christ," a "Eucharistic 'counter-politics.'"[143]

Chile had become, in the minds of the faithful, coterminous with the people of God. The *souls* of Chileans were nurtured by the institutions of the church, their *bodies* structured and protected by the nation-state. When Allende came to power, that *pax* seemed threatened. Pinochet's victory seemed at first to have been a defeat of the forces of evil. Once more the soul and the body of Chile seemed in tandem to be saved. When the violence of Pinochet's program beat and cut and broke the bodies of the people, there was no physician to give them care. The church had abandoned families and friends and neighbors. It had only an empty word to speak—and that to abstract, private souls. The church found itself to be in complicity with the atomization of its own "mem-

142. Cavanaugh, *Torture and Eucharist*, 230, 231–32.
143. Ibid., 252.

bers"—now no longer the organs in a network of organs, but excised, functionless, rotting masses of surgical waste.

At the moment when those institutions of the church that had served the national order so well were unmasked as the unwitting tools of death and despair, another order came to light, an order that had lain dormant, unheeded, and undone in the institutions of the church all along. And behold, the church came to life again—the life in which persons reduced to the isolation of individuality came once more to labor, to practice solidarity with the body of Christ and with the bodies of those he loves.[144] Eucharistic liturgy, now extending from long before the first word to long after the last word of a Sunday service, worked to "knit the people together."[145] This liturgy was once more performed as the movement of a people out into the exalted history of Christ and thereby out into the suffering lives of those with whom Christ was named. This liturgy was once more the movement of a people out into the bodies of the suffering, the poor, understood and performed as a true entry into the history of Jesus.

> Christ's true body is enacted here by the incarnation of the church in the bodies of the poor. The true body of Christ is the suffering body, the destitute body, the body which is tortured and sacrificed. The church is the body of Christ because it performs an *anamnesis* of Christ's sacrifice, suffering in its own flesh the afflictions taken on by Christ. In the church's communities of solidarity, the poor are fed by Christ but, insofar as they become Christ's body, they also become food for others.[146]

144. "Perhaps the most tangible way in which the church in Chile reappeared under the military regime was through the social program of COPACHI and the Vicariate of Solidarity. Offering a wide range of programs covering legal and medical assistance, job training, soup kitchens, buying cooperatives, assistance to unions and more, these organizations became the focus of church resistance to the regime. 'The church was almost a parallel state. It had its own health clinics, it had its own systems of food distribution.' In a moment when the state had outlawed base-level organizations and was atomizing the body politic, the church provided a space in which organizations could take place and social fragmentation could be resisted." Ibid., 264.

145. Ibid., 267.

146. Ibid.

No longer were a few individuals speaking and acting in outrage against the politics of torture. A whole body of people arose to lay down their lives for the poor and against Pinochet's machine: bishops, priests, laity—not for the sake of a generic "justice," but for the sake of the justice of God. And in the undeniable presence within the liturgical assembly of those who inflicted torture on the very people they were to call brother and sister, who thus violated the solidarity of the church, an anathema was pronounced. The church declared that those who would shatter the ecclesial fellowship by violence were excommunicate, already removed by their own acts. The sham of their bodily presence in the assembly was denounced. They would not be admitted cynically to the celebration of the coming reign and rule of peace.[147]

It is the Eucharist that shows that the separation between the sacred and the secular, the spiritual and the political, the soul and the body, is a lie. When the people of God take eucharistic bread and wine upon their tongues and into their bellies, they announce the coming of their crucified sovereign. It is in amnesia, a dis-membering of the church, that these people do not go with that body and blood to the oppressed. Of course, this is a different politics than that laid out by the modern nation-state. It is not occupying some niche carved out by the principalities and powers of this world. Indeed, the politics of the church is a politics of homelessness, of being in the world and yet always subversively out of place.[148] The politics of the church is a politics of what is to come, of the stigmatized Christ. The church is no static entity located here and now. The church is a texture of performances that an-

---

147. It is important to note that excommunication is taken very seriously by Cavanaugh precisely as an extreme response to a particular pattern of injustice. "My argument that torture, as an anti-liturgy of absolute power which attacks the body of Christ itself, should be met with excommunication is by no means an argument for the use of excommunication in general for other types of sin. This is *torture*, not theft or masturbation. If accepted, my argument would *limit* excommunication, to keep it from being used in the service of right-wing ecclesiastical politics. Furthermore, formal excommunication is not the only key to the church's visibility. It is not so much a solution as a recognition that something has gone terribly wrong. The church's own ecclesiology had contributed to making the Pinochet regime thinkable in the first place." Ibid., 264.

148. Ibid., 268–69.

nounces what is to come. It is alive with the question thrust into the present by the future. Note this:

> The body of Christ is not a perduring institution which moves linearly through time, but must be constantly received anew in the eucharistic action. Christ is not the possession of the church, but is always being given to the church, which in turn gives Christ away by letting others feed on its own body. . . . The Eucharist is therefore an "event" in the sense of an eschatological performance in time which is not institutionally guaranteed, but it is an event which is ontologically determinative; as Zizioulas says, the Eucharist is *"the reality which makes it possible for us to exist at all."* But the Christian in the world is never able to hold onto that reality as something which can be kept. It is not adequately characterized as a "deposit," nor does it produce virtue as a "sediment" in the human soul. Paradoxically, it must be given away in order to be realized.[149]

According to Cavanaugh, the church is a gift of the God who is alive with freedom. The church is no political party, no institution with its center of gravity in itself, no program among programs. It is in fact nothing in itself. It lives by the breath of the Spirit of God, each day gratefully receiving its bread. "Because the church lives from the future, it is a thing that is not. The church inhabits a space and time which is never guaranteed by coercion or institutional weight, but must be constantly asked for, as gift of the Holy Spirit."[150] The church is thus God's "no!" to the nation-state's imagination of violence. In the power of the Holy Spirit the church imagines a different order, one that no nation of violence, by violence, and for violence can excise from the earth. If such imagination is not to be a dream, it must be enacted. The church is not the church unless it bears witness bodily to the Christ. The church is the church only as a cruciform fellowship of martyrs. That is, the way to bear witness to the broken body and shed blood of the Christ in a world

149. Ibid., 269, 270. Emphasis in original.
150. Ibid., 272.

of torture is for the church to place its body—its bodies—in sacrificial solidarity with the suffering, that no one is to be made an isolated thing cut off from fellowship with the body of Christ, that every victim of the violent imagination of the nation-state is to be joined—muscles and blood and skin and bones—with the bodies of the church.

> The true body of Christ disrupts present historical time and opens a new space in opposition to the regime [of torture]. The bodies of those disappeared reappear in the reappearance of the visible body of Christ. . . . Christ's body reappears precisely as a suffering body offered in sacrifice; Christ's body is made visible in its wounds. But this body is also marked with future glory, for Christ has suffered in order to triumph over suffering and defeat the powers of death. The space it creates is therefore a space crossed by the [reign and rule] of God. We witness a liturgical anticipation of the end of history and the resurrection of the body.[151]

Of course, to lay one's body down in this present evil age is to believe that the "reality" of this world is not the truth. No one disciplined by the institutions of this world will come to more than a shadow-conviction by an individual decision of the will. It is the alternative cruciform discipline of the eucharistic church that enacts a different order, that enacts the imagination of the God who raised the tortured Jesus from the dead. Only God's imagination can inspire a martyr-church of the Christ.

> If torture is essentially an anti-liturgy, a drama in which the state realizes omnipotence on the bodies of others, then the Eucharist provides a direct and startling contrast, for in the Eucharist Christ sacrifices no other body but his own. Power is realized in self-sacrifice; Christians join in this sacrifice by uniting their own bodies to the sacrifice of Christ. Christians become a gift to be given away to others. . . . In giving their bodies to Christ in the Eucharist, a confession is made, but it is not the voice of the state that is heard. The torturer extracts a confession of the unlim-

---

151. Ibid., 277.

ited power of the state. The Eucharist requires the confession that Jesus is Lord of all, and that the body belongs to him.[152]

VI. What Might Engage Us in the Face of a Woman Who Stretches Out Her Hand?

God's grace and human faithfulness are thought to conflict only when God and human beings are thought to be in competition with each other. So long as God is placed within a universe of finite resources, any genuinely human act will require God to step back in self-limitation, to leave an energy reserve for humans to use. However, there is no competition with God in any act of human faithfulness. Indeed, the act of faithfulness claims for itself no native power or merit, no ground for boasting. It is only in sin that competition with God is posited. Bathed in the Spirit, alive with God's life in the gratitude that lives and moves in God's grace, one rejoices in God's liberating sufficiency. The God who saves is the God with the power to save, the power to hallow. Such power—which is finally the power of love—does not compete. The mystery of faith is the mystery of the transition from "will not"—and so "cannot"—to "may." One no longer thinks of God and God's relation to the world in the same way. One has undergone a *meta-noia*.

Human faithfulness and works are thought to conflict only when human faithfulness is thought to be a deep inner experience in one's private soul, an experience that is then perhaps to be expressed in some external form. The question then is, isn't faith enough? Why would works be necessary? However, if it is not some soul that is saved, but some-*body*, then everything is changed. If being saved were in some way comparable to what comes on Easter Sunday morning to the Jesus who lay dead in the tomb all of Holy Saturday, then perhaps we should think of it unexceptionably as a bodily event. No less than Adam, no less than Lazarus, no less than Jesus—all dust and ashes at the start of the day—the gifted body of the justified arises to come forth. "Faith without works is dead," because only the dead do not work (and in this sense even the thief on the cross worked in giving voice to the righteousness

152. Ibid., 279.

of his fellow sufferer). What then could Pauline texts mean when in them faith is said not to need works? Simply that it is only in faithful response to the Spirit's coming that a work is righteous. The graced work of faith is *given* to be done. Any other work is a work of death, a work in competition with God, knowing good and evil, aiming to hoard one's own glory, grounded in oneself, the god of one's own universe. And so, in that most apparently works-denying passage—"by grace you have been saved through faith, and this is not your own doing; it is the gift of God—not the result of works, so that no one may boast" (Eph 2:8–9)—the last word is "we are what [God] has made us, created in Christ Jesus for good works, which God prepared beforehand to be our way of life" (v. 10).

Furthermore, the gifting of salvation is the hallowing of our flesh by the coming of the life of the God who is love. To live a hallowed life is to love—not with good intentions, but with hands and backs and blood. To be hallowed by God's love is to give where God gives, to enter God's gift as it assumes vulnerable flesh, to be gifted with the *meta-noia* that is the mind of Christ. This work throws its center outside itself, as Christ threw his center outside himself. The work of love is given to the faces that we meet. A work that might have been one's own is in Christ the work of friends. The work of these people—the called, the gathered, the fellowship of the cross of Christ—is the work "which God prepared beforehand to be our way of life."

And so, Wesley tells us that the gift of God fills our lungs with the breath of life and we are to empty them, breathing words of praise—suffocating without the renewal of God's inspiration. And so, Schmemann tells us that God fills our bellies with the food of life and we are to empty them, performing works of praise—starving without the renewal of God's banquet. And so, Marion tells us that God comes to us in the iconic face of Christ: the one in which are inscribed the faces of those for whom Jesus yielded his breath and emptied his belly. And so, Cavanaugh tells us that we together as a church are to expend our bodies in a worshipful politics of love, giving our bodies to be broken, our blood to be shed—for one another in witness to the One at the right hand of God the Father almighty, the One who is forevermore our cruciform food and drink. And surely when they tell us this they speak the *a-letheia*.

When not solitary selves, not material forms frozen in a photograph, not the completed tasks of a crew of workers, not the good, the true, and the beautiful are saved, but a working body of people gifted in order to be gifted in the work of Christ—then the church emerges. But then the church is nothing but liturgy, the liturgy of the Eucharist.

The narratives of the gospels go to some pains to contrast the holiness of the Pharisees with the holiness of Jesus. The Pharisees in these narratives want no less than Jesus to be holy. They know no less than Jesus that to be holy is to be separate, to be different, to be set aside to the God who is radically other than the ways of this world. Yet the gospels tell us that the holy God to whom the Pharisees give their lives is different from the holy God to whom Jesus gives his life. Jesus proclaims the coming of God. Everything Jesus says and does has the coming of God all over it. And the God Jesus proclaims with his lips and his hands is coming to reign and rule precisely where the Pharisees will not be found: among the poor, the sick, the sinner, the dying, the dead, the damned. Jesus gives his life to the coming God who loves the very world from which Pharisees flee. To be holy according to the proclamation of Jesus is to be separated to God, and with God to be separated to the world.

Since the coming of God is a *basileia*, it is a politics, the politics of God. Where God's holiness is unrestrictedly manifested, where the God who is love is glorified, there is no solitude, no loneliness, no isolation of one body from another. Even the partial and fragmentary manifestation of God's holy love is political in this sense. It is always a sign of pride when the church forgets that it is not identical to "the kingdom of God." It is a sign of faithlessness when the church forgets that it lives from and to God's reign and rule. The church is a narrative politics that bears bodily witness to the story of the passion. Thus, the many are permeable and as such are one body—a work broken together for the life of the world, gratefully trusting in the gift of the Spirit that makes each new breath an occasion for prayerful, joyful, grateful labor.

What if faith had nothing to do with "experience," with the appearance of a phenomenon in the consciousness of an apprehending subject? What if faith were not found anywhere in particular *in me*? What if faith were an entry into something other, something different from and larger than any solitary "I"? What if faith were seeing in the mode of being seen, knowing in the mode of being known? What if faith were the gift of life, of an opening out into a future not to be achieved, but coming—coming for the weak, the lowly, the poor, the sick, the sinner, the dying, the dead, the damned? Then faith would be found among a people who in opening to God are sanctified to open to one another and to those who are not yet among them as good friends—traveling perhaps on the road to Jericho or to Santiago.

What it means to be sanctified is not to be learned by turning one's gaze to some deep, inner "spiritual" datum, some experiential idol. It is to be learned by turning to the broken body and shed blood of Christ, to whom the Spirit bears witness when we are gazed upon, say, by the face of a woman left beaten, broken, tortured in lonely despair—a woman, say, who stretches out her hand.

Part II Creaturehood

4

Holy, Holy, Holy

The World Need Not Have Been[1]

AMONG THE CLEAREST, MOST adamant, and most persistent creedal professions of the church's faith is that there is "one God, the Father, the Almighty, Maker of heaven and earth." Much of this doctrine was in fact inherited, woven as it is within the rich traditions of Israel. From at least the mid-second century, the church has affirmed it with the qualifier *ex nihilo*. It now accompanies readings of the creation accounts of the church's Old Testament as well as the gospels and letters of the New Testament. It is entangled in the apocalyptic vision of "the new creation." It has become all but self-evident to the church that God created everything from nothing.

Things Could Have Been Different

Things might have been otherwise. Genesis specialists frequently tell us that the first verses of the Holy Scriptures teach not *creatio ex nihilo*, but

1. A paper delivered to the forty-third annual meeting of the Wesleyan Theological Society, Duke Divinity School, Durham, NC, March 13–15, 2008. An earlier version of the present essay was first published in *Wesleyan Theological Journal* 44 (2009) 200–218.

God's mastery of preexistent chaos.[2] "In the beginning when God created the heavens and the earth, the earth was a formless void and darkness covered the face of the deep, while a wind from God swept over the face of the waters"—this is the way the NRSV translates Genesis 1:1–2. The church could have left its doctrine of creation there, a more accommodating and certainly less excessive route to take in a world in which both Jews and Greeks were at ease with the idea. Nonetheless, *creatio ex nihilo* may have been a happy doctrinal development, even if we must work hard to remember why. We grow daily more comfortable with one or another version of God as a "fellow sufferer who understands," a God tossed about alongside us in the relentless current of time, a God not wholly unlike us, one with whom we might have a "relationship." *Creatio ex nihilo* seems so "traditional."

Once an idea has been carved into the stone of an institution, it is easy to forget that at one time it was warm and supple and alive. Certainly, even the most morbidly rigid, institutionalized idea can stir to life again, but it is easier to deal with if it does not. And so, the doctrine of creation has often been reduced to a *proposition* to be made a *component* of a *cosmology* in which the idea "world" and the idea "God" drift smoothly from one to the other without interruption. Intellectuals within the church, alongside intellectuals without the church, have offered us new and stimulating ways to think about this world, with all the meaning we have found it to have, as suggesting or implying or demanding an Efficient or Formal or Final or (even) Material Cause, that is, a "God." In so doing, "the Father, the Almighty, Maker of heaven and earth" settles into a universal thought-world, a world in which the broad categories of power, meaning, property, race, class, and gender provide Him or Her or It with a home. And surely a Creator without a home would be much too uncanny, indeed unthinkable.

We read in his *Confessions* that Augustine first embraced the doctrine of creation because the church that taught it had been proven to have authority to declare such truths.[3] And we hear from the textbooks

2. See Brueggemann, *Theology of the Old Testament*, 153, 158, 163–64, 529; but see also Westermann, *Genesis 1–11*, 110.

3. Certainly Augustine had been experimenting with various doctrines of creation for some time before he came to give himself to the authority of the church. However, his concern now is less how he might come to some settled equilibrium

that Augustine was among the first to take up the proposition that God is Creator and make the case that this creation came into being by a creative fiat *ex nihilo*. We read that Augustine thus clenches the idea of divine omnipotence by arguing that a God who holds all the power could not be reduced to a demiurge who merely imposes order on recalcitrant preexistent matter, but rather exerts the authority to call a world into being out of what was unqualifiedly nothing at all.

Augustine does have a passion for rational order and is not embarrassed by propositions in the least. But when he says that the church taught him this doctrine, his words cut two ways. On the one hand, this is a doctrine to be understood. *Fides quaerens intellectum* is an Augustinian quest. But on the other, the church he knows is a people constituted by the grace of an elusive God who keeps them moving on a journey of hope.[4] It is significant that, in the *Confessions*, Augustine is inclined to find in the doctrine of creation a story of how we *in the church* are to live our lives. Much of its closing book is an allegorical interpretation that takes Genesis 1 as counsel to those who struggle to be faithful to God.[5]

(though Augustine does love equilibrium). His concern is now to give voice to the love and gratitude that have come to stir in him. "But now that my groaning is witness that I am displeasing to myself, You shine unto me and I delight in You and love You and yearn for You, so that I am ashamed of what I am and renounce myself and choose You and please neither You nor myself save in You. . . . I call upon Thee, O My God, my Mercy, who didst create me and didst not forget me when I forgot Thee. . . . You had not need of me, nor am I a being so good as to be of any aid to You, my Lord and my God: I do not exist to serve You as though to save You from weariness in action, or that Your power would be less for lack of my service: nor is the cult I pay You like the cultivation of a field, so that You would be the poorer for lack of it: but I serve You and worship You that I may be happy in you, to whom I owe that I am a being capable of happiness." Augustine, *Confessions*, 173 (10.2), 259 (13.1).

4. Augustine, "The Trinity" (Sermon 52), 57 (16): "So what are we to say, brothers, about God? For if you have fully grasped what you want to say, it isn't God. If you have been able to comprehend it, you have comprehended something else instead of God. If you think you have been able to comprehend, your thoughts have deceived you. So he isn't this, if this is what you have understood; but if he is this, then you haven't understood it. So what is it you want to say, seeing you haven't been able to understand it?" He adds a few pages later: "The Lord will be on hand to help; indeed I see he is on hand, from your understanding I understand that he is standing by" (60 [20]).

5. For example: "For among us also God has in his Christ created a *heaven and*

Could it be that even Augustine, the speculative theologian, is in
fact first and last a convert, a brother, a pastor, and a bishop presiding
before a eucharistic assembly, one who will not step outside the liturgy
into which he was baptized, even to conquer the rational schemes of the
civitas terrena, but who wants above all to remember the hope that God
elected not only him, the church in Hippo, Rome, and Corinth, but also
Israel, and most particularly the man Jesus? It is a difficult question to
answer, of course, since there are so many Augustines speaking in that
vast Augustinian corpus. The question is, however, not just a historical
one.

A Particular Story, People, and God

As metaphysically alluring as the doctrine of creation might seem,
thinkers of universal truths must contend with the no doubt faithful
reading that the Old Testament tells "a *particular* story about a *particular* people and their *particular* God."[6] As long as this threefold particularity—of story, people, and God—will not be subsumed under a larger
universality, we who have been trained to think always of the good, the
true, and the beautiful will be tempted to find in it an odd, if not scandalous, way of approaching God the Creator. The particularity of the
story and its people seems at most a preliminary, illustrative step toward
giving notice to all people everywhere to stop and look up to the God *a
se*, who demands adherence to a "truth" without storyteller, geography,
memory, or hope. Otherwise, it would seem that at the very least we are

---

earth, the spiritual and carnal members of His Church. And our 'earth,' before it received the form of doctrine, was *invisible and formless*, and wrapped in the darkness
of ignorance, for *Thou hast corrected man for iniquity and Thy judgments are a great
deep*. But because your Spirit moved over the waters, Your mercy did not abandon
our wretchedness; and You said: *Be light made; Do penance, for the Kingdom of God is
at hand. Do penance, be light made*. And because our soul was troubled within us, we
remembered you, O Lord, from the land of Jordan and from that mountain high as
Yourself but made low for us, and our darkness grew displeasing to us and we turned
our face to You and light was made. *And we were heretofore darkness, but now light in
the Lord*." Augustine, *Confessions*, 265 (13.12).

6. As Seitz puts it in *Word Without End*, 11; emphasis added. The sentence ends
this way: "who in Christ we confess as our God, his Father and our own, the Holy
One of Israel."

left with an implicit henotheism, if not relativism. That is, to persist in speaking of "a particular God" seems unwarranted, irresponsible, and primitive.

Admittedly, "the particular story" of the Old Testament has an eye to "all people." The early chapters of Genesis tell us of God's entry into the space of "humanity as such," that is, *'adam*. And yet quickly "humanity as such" fades from view. "The nations," particular nations, arise, at first with God's blessing, then through disobedience (Genesis 9–11). God responds to their godlessness after the flood with "gracious compassion and forbearance."[7] We learn in Genesis 12 that God comes "to bless" these nations by turning to *one* nation, to Abraham, Sarah, and their descendents. This particular nation is God's *one elect* people, possessed by God, addressed by God through God's law and prophets, the one elect people to whom God is made manifest by God's own particular deeds. The mightiest of these deeds is the exodus of the powerless Hebrew slaves from Egyptian bondage, the deed into which all the narratives of these people lean, even their creation narratives. That is, God's act of self-disclosure to *all* people comes into play in the election of *these* people. It is an event *there*, not elsewhere, and is not to be "abstracted or universalized." To receive God's self-disclosure, "one must be made privy [to it], through adoption or ingrafting."[8]

That is, this one God the Creator has not in this one story simply abandoned those outside this one nation. The Apostle Paul and the prophet Isaiah, for example, both agree that a way is made for Gentiles, too, that they might "grope" after and "find" God (Acts 17:27) where God has elected to come close to them: "God is with you [Israel] alone," the nations will at last say, Isaiah tells us (45:14). Though in their ignorant economic and military might they presume otherwise, it is through *Israel* that the nations, too, will be saved.[9]

7. Ibid., 19.

8. Ibid.

9. Isaiah 45:17–23: "Israel is saved by the Lord with everlasting salvation; you shall not be put to shame or confounded to all eternity. For thus says the Lord, who created the heavens (he is God!), who formed the earth and made it (he established it; he did not create it a chaos, he formed it to be inhabited!): I am the Lord, and there is no other. I did not speak in secret, in a land of darkness; I did not say to the offspring of Jacob, 'Seek me in chaos.' I the Lord speak the truth, I declare what is right. Assemble

As narrow-minded as Isaiah seems, the Paul of Ephesians is more so. "Gentiles" as such, he tells us, are "aliens from the commonwealth of Israel and strangers to the covenants of promise," they have "no hope" and are "without God in the world" (2:11–12). Good news appears here for them, but it carries its own temptation to offense: Gentiles may also enter God's promise, Paul says, but they do so not as a de-particularizing of God's work.[10] Rather, they come to be "*with* God in the world" through the peasant Jesus, through whom they, too, come to the God and Father of the prophets, the priests, and the sages. Bathed in the promises of Abraham, Isaac, and Jacob, of *their* God, Jesus opens to the outside. However, by passing through this narrow gate and down this narrow path, Gentiles break from the promises of *their* ancestors, of their *gods*. "So if anyone is in Christ, there is a new creation: everything old has passed away; see, everything has become new!" (2 Cor 5:17).[11]

---

yourselves and come together, draw near, you survivors of the nations! They have no knowledge—those who carry about their wooden idols, and keep on praying to a god that cannot save. . . . There is no other god besides me, a righteous God and a Savior; there is no one besides me. Turn to me and be saved, all the ends of the earth! For I am God, and there is no other. By myself I have sworn, from my mouth has gone forth in righteousness a word that shall not return: 'To me every knee shall bow, every tongue shall swear.'"

10. Seitz, *Word Without End*, 6, 20, 21: "Paul's point has to do with revelation and election, which becomes adoption for those in Christ. . . . The foundation of the house to which Christians belong remains the witness of the prophets, joined by that of the apostles. 'Prophets' is shorthand for the testimony of God to Israel, by which God's character was once known and is now to be shared with fellow citizens, for their illumination and instruction, now that they have been brought near by Christ. . . . [The] Word made flesh is 'in accordance with the scriptures,' in accordance with the God who calls his elect people, Israel. . . . God is the Holy One of Israel, and his son gives us access to him. The witness to Jesus Christ in the New Testament is joined to the Old as Christ is joined to the Father. . . . [Outsiders] read the Old Testament Christologically . . . acknowledging that what we know of God there is related to what we know of God in Christ, who is our only point of access."

11. Ibid., 26–27: "Not only is our *per se* witness of the Old crucial to our understanding of the New's witness; so too our understanding of the holiness of the Son and the life he calls us to is derived by reference backward to what Israel knew of God in tent, temple, pillar of fire, and cloud. We who stood apart from the law now glimpse there, beyond the veil of our former outsiderness, the abiding theological witness of the Old Testament, a witness to the Holy God of Israel, with whom in Christ we have to do."

Certainly, it becomes new for the Jews, too, but differently (cf. 1 Cor 1:23).

The Holy God Who Is and Comes

The God of Abraham, Isaac, and Jacob is holy. Far from being a kind of deep, self-evident feeling of the numinous proper to human consciousness as such, this holiness *has to be made known.* The children of Israel are the elect people, only because it *has* been made known to *them.* To them the holy God has come no longer simply to be "other." They have been invited *in.* Daily life is interrupted, work stopped, productivity called into question, a Sabbath declared.[12] "You shall be holy to me; for I the Lord am holy, and I have separated you from the other peoples to be mine" (Lev 20:26). For every nation outside the elect people, God *is* simply other. God need not have come alongside Israel, but God *is* alongside them (cf. Deut 7:6–8). Thus it has *come to pass* that these people know the holy God. Their neighbors do not.[13]

Though it might have been otherwise this one God comes *here,* precariously here, no doubt, but here nonetheless. God is not *simply* here, of course. God *comes* here by the holy word of manifestation, a word that may be withdrawn (cf Ps. 28:1).[14] It is the one holy God who

---

12. "Observe the sabbath day and keep it holy, as the Lord your God commanded you. . . . Remember that you were a slave in the land of Egypt, and the Lord your God brought you out from there with a mighty hand and an outstretched arm; therefore the Lord your God commanded you to keep the sabbath day" (Deut 5:12, 15). Brueggemann, "The Book of Exodus: Introduction," 679–80, writes: "This God, however, is not casually or easily available to Israel, and the emerging problem is to find a viable way in which to host the Holy. . . . [The Book of Exodus makes] the poignant claim that Israel is a profound *novum* in human history. It is a community like none that had yet been—the recipient of God's liberating power, practitioner of God's sovereign Law, partner in God's ongoing covenant, and host of God's awesome presence. This astonishingly odd community is, of course, made possible only by this incomprehensible God who dares to impinge upon the human process in extravagant and unprecedented ways (see 36:16)."

13. Seitz, *Word Without End,* 22–23.

14. Ibid., 23: "God is holy. For this reason he guards his character, revealing it only to an elected people, and therefore that people is charged and held accountable for infringement against God's holiness in a direct sense, while the nations experience

is to have priority in all the actions and passions of these people, and only subsequently and dependently may *they* be said to be holy. They are what they are, only because God has spoken. Even their leaning into God's word entails their holiness only secondarily, only as an obedience that refuses to take credit. "Do not presume to say to yourselves, 'We have Abraham as our ancestor'; for I tell you, God is able from these stones to raise up children to Abraham," John the Baptist says with the traditions of his people (Matt 3:9). Thus, the holiness of Israel is a gift and a command.

Far from being a proprietary identity, holy election is an occurrence, an occurrence that is to *recur*—to recur in memory and hope. The celebration of the Passover rehearses the elective coming of the one God to this one people. In an annual celebration of Passover, one lives the event, however far away entropic chronology might insist one is from it. "When your children ask you in time to come, 'What is the meaning of the decrees and the statutes and the ordinances that the Lord our God has commanded you?' then you shall say to your children, 'We were Pharaoh's slaves in Egypt, but the Lord brought us out of Egypt with a mighty hand'" (Deut 6:20–21). *We* were slaves. The one God brought *us* out of Egypt. That is, *we* are elected even now by God's good pleasure. *We* are to be holy, for God is *this* holy God, the God whom the nations do not know, the God whom we know only because this God has heard *our* cry (cf. Exod 3:7–9).[15]

It is no mean task to be a holy people, step by step in everything to depend on the freely electing God, to live a life of purity, justice, wisdom, and hospitality. Not only might one fall prey to faithlessness; even

blessing and curse in some more indirect sense. . . . Strange as it may seem, Balaam's ass and Cyrus the Persian have more in common than either do with Israel."

15. Brueggemann, "Book of Exodus," 684–85: "Because this text [i.e., Exodus] refuses to remain 'history,' but insists on contemporary liturgical engagement . . . [even in our time] hearers of this text [may be] like youths entering into the Passover liturgy and hearing with our own ears the wonder of God's power over Pharaoh. Or we are like children in a ritual of covenant renewal, watching again the frightful theophany, frightened to death, hearing the law proclaimed afresh, claimed in innocent obedience. Or we are like children dazzled by the 'pattern of presence,' free to imagine how the glory comes and where it dwells, in our midst. Then, upon hearing the wonder of liberation and the poignancy of the law proclaimed, and being dazzled by the presence, we break out in an innocent *Te Deum*, when it is all 'finished' (39:32; 40:33)."

under the best of circumstances, encounters with the holy God may in fact be profoundly hazardous. Thus, even Abraham, the father of faith, bold to speak to God on behalf of Sodom, does so with humble obeisance: "I who am but dust and ashes" (Gen 18:27).[16] Moses shudders before the flaming bush as God speaks: "And Moses hid his face, for he was afraid to look at God" (Exod 3:6). Isaiah 4 imagines the chosen people purified "through blasts of burning justice"[17] and made holy, set apart from the corrupt, unjust, and unresponsive people the holy God has justly ravaged. It is, however, Isaiah 6 that most comes to mind, a chapter in the story of an elect people in grave peril, because they have not been faithful to their task.

Isaiah enters the temple that sits high on its mountain above an unjust nation. He, too, one of these faithless people, is thus unclean, thus unholy. The seraphs covering their faces and feet and flying above him shout, "Holy, holy, holy is the Lord of hosts; the whole earth is full of his glory" (6:3). The temple shakes and is filled with smoke, as above Isaiah the electing, holy God sits enthroned. Isaiah, no less shaken, in terror, cries out, "Woe is me! I am lost, for I am a man of unclean lips, and I live among a people of unclean lips; yet my eyes have seen the King, the Lord of hosts!" (6:5).

The shout of the seraphs is particularly excessive. It would have already been a superlative had they announced that the sovereign is "holy, holy," that is, that this God is in every way other. The trisagion, however, goes beyond this. God's difference—God's difference from the gods, and especially God's difference from *this* unholy nation—is focused and intensified beyond limit: "You who are to be holy, you who have forsaken your promise, you will now see what it is to encounter the holy God!"[18]

---

16. When Sodom's outrages persist, it becomes clear to the hearer of the tale just how bold Abraham was: "Abraham went early in the morning to the place where he had stood before the Lord; and he looked down toward Sodom and Gomorrah and toward all the land of the Plain and saw the smoke of the land going up like the smoke of a furnace" (Exod 19:27–28).

17. This is R. W. L. Moberly's translation of Isaiah 4:4; see his "'Holy, Holy, Holy': Isaiah's Vision of God," 124.

18. See ibid., 126–28. Isaiah "now sees himself as being at one with the people of Israel as 'unclean' (*tame'*), a condition far removed—perhaps as far removed as it possibly could be—from that of holiness" (127–28).

When the prophet's lips are by a burning coal made pure, and they open to speak the trisagion with the seraphs, he has not had an "experience," but has been made something he was not before. He now takes in the very word of God—a call he hears spoken directly to him, a call to a task to which he gives himself: "Whom shall I send, and who will go for us?" His response, "Here am I; send me!" (6:8), signifies that Isaiah has undergone an "unreserved reorientation of his life in relation to God." He steps into God's call, gifted with boldness to live and speak "both *from* God and *for* God."[19] He is told by God, "Go and say to this people: 'Keep listening, but do not comprehend; keep looking, but do not understand.'" He is told to "stop their ears and shut their eyes," so that as they are, they will be thrust back, bewildered (6:9–10). In this call and response, Isaiah recapitulates the election of the nation and voices God's rage toward the nation commanded once more to be the people who remember and hope for the coming of the holy God. Having himself been purified by fire, his task is similarly to confront the nation with a strange prophecy until a purifying fire burns it—as a tree is burned, and burned again, its smoldering stump now a "seed" that is to grow into the nation it all along was to be, unreservedly given to the one electing God.[20]

Holiness is "narrow and is difficult to walk as a razor's edge."[21] One—people or prophet—walks it borne from the outside, by gift and

---

19. Ibid., 130–31.

20. This is Moberly's argument ("'Holy, Holy, Holy,'" 132–40). He says this of the destiny of Israel (135–36): "Israel is understood to be the offspring of YHWH (Isa. 1:2, *banim*), and so in some way partakes of the nature of the divine parent, in this instance in terms of holiness. The problem, however, is that Israel fails to realize in its life that which it intrinsically is through its generative divine vocation—it fails to live in a holy way, as its God is holy (cf. Lev. 19:2). Israel has become unclean (Isa. 6:5), and so needs God's purifying fire to engender holiness. . . . [Because] YHWH is holy, and because Israel is intrinsically holy, but fails in practice to be holy, the text pictures purification as in effect also intrinsic to the relationship between YHWH and Israel, and as such a potentially unceasing process." Surely that Israel's holiness is an event dependent on the call of the holy God means that it is not "intrinsic" to Israel, but rather to the call as the word of God.

21. The Katha-Upanishad epigraph from W. Somerset Maugham's *Razor's Edge*: "The sharp edge of a razor is difficult to pass over, thus the wise say the path to Salvation is hard," is rephrased and put in the mouth of a Tibetan monk as "The path to salvation is narrow and is difficult to walk as a razor's edge." *Razor's Edge*, directed by John Byrum.

command, by wind and fire. It is never the property of the chosen, because it is in the end only the one God who without qualification is holy. The holiness that comes to earth—to Israel—comes out of nowhere as freely as an act of election, as freely as the irruption of the countenance of One terrifyingly other who will not be appropriated or assimilated, as freely, that is, as an act of creation.

The Electing and Creating God

It is not surprising that Israel came to believe that this mighty, holy God, is the Creator. The ancient Near East was awash with accounts of gods making worlds. Israel's discourse, however, has significance within its larger testimony to the concrete and practical faithfulness of God to these people.[22] That is, there is no departure from the narrative logic of particularity as Israel articulates its "creation faith." It, too, emerges from its primal testimony that God has *elected* Israel and is thus *its* Maker (see Isaiah 43). It is a rhetorical move that rises in the strength and magnitude of a *hope* that would counter and exceed the strength and magnitude of the forces that are bent on *crushing* its hope. Thus, it is not surprising that the mode of speech that announces that Yahweh is Creator "is *exuberant and effusive*, . . . doxological and lyrical," a testimony that "refuses to be restrained, but must be cut free to match the subject of extravagance."[23] The testimony that God created and creates does not extrapolate from inexorable, extant cosmic patterns. This testimony certainly remembers what was and is. There is nothing that it must forget, nothing that it must not see. However, it is to a future that cannot be seen, one that is not, one that no past or present could make, that its testimony points, even as that future is declared to be congruent with God's liberating work long ago.

It is in the Isaiah of the exile that God is most forcefully announced in the Old Testament to be Creator. In bondage to an overwhelming alien power, threatened by despair, the Hebrew children are tempted to run to the gods of Babylon, who had so effectively swept them into

22. Brueggemann, *Theology of the Old Testament*, 149.

23. Ibid., 157. He continues: "It is most likely that these utterances are situated in liturgy, so that they are utterances in the construction of a contrast-world . . ."

Babylon's tight grip. From all immediate appearances, the God of Israel had failed to withstand their onslaught. Yet, flying in the face of obvious facts, a word rings out in Isaiah "that Yahweh is stronger than the Babylonian gods, and therefore that Israel's capacity for liberated action is stronger than the restraining coercion of the Babylonian regime."[24] It is out of this audacious hope, woven as it is upon an audacious memory, that the prophet cries out that *Yahweh*—the God who elected the slave forebears of *these* slaves—is Creator. That is, this conquered people, raised on the story of the God who had chosen them, the God who will fight for them, hears their prophet announce that Yahweh alone is Creator and that all others are sham gods. Thus, the day is coming when Babylon and its wooden idols will be shattered by Yahweh's hand. The Maker of heaven and earth is the Maker of Israel, to whom this God is abundantly faithful.[25]

> Thus says the Lord to his anointed, to Cyrus . . : I will go before you and level the mountains, I will break in pieces the doors of bronze and cut through the bars of iron . . . For the sake of my servant Jacob, and Israel my chosen, I call you by your name, I surname you, though you do not know me. I am the Lord, and there is no other; besides me there is no god. . . . I form light and create darkness, I make weal and create woe; I the Lord do all these things. Shower, O heavens, from above, and let the skies rain down righteousness; let the earth open, that salvation may spring up, and let it cause righteousness to sprout up also; I the Lord have created it. Woe to you who strive with your Maker, earthen vessels with the potter! . . .Thus says the Lord, the Holy One of Israel, and its Maker: Will you question me about my children, or command me concerning the work of my hands? I made the earth, and created humankind upon it; it was my hands that stretched out the heavens, and I commanded all their host. (Isa 45:1–2, 4–9, 11–12)

24. Ibid., 149–50.

25. Ibid., 149–51. "This God created not only heavens and earth, as the other gods could not; this God created Israel as a special object of Yahweh's attentive faithfulness" (151).

The God who elects Israel and therefore calls heaven and earth into being is the God who has ordered Israel's life covenantally and therefore orders the cosmos covenantally. The entire world is gifted; because gifted, it is to be grateful; because grateful, it is to be merciful.[26] And yet this is not just any order, an order, say, of cause and effect, an order that clever men have the power to exploit. God elected Israel when it was a stranger in a strange land. In electing Israel God has sided with the stranger, the oppressed, the hungry, the prisoner, the blind, the bowed down, the widow, and the orphan, that is, with the poor. The proclamation (for example, in Psalm 146) that God has created this world signifies that every event, far from being an empty act of sheer divine power, is for the very ones whom the wicked, who hoard power, would bring to ruin.[27]

In the opening of Genesis, a narrative to be imagined within Israel's liturgical life and in the light of Isaiah's stunning creation prophecies, God creates *freely*. God does not by a cosmic battle wrest control from some cosmic insurgent, but moves without obstacle or distress, step by effortless step from the work of the first day in verse 1 to the Sabbath moment of the seventh day early in chapter 2. The Sabbath is inscribed into the texture of the world, but precisely as the seventh day set apart week after week, weeks now set apart, too, for these holy people. Gifted by the God who creates without anxiety, creatures, too, are destined to live without anxiety, to work all week long in anticipation of the liturgical moment that acknowledges overtly that to be is to let one's full weight come down into the hands of the God before whom there is nothing to lose or win.[28] The creation of rocks, trees, quarks, and quasars has its theological significance in the memories and hopes of these people of promise. It may come to have another kind of significance, as well, if contextualized, for example, in the troubled dreams of a eu-

26. Brueggemann, *Theology of the Old Testament*, 157–58.

27. Ibid., 155.

28. Ibid., 153–54: "This Sabbath rest is ordained into the very fabric and structure of created life. But even if Sabbath is thereby given cosmic significance, the observances of the day of rest still remain concretely and precisely a Jewish enactment, whereby Jews in Babylonian exile (and in every other circumstance) visibly and publicly distinguish themselves from a world that is too much given to the power of restless anxiety and control."

genesis of dominion that haunt the dark night of modern technology. But the testimony that the God of the story of Israel is Creator calls into question this and all other images of creation.

A Truly New Creation

God's holy declaration, "you are mine!"[29] directly determines the particularity of the people of Israel, their story, but especially the particularity of the God who elects these people. It is *this* God, not Baal or Ishtar, who has laid claim to them. It is to *this* God that they are to give themselves and not to another. It is *this* God who made them, who otherwise were no people at all. It is in the consciousness of the predictable devastation of *this* people in Babylon that the doctrine of creation is worked out in Isaiah and in its train in Genesis. In the end, the God who made Israel is the God who, against all odds, will deliver Israel. Such a God has sovereignty against which no king, no military power, no empire, no *chaos* can prevail. Such a God has a sovereignty that without effort may and does create heaven and earth. It is in the face of obviously irresistible necessity that the political resistance literature of creation emerges among an oppressed people. Could there ever be a more excessively radical doctrine?

Without explicit reference to the creation of the universe, Paul sternly counsels members of the Corinthian church engaging in factionalism, closed circles jockeying for positions of superiority over one another. It is explicitly in view of the crucifixion of Christ that he speaks (cf. 1 Cor 1:23; 2:2): "God chose what is low and despised in the world, things that are not, to reduce to nothing things that are, so that no one might boast in the presence of God. He is the source of your life in Christ Jesus, who became for us wisdom from God, and righteousness and sanctification and redemption" (1 Cor 1:28–30). Using similar language while slowly moving to declare again the grace of God in Christ, Paul speaks to the Romans of the way Abraham, open to a future held inscrutably in God's hands, trusted God's promise to make of him a mighty nation, that is, trusted before "the God . . . who gives life to the

29. Cf. God's designation of the Hebrew slaves in Egypt in the narrative especially of Exodus 8–9.

dead and calls into existence the things that do not exist" (Rom 4:17). Paul continues: "Therefore his faith 'was reckoned to him as righteousness.' . . . It will be reckoned to us [as well] who believe in him who raised Jesus our Lord from the dead . . ." (Rom 4:22, 24). 🗸

When we remember the way Isaiah's soteriological vision grows and intensifies to give voice to a vision of God's unrestrained creation of the world, we may begin to hear in these Pauline passages, which continue to live in the story of Israel, the hint of that most interruptive of creation pronouncements, namely, the *creatio ex nihilo*. Israel in Babylon faced a chaos that *threatened* its very existence. Jesus, the elect of the elect of God, *was*—the definiteness of the past tense must not lose its force—*was* reduced to *nothing*. "For our sake he was crucified under Pontius Pilate; he suffered death and was buried," as the creed puts it. This is a dense and grave event. The living body that had healed the sick and raised the dead was *an-nihilated* on the cross; the dead weight of a lifeless corpse hung limply in its place.[30] The entombed carcass of Jesus was not a latent potency waiting to be drawn to some proper entelechy. It was devoid of all "can"—in relation to the living Jesus, a pure nothing.

What comes out of the tomb on Easter Sunday morning is not Jesus-revived, but a new creation, out of nothing. He is Jesus, certainly, the son of Mary, the Nazarene peasant, the itinerant Jewish wonderworker and prophet. And yet he has come to be this by an act that irrupts into what could never have yielded it. Resurrection is God's creative deed. In it the apocalyptic sovereignty of God transgresses every cosmological, ontological, and theological limit. The world is made anew when Jesus walks out of the tomb.[31] In him everything begins again. "So if anyone is

30. Wolff, *Anthropology of the Old Testament*, 106–7: The dead are "beings who have been expelled from Yahweh's sphere of influence. . . . In the world of the dead, Yahweh's work, Yahweh's proclamation, and Yahweh's praise no longer have any place. . . . This definition of death in the Old Testament is of fundamental importance for the understanding of the death of Jesus in the New. Jesus dies a completely and utterly untransfigured—indeed a radically profaned—death. Here too every nimbus is completely missing. He dies man's most horrible death and is thus present for man in the midst of complete alienation from God."

31. "Thus it is written, 'The first man, Adam, became a living being'; the last Adam became a life-giving spirit" (1 Cor 15:45).

in Christ, there is a new creation: everything old has passed away; see, everything has become new!" (2 Cor 5:17).

Jesus is reduced to nothing by the principalities and powers that hold us in their grip, like slaves held in Egyptian bondage. Jesus is reduced to nothing by the calculative powers for which "justice" means getting even, the ones for whom *shalom* is written off the ledger by a *pax* of indifferent tolerance enforced by the threat of violence. Jesus is reduced to nothing by the ideologies that keep us apart, that make strangers, widows, orphans, and the poor, the ideologies that rise to heaven to keep "the good" safe by excluding "the evil." Jesus is reduced to nothing by the architects of a future that builds on a settled past, those who know, like the board of a world bank, how to turn a profit before mountains of debt, the forgiveness of which would constitute a leap into the abyss of certain economic ruin. Jesus is reduced to nothing by the same death-dealers who break the backs of the inefficient, the insufficient, the unproficient, the deficient—the "least" whom the champions of progress recognize intuitively as the sisters and brothers of the Jesus whose body they break and throw into the ditch with theirs. When this Jesus is created anew, he emerges from the depths of the darkness into which they have plummeted—made the redeeming, justifying, reconciling, forgiving sacrifice by which God has entered into creative, life-giving solidarity with the children whose dead bodies cry out mutely from the grave.[32]

Jesus, crucified and raised, is the particular, human—all too human, all too particular—locus of God's creation of all things. In his crucifixion and resurrection are simultaneously the *nihil* and the *creatio* of every event of heaven and earth. Nothing is left out of this fiat. This is the manifestation of the mystery hidden "from the foundations of the world" (cf. Col 1:26).[33] There is nothing more primal, nothing "prior to" this event. There is before it no chaos, no prime matter, no simple physical feelings; indeed no *khora*. There is only "Christ and him crucified" (1 Cor 2:2) and the *Spiritus Creator* who raises him from the dead.

32. Cf. Gorringe, "Atonement," 363–76.

33. For this important phrase, "from/before the foundation [*apo/pro katabolēs*] of the world," cf. Matt 13:35; 25:34; Luke 11:50; John 17:24; Eph 1:4; Heb 4:3; 9:26; 1 Pet 1:20; Rev 13:8; 17:8.

With the history of the elect people of God all over him, this elect one, this "slaughtered Lamb," this "Lion of the tribe of Judah, the Root of Jesse," opens to take in all things (Revelation 5). He is capacious enough to hold the whole universe. Everything is created through him (John 1:3), in him, and for him (Col 1:16). This is not a theory that has some degree of certainty or probability, which a good argument might make compelling. It does indeed call for a re-pentance, a *meta-noia*, that is, an overflow of mind, but one that is an act of the body.[34]

> Do you not know that all of us who have been baptized into Christ Jesus were baptized into his death? Therefore we have been buried with him by baptism into death, so that, just as Christ was raised from the dead by the glory of the Father, so we too might walk in newness of life. (Rom 6:3–4)

The nothing that swallowed him swallows us all: "hardship . . . distress . . . persecution . . . famine . . . nakedness . . . peril . . . sword . . . we are being killed all day long; we are accounted as sheep to be slaughtered" (Rom 8:35, 36). A radical newness occurs as his resurrection opens into us all and into all the worlds we presume to inhabit.

The *creatio ex nihilo* that emerges from the story of Jesus is political resistance literature, even more so than Isaiah's. In the face of the Empire and its Whore, of Roman military might and its economic system,[35] this doctrine is bold to say that *nothing* "will be able to separate us from the love of God in Christ Jesus our Lord" (Rom 8:39).[36] Indeed, this is a

34. "I appeal to you therefore, brothers and sisters, by the mercies of God, to present your *bodies* as a living sacrifice, holy and acceptable to God, which is your spiritual worship [*logikēin latreian*]" (Rom 12:1).

35. See Bauckham, *Theology of the Book of Revelation*, 35–36.

36. Gorringe, "Atonement," 376–77: "The cross began as a political symbol and remains one. In a world where the poor are routinely sacrificed on the altars of corporate capital, it speaks of the once-for-all abolition of all sacrifice; in a world where the poor are disproportionately imprisoned and executed, it calls all judicial punishments into question; in a world of manifold alienations, it is a standing proclamation of the possibility of reconciliation; in a world dominated by the powers, it continues to provide, as it did for the first-century communities, a critique of their delusionary assumptions. In this sense it is possible to agree with the ancient tradition of the church: *Ave crux, unica spes.*"

creation that embraces all those who had been, but whom death would consign to oblivion. When Jesus is created out of nothing, there are in his resurrected body the faces and bodies of harlots and slaves; the thief on the cross; the Gadarene demoniac; the peasant girl Mary; the woman with an issue of blood; the Syro-Phoenician woman; Jairus's daughter; Rahab, Tamar, Ruth, and Bathsheba; Moses and Elijah; Abraham, Isaac, and Jacob; and Adam (cf. Matthew 1 and Luke 3). Indeed, "before Abraham was, I am" (John 8:58). Jesus is the creative Word God speaks that calls all things into the light and life of an insuperable future that irrupts into and beckons from the foundations of the world. "In the beginning was the Word, and the Word was with God, and the Word was God. He was in the beginning with God. All things came into being through him, and without him not one thing came into being. What has come into being in him was life, and the life was the light of all people" (John 1:1–4).

Christ carries the elect people with him through a breach in the dividing wall that would have kept them and him separate from outsiders. That wall is breached by an act of God, when the crucified Jesus is raised. There is no loss of particularity here. The particular story of the particular people and their particular God is still remembered and recited, but now within the particularity of the story of one human being, Jesus, the Messiah of Israel (cf. Mark 15:32). Just as God freely elected the people of old, God has freely elected Jesus and all those entangled in his story: a story of a Jew entangled with Greeks, a free male entangled with slaves and women (cf. Gal 3:27–29). This is an act the mystery of which remains elusive even as it is revealed: here in particular *Deus Revelatus* is *Deus Absconditus*. There is about it a love that is neither sentimental nor impulsive. It is love as creative fiat, the fiat in which what is in every respect other than the living God, including that which *is not*, is addressed: "you are mine!"[37] Because the *creatio ex nihilo* of Good

---

37. Burrell, *Faith and Freedom*, 137–38: "Our temptation . . . will be to model [God's free act of creation] after a *decision*, or what is even more banal, a *choice* among 'possible worlds.' . . . Our freedom, of course, includes the possibility of refusing to acknowledge and to pursue that discerned good, and to that extent answers to a 'libertarian' paradigm. But to refuse is to fail, and it should count decisively against a libertarian account of freedom that it would propose a failure as the very paradigm of a free act. Again, what Aquinas' cryptic reference to the creator's inner Trinitarian

Friday and Easter Sunday embraces difference without indifference, it is an act of reconciliation—between us and God, and thus between us and all those entangled in the body of the resurrected Jesus, that is, the crucified Jesus in whom God embraces us all (cf. Rom 5:8–11).[38]

It is in the liturgical life of the church that the doctrine of creation has significance. In the baptismal waters we who had claimed to *be* have been reduced to nothing in solidarity with Christ; but we emerge from those waters as new creatures in a new creation. Week after week we are fed on the broken body and shed blood of Christ. This is "heavenly food," of course, saturated by the resurrecting vitality of the Spirit. And yet it has about it the scars of crucifixion. To eat and drink this food is to live in the glorious moment of the one unprecedented creation which has called into "existence the things that do not exist" (Rom 4:17). It is in the memory of the particularity of the election of Israel, of Jesus, and of those who have been, are, and will be baptized into his body that the church invokes "before the moment of eucharistic unveiling what the seraphim exclaim in Isaiah's temple vision: 'Holy, Holy, Holy, Lord God of Hosts, Heaven and Earth are full of thy glory' (Isa 6:3)."[39] The holy God who shatters the wooden idols of Babylon and calls heaven and earth into being is in Christ the God before whom not even the *nihil* of godlessness is to be locked outside. In the end, the God who made and delivered Israel is the God who, against even possibility, made and delivered Jesus, reached into the pit and pried him from the grip of death and damnation. Such a God has a sovereignty against which no king, no military power, no empire, no grave, no *nothing* can prevail. Such a God has a sovereignty that without effort may from nothing create (a new) heaven and (a new) earth.

God's holy declaration, "you are mine!" directly determines the particularity of the people of the body of Christ, and thus of the God who calls out to them, even when the scent of death exudes from their

---

life suggests is that creating is a fully gratuitous act, operating out of a fullness that needs no further completion. . . . What proves significant here is the way in which this presumption is shared by Jewish and Muslim thinkers as well. . . . [Thus] the Qur'an's repeated avowal: 'God said "be" and it is' . . ."

38. God "is the source of your life in Christ Jesus, who became for us wisdom from God, and righteousness and sanctification and redemption" (1 Cor 1:30).

39. Seitz, *Word Without End*, 24.

bodies. It is to *this* God that they are to give themselves and not to any other. It is *this* God who made them, who otherwise were no people at all, and before whom they are to cast the crowns of their inevitability. It is *this* holy, holy, holy God who creates in Christ (whose body they have been given to enact) a world that need not have been, *but was and is and is to come*—by the boundary-shattering mercy of One whom only those created *ex nihilo* will ever know in their bones to be love.)

> And the four living creatures, each of them with six wings, are full of eyes all around and inside. Day and night without ceasing they sing, "Holy, holy, holy, the Lord God the Almighty, who was and is and is to come." And whenever the living creatures give glory and honor and thanks to the one who is seated on the throne, who lives forever and ever, the twenty-four elders fall before the one who is seated on the throne and worship the one who lives forever and ever; they cast their crowns before the throne, singing, "You are worthy, our Lord and God, to receive glory and honor and power, for you created all things, and by your will they existed and were created." (Rev 4:8–11)

5

Homo Precarius

Prayer in the Image and Likeness of God[1]

Nearly all the wisdom we possess, that is to say, true and sound wisdom, consists of two parts: the knowledge of God and of ourselves. But while joined by many bonds, which one precedes and brings forth the other is not easy to discern.[2]

—John Calvin

Theology is anthropology.[3]

—Ludwig Feuerbach

How Majestic Is Your Name in All the Earth!

It is interesting that we *homo sapiens*—we who claim to have risen beyond the earth from which we were scraped, who claim to be so discern-

1. A paper delivered to the thirty-first annual meeting of the Wesleyan Theological Society, Wesleyan Theological Seminary, Washington, DC, November 1–2, 1996. An earlier version of the present essay was first published in *Wesleyan Theological Journal* 33 (1998) 128–50.

2. Calvin, *Institutes of the Christian Religion*, 35 (I.1.i).

3. Feuerbach, *Essence of Christianity*, xxxvii.

ing, so wise—it is interesting that we who know so much know so little about ourselves. And yet we want to know; and despite the shortness of our reach, despite the emptiness again and again of our hands, we grope for the slightest trace of what it might be that makes us—makes me and you—distinctively human. It is a kind of preoccupation that we have, and have had especially since the time of that Königsberger, Immanuel Kant (1724–1804). But we have always (as far as our backward self-scrutiny can tell) wanted to know who we are; and we have always, even if secretly, wanted to know that we are not to be taken lightly—not by Trojans, not by seductive sirens, not by the strong men of Ithaca, not by Poseidon. Is it any surprise, then, that when we come upon Genesis 1:26–27 at the very beginning of our holy book, we straighten up and take notice? "And God . . ."—"God," who has just called the universe into being merely by the force of a word, "God" who is sovereign over light and darkness, waters and sky, earth and world, and the living things that move where these contend—"And God said, 'Let us make humankind in our image, according to our likeness . . .'"[4]

Indeed, we have not only taken notice, we have read this passage with great energy, struck as we have been by its unusual import. We have read it and read it and read it and, when our various interpretive labors have been done, we have found and brought to one another not the same meaning or even a complex unity of harmoniously different meanings, but a welter of often conflicting ones. Claus Westermann counts altogether nine different prominent interpretations of Genesis 1:26–27.[5] Which is it? Does this verse affirm that human being as such is

---

4. "Since biblical interpretation came in contact with Greek thought and the modern understanding of humanity, scarcely any passage in the whole of the Old Testament has retained such interest as the verse which says that God created the person according to [God's] image. The literature is limitless. The main interest has been on what is being said theologically about humankind: what is a human being? What is striking is that one verse about the person, almost unique in the Old Testament, has become the center of attention in modern exegesis, whereas it has no such significance in the rest of the Old Testament and, apart from Ps 8, does not occur again." Westermann, *Genesis 1–11*, 148.

5. Ibid., 148–58. These are not all mutually exclusive. At times the same writer will put two or more of them together. However, there is a diversity here that itself speaks of the difficulty of reading this little verse.

God's representative, viceroy, vizier, attorney in this world?[6] Or is it that "image" here is a more pointed power-term, indicating human exercise of "dominion," as Genesis 1:28 says, over the rest of God's creatures?[7] Or is the divine image a kind of minimal "natural" similarity to God that is to be distinguished from a loftier *supernatural* divine likeness that was added to it in our first parents?[8] Or is the image the "spiritual qualities or capacities" that make us humans at least relatively unique, capacities such as freedom, personality, understanding, self-consciousness, intel-

---

6. Ibid., 153–54. Westermann deals very seriously with this view, noting that there is considerable evidence that the phrase "image of God" occurs in the broader world of which the ancient Jews were a part. There are extant Egyptian and Mesopotamian records that speak of a king as the image of a god. It is clear in these texts that the king is being described as the representative of the god. And so, the argument goes, Gen 1:26, too, says that human being is God's representative in this world. However, Westermann comes finally to reject this reading of the passage. A representative represents another before some third. The only way that human being (and not *a* human being) could be God's representative is before the rest of God's creation. "But," Westermann says, "that is certainly not the meaning here." Further, the passage stands within a broader literary whole ("P") with a specific conception of the holy God, and, it is "inconceivable that P could have meant 'wherever a human being appears, there God appears.' . . . P could conceive of an appearance, manifestation, or representation of God only as a holy event, completely outside the range of ordinary events. He could not possibly think of a human being as standing in the place of God on earth" (153). Finally, there are also to be found a few Egyptian and Mesopotamian references to the creation of human being as such in the image of the god. Although these do little to show positively what Gen 1:26 means, they are different enough from what is said about the king to be a rather strong warning against hasty generalization.

7. Westermann considers this to be one of the less convincing interpretations of the passage. His rather summary dismissal is this: "A whole series of studies has shown quite correctly that this opinion is wrong, and that according to the text dominion over other creatures is not an explanation, but a consequence of creation in the image of God." Ibid., 155.

8. Westermann dismisses this interpretation: "It is generally acknowledged that Gen 1:26f. is not speaking of a distinction between the natural and the supernatural and that such talk about the person does not accord with the Old Testament. There is unanimity in the abandonment of the distinction." Ibid., 149.

ligence, or immortality?[9] Or is it simply our external, bodily form?[10] Or is the image neither "spiritual qualities" nor bodily form in isolation from one another, but more broadly "the person as a whole"?[11] Does the verse have a more specifically christological significance, indicating that humans were created long ago, with the coming Christ as their destiny?[12] Is the image of God a yet unobtained goal toward which we were created to move?[13] Or is it our being "God's counterpart" (*Gottes*

---

9. At times these "spiritual qualities" have been taken as the "natural image" in us to which supernatural likeness may be added. Westermann rejects this interpretation of the verse as well as the contrasting interpretation to follow ("the image of God" as "the external form" of the human) because in his view the Old Testament refuses to split human beings into a spirit and a body. See below.

10. Of course, this would be very difficult for later participants in the Judeo-Christian tradition to affirm. However, at this early stage of development, the argument runs, abstraction has not yet overcome the concrete thinking that looks to "external form."

11. In other words, a human being is simply a human being, certainly with various dimensions and modes of action and passion, but a whole human being nonetheless. And so, to look for a spirit distinct from a body or a body distinct from a spirit is to look for what is not there. Westermann quotes W. H. Schmidt with approval: "The most recent exegesis has managed to pry the phrase 'in the image and likeness of God' free from an idea foreign to the Old Testament, namely the separation of the corporeal and the spiritual." Westermann adds: "The discussion whether the image and likeness of God referred to the corporeal or the spiritual aspect of the person has brought us to the conclusion that the question has been placed incorrectly. Gen 1:26f. is concerned neither with the corporeal nor with the spiritual qualities of people; it is concerned only with the person as a whole." He concludes: "There can now be basic agreement that when Gen 1:26 talks of the image and likeness of God, it envisages the whole person, and not just the corporeal or the spiritual side." Westermann, *Genesis 1–11*, 150. Westermann nonetheless maintains that the point of the verse is not to focus attention chiefly even on the wholeness of the human being.

12. This is another of the interpretations that Westermann takes to be relatively minor. His rejection of it is accounted for in this way: "Such an explanation however is forced to say that fallen humanity is not the image of God." Ibid., 155. In other words, Westermann is saying that according to this view those who have failed to conform to Christ are cut off from God's image (which, he would maintain, is untenable). However, there are other ways of thinking this christological notion of the *imago dei*.

13. Westermann spends almost no time with this reading of the text. He does note that, since the time of the fathers of the church, it has gone out of fashion (and we should add "in the West"). He is willing to quote a more recent (again, Western) advocate (A. M. Dubarle): "The image of God is not a static quality conferred once

Gegenüber), the one whom God addresses as "you," the one who can reply as "I"?[14]

But what if we have miscalculated in our analyses of ourselves and this verse? What if we have prepared ourselves so much for a certain kind of answer to our questions that we have missed a very different one, an answer that one might yet read in our holy book? Westermann thinks that this is precisely what has happened:

> This survey . . . reveals a common trait: all exegetes from the fathers of the church to the present begin with the presupposition that the text is saying something about people, namely that people bear God's image because they have been created in accordance with it. The whole question therefore centers around the image of God in the person . . . Scarcely one of the many studies of the text asks about the process that is going on. . . . There can be no question that the text is describing an action, and not the nature of human beings. Most interpretations presume without more ado that the verb "create" can be understood in itself and apart from the context in which it is set. But the text is speaking about an action of God, and not about the nature of humanity. . . . In any case, what the Old Testament says about the creation of humanity in the image of God has meaning only in its context, namely that of the process of the creation of human beings. . . . [The point of the passage is that] the creation of humanity has as its goal a *happening between* God and human beings. . . ; it is not a question of a *quality in* human beings. . . . God has created all people "to correspond to [God]," that is so that something can *happen between* creator and creature.[15]

---

and for all, it is a call to imitate in action the one whose image is carried. It is a call to live a life of religion: 'Be holy, because I am holy.'" Ibid., 155. Perhaps this view can yet be rehabilitated and made ingredient to a more adequate understanding of the *imago dei*.

14. This is the position of Karl Barth and in a certain way of Westermann himself. Although his critical remarks are framed in such a way that they seem to be directed at all nine interpretations of the *imago*, obviously he is not attacking himself.

15. Westermann, *Genesis 1–11*, 155, 157, 158; emphases added.

Westermann's reading of Gen 1:26–27 provides an intriguing alternative to the typical approach to the text. Here we have the notion that the image of God is not to be located *in* the human being, but rather in the region *between* the human being and transcendent God, in the region opened up by God's movement to the one who is irrevocably God's creature. Thus the image is very much the image of the God who approaches and addresses the human and only thereby sets the human apart as unique. This means that no matter how hard one looks at the human being, it is only as one's gaze slips from the human to the God who addresses the human that one comes to find the uniqueness that constitutes the *imago dei*. The image of God is not simply there in us or about us, a brute matter of fact lodged, located statically in place. The image rather *comes*; it comes as a gift that never becomes a possession, that never ceases being a gift. Genesis 1:26–27, therefore, speaks first of the God whose movement yields that which is most distinctive in the human being, and only then, derivatively, speaks of that human to whom God moves. Westermann is saying that the address of God is an event that calls, that challenges us to respond. Thus, it is not so much that the human "images God." It is much more that the human is "imaged by God."

This in turn means that the human is the one who answers the call of God, who lives from the insuperable gift that God gives, who turns to the God who first turns to humans, who thus *is* only in the space opened by God's image. It means that this human prays. The implication of Westermann's argument is that the human being, according to Gen 1:26–27, is to be thought of as the prayer invited by God, is to be understood as *homo precarius*. That is, insofar as being human is being in the image of God, prayer is not something added to the human being as if without it the human would remain essentially unchanged. Rather, prayer, specifically the prayer called forth by God's address, makes us human.

The one theologian cited again and again by Westermann as having understood the passage,[16] as having avoided the "false start" that

---

16. That is, the theologian who understood that it concerns human being holistically, that it concerns human being as God's counterpart, as having understood that it concerns not a quality *in* human being but an event for which we were created, etc.

has taken almost all interpreters down a path away from the text, is Karl Barth, whose now classic treatment of Gen 1:26ff. is found in the *Church Dogmatics* III/1. Although Westermann would not, of course, embrace all that is said in that section—indeed, he rejects the christo-logical-Trinitarian reading of the text that is essential to it—his weighty words of approval invite a closer examination of what Barth has to say. Barth's understanding of human life lends itself precisely to the notion that the human being is prayer, that is, an openness to the openness of God. However, the position advocated by Barth and Westermann is not entirely new. Its continuity with older Protestant thought is illustrated, for example, by John Wesley's notion that salvation is simultaneously an event of prayer ("prayer without ceasing") and the restoration of the human being in the image of God. Both of these positions will be examined in what follows.

Where the Spirit of the Lord Is, There Is Freedom

The theology of Karl Barth is a theology of revelation. It is certainly also a theology of the wholly other; but Barth speaks of the wholly other only as he speaks of the apocalyptic event in which God makes God known, in which God is opened, is bared.[17] Indeed, everything Barth says, whether of the finite or the infinite, the temporal or the eternal, the human or the divine, emerges finally from that event in which two utterly alien realities, one creature, the other creator, become one. All theological utterances are to be received here.

It is because of the exhaustively constitutive nature of God's self-revelation in Barth's theology that late in his career he could (to the surprise of many) write of "the humanity of God."[18] The wholly other comes close, so close that one cannot speak of God in isolation from God's coming: and God's coming entails us. To understand who God is, is to understand who God is in the event of God's self-revelation. But it is equally true that to understand who *we* are as humans is to understand who we are in that same event. Where God and human being are

17. Karl Barth, *KD*, I/1, 314–15 (*CD* I/1, 298). "Dieser Gott selbst ist gerade nicht nur er selbst, sondern auch sein Sich-Offenbaren" (315).

18. Barth, *Humanity of God*, 37–65.

one is where God is most really God and human being is most really human being. Thus Barth refuses to speak in abstraction from revelation either when he speaks of God or when he speaks of human being: they are equally inseparable from that revelation. Anthropology is theology: in order to speak of human being, one must first and last speak of God. And so, when Barth explains the doctrine of the image of God, he does so by thinking human being at the place where the outgoing reality of God occurs.

Further, the revelation of God, according to Barth, is the history of Jesus Christ, the concrete history of this concrete human being. This is the history of God's radical grace; this is the space opened as God goes out to what God is not, to what is radically other than everything God is, and here gives Godself unreservedly.[19] God is utterly laid bare here, and so is human being. What occurs here has no referent beyond itself that gives it meaning and worth. This God is God. This human being is human being. All purported divine events as well as all purported human events are to be judged here. There is no higher court of appeal. Since it is God's outgoing that takes place as the history of this human being—a human being who is in all things oriented to God's outgoing— this human history, as particular as it is, takes place as that to which all human histories are to be referred; that is, because God is radically here as this history, it is constitutive of human being as such, it defines human being.

Moreover, the presence of God as this history is not a casual and static presence. It is not simply there like a marble in a jar. Rather, the unity of this history occurs as two radically different natures concur in the heat of their difference, as an act, a movement, of mutual self-giving, of mutual kenotic love. This history, which is this human being and is this God, is the "yes" spoken by each to the other. Therefore, what happens in the profound relation between this human and the God who is here revealed is that human being is made known as the creature utterly given over to God (*der Mensch für Gott*). What occurs as Jesus Christ is the reality of every human being (*er ist . . . der wirkliche Mensch*). Everything human *is* human only here, in him, in his life and death. In other words, human being is created to occur precisely as Jesus occurs:

19. Barth, *CD* I/1, 315; see idem, *CD* II/1, 257–321.

as the event of absolute openness to the God who is absolutely open to him, as the history of God with us and of us with God, as the history in which there is no distinguishing what human being is about from what God is about.[20] Jesus Christ is the concrete history of human being utterly given over to God; the entirety of his history is human being corresponding (*entsprechend*) to God.[21]

If the history of Jesus Christ is the defining event of human being, then human life is to be understood in relation to him from the very beginning. Indeed, since God is at work here, the history of Jesus Christ must be traced beyond the very beginning to the heart of God. The outgoing of God that occurs with us as a human history, the outgoing of God that lays God bare to us, the outgoing of God that is indistinguishable from the what and who of revelation, is an outgoing at work already transcendently *within* the divine reality. God not only appears to be love; God *is* love from all eternity. The history of Jesus reveals that God *in Godself* is never *simply* in Godself, but is even there an outgoing movement of self-giving. For example:

> Among all other [human beings] and all other creatures
> He [Jesus] is the penetrating spearhead of the will of God
> their Creator: penetrating because in Him the will of God
> is already fulfilled and revealed, and the purpose of God
> for all [human beings] and creatures has thus reached its
> goal; and the spearhead to the extent that there has still to
> be a wider fulfilment of the will of God and its final con-
> summation, and obviously this can only follow on what

20. Barth, *KD* III/2, 64–241 (*CD* III/2, 55–202). "God acts as Jesus acts. The divine work is accomplished in the work of this [human being]. And the work of this [human being] consists in the abandonment of all other work to do the work of God" (*CD* III/2, 62). "In Jesus Christ there is no isolation of [the human being] from God or of God from [the human being]. Rather, in Him we encounter the history, the dialogue, in which God and [human being] meet together, the reality of the covenant *mutually* contracted, preserved, and fulfilled by them" (idem, *Humanity of God*, 46).

21. Barth, *CD* III/2, 70–71: "To sum up, the distinctiveness of this creature consists in the fact that it is for God. That it is for God means that it is for the divine deliverance and therefore for God's own glory, for the freedom of God and therefore for the love of God." This means that his identity as this specific human being *is* his mission from and to God. However, he is not dissolved into the divine work. There are two natures here in this one history, this one person.

has already been achieved in this [human being]. . . . And if the [human being] Jesus is the penetrating spearhead of this will of God . . . His existence is determined from the beginning, before the foundation of the world. This can be said only of Him. For He alone is the [human], the crea-ture, in whom the will of God has already been fulfilled and by whom the enemy of being has been slain and the freedom of being attained. He alone is the archetypal [hu-man being] whom all threatened and enslaved [human beings] and creatures must follow. He alone is the promise for these many, the Head of a whole body. . . . If now in the vast sphere of human fellowship and history we have to do with the [human] Jesus, it is because His existence was eternally resolved in the sovereign will of God to save us and all creation: resolved before all things, before being was even planned, let alone actualised, before [human be-ing] fell into sin, before light was separated from darkness or being from non-being, and therefore before there was even a potential threat to being, let alone an actual; re-solved as the very first thing which God determined with regard to the reality distinct from [Godself]; resolved as the all-embracing content of [God's] predestination of all creaturely being.[22]

The resolution of God, therefore, occurs in the inner life of God. God goes out because God is essentially outgoing even in Godself. That is, the revelation of God to God's other is grounded in the inner divine life. God is alive and moves precisely as Godself; that is, there is an other at work within God.[23] God is God only because God's unity occurs in this movement of othering. This, Barth maintains, is the implication of God's revelation in Jesus Christ. From here Barth moves to Gen 1:26–27. He of course knows that the history of the christological interpretation of Genesis has not been an altogether pretty sight. Yet he does not on that account draw back from letting the implications of the notion that

22. Ibid., 143–44.

23. In other words, the revelation that occurs as the history of Jesus Christ means that there is a trinitary movement in the transcendent reality of God, there is a You addressed by the divine I—here is a Son to the sovereign Father.

Jesus is the Christ, the hope of Israel and the world, the eternal Son of the Father, unfold even here.[24]

The creation of human being is an event in which God moves to the outside. In that event, Barth argues, human being is set in motion in the direction of the movement of God.[25] We are created toward the creator who comes to us. Again, there is in God an outgoing, and it is to this outgoing that human being is created to move. The outgoing of God is not something separate from God. God indeed remains the mystery, the wholly other, the transcendent one, high and exalted, precisely when God is closest. Thus the outgoing of God is a kind of repetition of the hidden one, a kind of "over-against" (*Gegenüber*[26]) of God to God, a kind of *image of God*. Again, God moves to what God is not without ceasing to be what God is. God's moving to what God is not is still true God. Yet it is the one God *again*, as the image of God. God, whom we confront as we are formed from the ground, is the transcendent one come close, the true, utterly undiluted, undiminished image of the true God. Human being is created to move to this outgoing, to this image, to stand out in it, to go after it.[27] In other words, human being not in itself

24. "Here, too, we can only say that, if the hope of the Old Testament was not meaningless, if its covenant-history really had a supremely definite and concrete goal, if Jesus Christ really was Israel's Messiah, the Son of God and therefore the fulfilment of Israel's own existence, the meaning and goal of its whole course, and therefore the answer to the enigma of Gen. 1: 26f., Paul did not represent any innovation in relation to the Old Testament but pointed to its fulfillment." Barth, *CD* III/1, 202.

25. It might be helpful at this point to remember the title of Eberhard Jüngel's fine book on Barth's doctrine of the Trinity, *Gottes Sein is im Werden* [*God's Being Is in Becoming*].

26. Though translated (in Barth *CD* III/1, 184 and passim) as "counterpart," the literal meaning of *Gegenüber* is "over-against," "that which is opposite." Consequently, it is often translated in other contexts as "object." The meaning here is that there is in God not homogeneity, but a living movement, a *vis-à-vis*, a reciprocal outgoing. Explicating this idea yields, of course, Barth's doctrine of the Trinity.

27. Barth's German translation (*lasset uns Menschen machen in unserem Urbild nach unserem Vorbild!*) centers on the phrases "in our image" (*in unserem Urbild*) and "according to our likeness" (*nach unserem Vorbild*). These German nouns, *Urbild* and *Vorbild*, are not easy words to translate. The prefix *ur-* indicates that which is primordial, originary. The prefix *vor-* indicates that which is or goes before. Since *Bild* simply means image, these prefixes say something subtly important about the kind of image in relation to which human being is created. That is, humans have

the image of God, "is created in *correspondence [entsprechend] with* the image of God,"[28] is created speaking (*sprechend*) out (*ent-*)[29] in answer to the divine image; speaking freely with what it is and is called to be, and only thus being human.[30] The image of God is God's being that in going out calls to us. The human "correspondence" with the image of God is our being the answer to that very image which is Godself as God's call, God's voice, God's word.[31]

It is, Barth says, this complexity in God that moves behind the Pauline understanding that Jesus Christ, unlike Adam, *is* the *very image* (*eikon*) of God.[32] His history is identified with God's image not because he exceeds human life, but because he is human life in its most comprehensive sense. God created Adam and Eve to correspond to, that is, to answer God's call, God's image. What the early chapters of Genesis lay out as failing to occur in their history is precisely what happens as the history of Jesus Christ. However, the correspondence of Jesus Christ to God's image is unrestricted: whatever he is about is what God's outgoing is about. Therefore, to say "Jesus Christ" is to say "the image of God."[33] In this way, Jesus Christ, *qua* the image of God, is the point of the creation of human life. Adam and Eve were called into being as a hope

---

not been created with God's image *in* them, they have been created with a certain *direction to* an image that is originary in God, with a certain direction to an image that is happening already in God. Thus human being is called *ein Abbild* (in contrast to the divine *Urbild*) and *ein Nachbild* (in contrast to the divine *Vorbild*): literally that which is lower than the image and that which goes after the image, respectively. The image that is originary in God, the image that goes before in God, is an otherness (*ein Gegenüber*), a divine You to the divine I, at work at the heart of the divine life. See Barth, *KD* III/1, 221; cf. 211–14 (*CD* III/1, 197; cf. 188–91).

28. Barth *CD* III/1, 197 (*KD*, III/1, 222); emphasis added.

29. "Ent-, insep. and unaccented prefix; in composition with other words indicates establishment of or entry into a new state or abandonment of an old state." Betteridge, ed., *New Cassell's German Dictionary*, s.v. "ent-."

30. Rather like Martin Buber's prayerful "I-You." See Buber, *I and Thou*, 54 and 122–82.

31. See Jüngel, "Truth of Life," 231–36; idem, "Humanity in Correspondence to God," 124–53.

32. Barth, *CD* III/1, 202: "Paul's daring equation of the man Jesus . . . directly with the divine image, is an unprecedented and radical innovation."

33. Barth *CD* III/2, 62, 64; *CD* III/1, 201–3.

that opens to the coming history of the fullness of God with us. That is precisely what the history of Jesus is. Therefore, it is to this that they are essentially related; when God created Adam and Eve, it was to the coming Christ that God looked.[34]

This remains the destiny of human life, whether or not one turns from God, whether or not one "falls." Since it is not a human possession but a gift—and a gift of a most persistent giver—the image, the voice of God, cannot be lost. It continues to call to every child of Adam and Eve, whom the gracious creator will never leave or forsake.[35]

The being of the human is, therefore, that which acknowledges its source, ground, and object as that which lies outside itself and yet has come in mercy and grace.

> We may thus say that the being of [humankind] is a being
> in gratitude. [Humankind's] history as constituted by the
> Word of the grace of God, [humankind's] being therefore,
> continues and must continue in the fact that it is a being in
> gratitude. . . . The Word of grace and therefore grace itself,
> it can only receive. But as it does this, as it is content to

34. Barth, *CD* III/1, 191, 204–5. This exposition of Barth's conception of the image of God has left aside his famous discussion of the *analogia relationis*, the notion that involved in our being created in God's image is our being created in relation as male and female (a discussion owing much to Bonhoeffer's work). This has not been drawn into this study, for two reasons: (1) it is not directly related to the main line of argument of the paper, and (2) it is not central to Barth's own discussion. Barth makes clear that when placed outside the more important notion of the *analogia fidei* (our being created *in* and *for* God's image, related to [*ana-*] the image [*logos*]), our being male and female merely makes us akin to the animals, which are similarly differentiated (194–97). Thus on this point Barth is not quite as far removed from the position of Phyllis Bird as she thinks. See Bird, "Sexual Differentiation and Divine Image in the Genesis Creation Texts," 5–20.

35. Barth, *CD* III/1, 200.Westermann quotes Horst's positive reading of Barth: "When he speaks of human existence he is not speaking of a quality in the person, or of something which the person, cut off from God, can dispose of, or of something or other which might be counted among one's possessions. He is speaking rather of human existence as blessed by God, who in his sovereign freedom has ruled that the human being alone out of all creatures is to be [God's] counterpart and to correspond to [God], and with whom [God] will speak and share and who in turn must talk to [God] and live 'in [God's] presence' (lit. before [God's] face)." Westermann, *Genesis 1–11*, 151.

be what it is by this Word, as it thus exists by its openness towards God, the question is decided that it is a being in gratitude. It has not taken the grace of God but the latter has come to it; it has not opened itself but God has opened it and made it this open being. And it now is what it has been made. But it cannot be without itself actualising this event. It is, as it is under an obligation to the God who has seized the initiative in starting this history; as it is re-ferred to [God] in respect of its whole attitude. It is in the strength of its promise which God makes to it, that [God] is its Helper and Deliverer. As God comes to it in [God's] Word, it is a being open toward God and self-opening, transcending itself in a Godward direction.[36]

Such gratitude is the essence of prayer.[37] To be human for Barth is to move in the open relation that is initiated by God. That is, to be human is to be responsive before God, in all the concreteness of daily life, in all the complexity and confusion of an uncertain world. Yet it is to be responsive in the gratitude that is joy and freedom before the mercy and love and openness of the God who in Jesus Christ has said a resounding "yes" to human being, and thus has called to the newness of life what otherwise would be swallowed by death. Thus, for Barth, to take human being as something approachable and knowable apart from the history of Jesus is to fail to understand what his history in fact signifies for those who have the hope of being human only in his death and resurrection.

36. Barth, *CD* III/2, 167–68.

37. Cf. what Barth writes of theology as prayer: "Human thought and speech can-not be *about* God, but must be directed *toward* God, called into action by the divine thought and speech directed to [human beings] and following and corresponding to this work of God. Human thought and speech would certainly be false if they bound themselves to a divine 'It' or 'Something,' since God is a person and not a thing. But human thought and speech concerning God could also be false and would at any rate be unreal if they related themselves to [God] in the *third* person. What is essential for human language is to speak of [human beings] in the first person and of God in the *second* person. True and proper language concerning God will always be a response to God, which overtly or covertly, explicitly or implicitly, thinks and speaks of God exclusively in the second person. And this means that theological work must really and truly take place in the form of a liturgical act, as invocation of God, and as prayer." Barth, *Evangelical Theology*, 164.

Christ Is All and in All

The ideas at work in Barth's account of Gen 1:26–27 resonate with many of the ideas at work in the theology of John Wesley: God's grace is precisely God lovingly at work in the lives of God's creatures; God is prevenient, going out to us before we are in any position to respond; God addresses the human being as a whole; God's address liberates us to the Christ who is the human reality that we, too, are created to be; in Christ we find our destiny. However, Wesley's explicit account of the meaning of the *imago dei* clashes with Barth's. Indeed, it is striking how much he draws attention to the human being as a reality whose meaning is found in itself, as a proper substance in which proper qualities reside. Thus it is also striking how much his position falls prey to the critique of Westermann. However, there is something more at play in Wesley, something that eludes the simple definitions that he had been taught so well and that were part of the stock-in-trade of every learned divine of his time.

As one would expect, there is in the more than sixty years of Wesley's commentary on the doctrine of the *imago dei* a great deal of traditional material.[38] He is doing little more than repeating classic treatments when he speaks of the doctrine in 1730 as "a truth that does so much honour to human nature"[39] and in 1790 as indicating "the greatness, the excellency, the dignity of [human being]";[40] or when he speculates about the strength, clarity, infallibility, justice, and speed of human understanding, will (or "affections"), and "liberty" in their original, paradisiac state;[41] or when he describes undefiled human being as

---

38. One of the most significant recent treatments of the history of the notion of the *imago dei* is Børresen, ed., *Image of God*. The essays by Børresen and Jane Dempsey Douglass in particular help provide a context for understanding Wesley's thought on the doctrine.

39. Wesley, "Image of God," in *WJW*, 4:292 (§1).

40. Wesley, "Heavenly Treasure in Earthly Vessels," in *WJW*, 4:162 (§2).

41. Wesley, "Image of God," 293–95 (I.1–4); idem, "The New Birth," in *WJW*, 2:188 (I.1); idem, "The General Deliverance," in *WJW*, 2:437–50 and passim; idem, "On the Fall of Man," in *WJW*, 2:409–10 (II.6); idem, "Heavenly Treasure in Earthly Vessels," 163 (I.1).

"resembling" God,[42] as "an incorruptible picture" of God,[43] as "like" God.[44] Even when Wesley speaks of the "total loss" of the image,[45] or more moderately of the loss of "the moral image,"[46] he is repeating a familiar Protestant notion.

Though making use of these ideas (however ineffectually), Wesley writes with considerably more energy and interest when he attends less to the human subject, its powers and dignity, and more to the gracious God who in Christ delivers us. The work of God in Christ is a liberation for Wesley, viz., *from* the darkness and despair of sin, and *to* the God who thus "restores" and "renews" us in God's own image.[47] Even as he affirms the notion that the image of God can reside *in* us, Wesley shifts attention *away from* us to the God who—in loving—comes to us.[48] Further, though the terms that he inherits make the *imago* proper to the human subject, the vision within which Wesley locates these terms is profoundly expropriating: "It is of his mercy that he made us at all. . . . But if he has made us, and given us all we have, if we owe all we are and have to him, then surely he has a right to all we are and have, to all our love and obedience."[49] There is finally no claim to possession in Wesley. What God does in us is not our property. Indeed, the hallowing that is our being restored in the image of God is a "living sacrifice" in which whatever I am is yielded to God.

---

42. Wesley, "Image of God," 293 (I.1).

43. Wesley, "The One Thing Needful," in *WJW*, 4:354 (I.2).

44. Wesley, "On the Fall of Man," 409 (II.6).

45. Wesley, "Original Sin," in *WJW*, 2:185 (III.5); idem, "Heavenly Treasure in Earthly Vessels," 162 (§2).

46. Wesley, "On the Fall of Man," 410 (II.6).

47. Wesley, "Image of God," 293, 300–301 (§4, III.3); idem, "One Thing Needful," 353–57 (I.1–II.5); idem, "Original Sin," 185 (III.5); idem, "On Working Out Our Own Salvation," in *WJW*, 3:204 (II.1).

48. The favor of God is greater, for Wesley, even than life itself: "[T]he best, indeed the only means under heaven given to man whereby he may regain the favour of God, which is better than life itself, or the image of God, which is the true life of the soul, is the submitting to the 'righteousness which is of faith,' the believing in the only-begotten Son of God." Wesley, "The Righteousness of Faith," in *WJW*, 1:214 (II.9).

49. Wesley, "The Deceitfulness of the Human Heart," in *WJW*, 4:153 (I.2).

Moreover, Wesley's elucidation of the *imago dei* is not all talk of substance and quality. It can also be explicitly and profoundly relational. Life in God's image is, for Wesley, "[human being] dwelling in God and God in [human being], having uninterrupted fellowship with the Father and the Son through the eternal Spirit."[50] That is, human being in God's image is an eccentric being, a being whose center is shifted to the outside, to the one who in love has come first to us. Such eccentric love is an outgoing granted by the outgoing grace of God. Again:

> O trample under foot . . . all the things which are beneath the sun—"for the excellency of the knowledge of Christ Jesus"; for the entire renewal of thy soul in that image of God wherein it was originally created. . . . Let nothing satisfy thee but the power of godliness, but a religion that is spirit and life; the dwelling in God and God in thee . . .[51]

Wesley in his last years by no means abandoned the categories he had used for decades to explicate the *imago dei*. However, he began to describe the doctrine in a rather different way. It became clear to him that phenomenal human qualities (the understanding, the affections, freedom of will, etc.) are shared with animals and that the distinctiveness of human life is to be found elsewhere. Such qualities remain part of the meaning of our being created in God's image, but they are not constitutive of "the supreme perfection" of the human being. That which is most uniquely human, that which when lost most deprives us of what we essentially are, is our being "capable of God," "capable" of knowing, loving, obeying, and enjoying God.[52]

This term "capable of God," however, is by no means clear. At first sight it seems to affirm that human beings, at least when not ravaged by sin, have resident within them a power that makes them able to grasp

50. Welsey, "End of Christ's Coming," in *WJW*, 2:475–76 (I.7); see idem, "Justification by Faith," in *WJW*, 1:184 (I.1).

51. Wesley, "Upon our Lord's Sermon on the Mount, II," in *WJW*, 1:498 (II.6). The word *dwell* has an etymology that adds a certain twist to what Wesley is saying here. The word comes from a root that means "to lead astray." See *Oxford English Dictionary*, s.v. "dwell."

52. Wesley, "General Deliverance," 439 (I.2), 441 (I.5), 449–50 (III.11–12); idem, "Deceitfulness of the Human Heart," 153 (I.2).

the divine reality.[53] Yet the term as used by Wesley can be read differently. If one thinks of the word *capability* in the light of its history, it begins to speak not of a quality *in* the centered human subject, but of an openness, a capaciousness, that calls the centered subject into question.[54] In other words, in our time the word *capability* carries about it connotations of a kind of native potency that under the right circumstances might be actualized. The word, of course, does not in fact have such a narrow denotation, and indeed (here is nothing in the theology of Wesley that would lead one to expect him to maintain that even the most godly creature has an inherent power to grasp the divine.)"None feel their need of Christ," he writes, "like these [who live without sin]; none so entirely depend upon Him";[55] and "it is pride . . . to ascribe anything we have to ourselves."[56] If Wesley again and again maintains the utter dependence of the redeemed upon the Redeemer, of the sanctified upon the Sanctifier, then it is unlikely that his conception of the human "capability of God" would be attributed to inherent human nature as it exists in itself, even under the power of the Spirit. (His is a theology of grace which struggles to expropriate what we otherwise are so inclined to claim as our own.) The work of the Spirit is not to deposit new goods into our storehouse of property. (The Spirit "fills" us with the love, the openness of God.)

This is not to say that being "capable of God" is merely a passivity, something that comes to us as if we were not involved. Wesley's usage is far richer than that. For Wesley a "capable" human being receives from God, certainly; but the receiving human also restores to God what has been received. In that sense, capability is a gratitude, a thanksgiving,

---

53. Indeed, the *Oxford American Dictionary*, Eugene Ehrlich et al., eds. (New York: Avon, 1980), defines the word as "1. competent. 2. having a certain ability" (s.v. "capable").

54. "F., Late L., *capabilis*, receptive, in early theol. use, from *capere*, to hold." Weekley, *An Etymological Dictionary of Modern English*, s.v. "capable." See also the *Oxford English Dictionary*, s.v. "capable." Further, the suffix "-able" is a much more ambiguous term than its spelling might first suggest. It has the sense of "given to, tending to, like to, fit to, able to." The adjective *able* (used, of course, at the end of this string of terms) grows from an entirely different root (*Oxford English Dictionary*, s.v. "able," "-able," "-ble"). Neither *capere* nor *-ble* is a power-word.

55. Wesley, *A Plain Account*, in *WJWJ*, 11:395.

56. Ibid., 427.

a joy, *eine Entsprechende*, a prayer—fluctuating in its facility *between* the passive and the active. To be "capable of God" means to be utterly yielded to God, to be *agape*—heart, soul, mind, and strength. To be "capable of God" is to be "capable of being filled" by God. Thus:

> When we have received any favour from God, we ought to
> retire . . . into our hearts, and say, "I come, Lord, to restore
> to thee what thou hast given; and I freely relinquish it, to
> enter again into my own nothingness. For what is the most
> perfect creature in heaven or earth in thy presence, but a
> void capable of being filled with thee and by thee; as the
> air, which is void and dark, is capable of being filled with
> the light of the sun, who withdraws it every day to restore
> it the next, there being nothing in the air that either appro-
> priates this light or resists it? O give me the same facility
> of receiving and restoring thy grace and good works! I say,
> *thine*; for I acknowledge the root from which they spring
> is in Thee, and not in me."[57]

57. Ibid., 441. The whole remarkable passage from which the selection above has been taken is as follows: "Charity cannot be practiced right, unless, First, we exercise it the moment God gives the occasion; and, Secondly, retire the instant after to offer it to God by humble thanksgiving. And this for three reasons: First, to render [God] what we have received from [God]. The Second, to avoid the dangerous temptation which springs from the very goodness of these works. And the Third, to unite our-selves to God, in whom the soul expands itself in prayer, with all the graces we have received, and the good works we have done, to draw from [God] new strength against the bad effects which these very works may produce in us, if we do not make use of the antidotes which God has ordained against these poisons. The true means to be filled anew with the riches of grace is thus to strip ourselves of it; and without this it is extremely difficult not to grow faint in the practice of good works.

"Good works do not receive their last perfection, till they, as it were, lose them-selves in God. This is a kind of death to them, resembling that of our bodies, which will not attain their highest life, their immortality, till they lose themselves in the glory of our souls, or rather of God, wherewith they shall be filled. And it is only what they had of earthly and mortal, which good works lose by this spiritual death.

"Fire is the symbol of love; and the love of God is the principle and the end of all our good works. But truth surpasses figure; and the fire of Divine love has this advantage over material fire, that it can re-ascend to its source, and raise thither with it all the good works which it produces. And by this means it prevents their being cor-rupted by pride, vanity, or any evil mixture. But this cannot be done otherwise than by making these good works in a spiritual manner die in God, by a deep gratitude,

Being capable of God is an openness to God which receives whatever God gives and receives it without laying claim to it. Being capable of God is being a "void," a "nothing," which waits in active anticipation of what is to come. It is a rhythm that is gifted, that is and remains grace-gift.

Further, this is not for Wesley a private matter between the Spirit of God and me. Restoration in the image of God comes to me only in the Christ who threw his life open and thus is prophet, priest, and king. That is, to be filled with God is, according to Wesley, to be filled with God in the Christ who enlightens, hallows, atones:

> The holiest of men still need Christ, as their Prophet, as "the light of the world." For He does not give them light, but from moment to moment; the instant He withdraws, all is darkness. They still need Christ as their King; for God does not give them a stock of holiness. But unless they receive a supply every moment, nothing but unholiness would remain. They still need Christ as their Priest, to make atonement for their holy things. Even perfect holiness is acceptable to God only through Jesus Christ.[58]

---

which plunges the soul in [God] as in an abyss, with all that it is, and all the grace and works for which it is indebted to [God]; a gratitude, whereby the soul seems to empty itself of them, that they may return to their source, as rivers seem willing to empty themselves, when they pour themselves with all their waters into the sea.

"When we have received any favor from God, we ought to retire, if not into our closets, into our hearts, and say, 'I come, Lord, to restore to thee what thou hast given; and I freely relinquish it, to enter again into my own nothingness. For what is the most perfect creature in heaven or earth in thy presence, but a void capable of being filled with thee and by thee; as the air, which is void and dark, is capable of being filled with the light of the sun, who withdraws it every day to restore it the next, there being nothing in the air that either appropriates this light or resists it? O give me the same facility of receiving and restoring thy grace and good works! I say, *thine*; for I acknowledge the root from which they spring is in Thee, and not in me'" (440–41).

This passage does not harmonize well with those in Wesley that suggest the placement of the image of God *in* the human subject. Here, whatever the human is or has is given back to its source in God. The implication is that the restoration in the image of God is restoration of oneself away from oneself and to God.

58. Ibid., 417.

Such giving retains the precariousness of every gift *qua* gift. Christ as love bestows love. He gives himself and, as we receive him, we take on his nature. In this way *we* come to give. To grasp after the light, to hoard the holiness given by the holy one, to take that holiness as holy in itself, is to fail to understand that light and holiness are Christ and Christ is *agape.* Only in the crucified one is there the free resurrection life of joy, thanksgiving, and prayer. Moreover, to be filled with God in Christ is to be filled with the Holy Spirit:

> [T]he life of God in the soul of a believer . . . implies a continual inspiration of God's Holy Spirit: God's breathing into the soul, and the soul's breathing back what it first re-ceives from God; a continual action of God upon the soul, the reaction of the soul upon God; an unceasing presence of God, the loving, pardoning God, manifested to the heart, and perceived by faith; and an unceasing return of love, praise, and prayer, offering up all the thoughts of our hearts, all the words of our tongues, all the works of our hands, all our body, soul, and spirit, to be an holy sacrifice, acceptable unto God in Christ Jesus.[59]

"Restoration in the image of God" is the restoration of a capability of God which opens us to God the way lungs are opened to fresh air. We receive and we yield what we have received in the rhythm of love, praise, and prayer. Restoration in the image of God is bringing back to God what God has given; it is releasing one's grip, emptying one's pockets, yielding one's very life as a sacrifice to the One to whom the crucified one prayed.

It would have been all but impossible for Wesley to abandon the tradition that for over a millennium and a half had located the image of God *in* the human being. However, though the *imago* is dear to him, though he refers to it time and time again, he looks finally not to something we can get, something that can be made proper to us, but to something we can give. Oddly, what makes us most truly human is adherence to Jesus, who in his absolute human perfection, in his being

59. Wesley, "The Great Privilege of those that are Born of God," in *WJW*, 1:442 (III.2).

all that a human is to be, emptied himself, gave himself away, with his eyes and ears trained on a silent sky. Though Christ utters a prayer from the cross, it is perhaps better to say that the crucifixion as a whole is one long, uninterrupted prayer that begins with his first cry in that dirty stable in Bethlehem. Wesley calls for us to turn to God and to trust God even as we hang abandoned and alone. This is finally what it means to be a creature in the image of God.

The One Who Calls You Is Faithful

The term "restoration in the image of God" is a synonym in Wesley for the hallowing of human being.[60] It is, therefore, not without significance for the meaning of the *imago dei* that Wesley explicates the idea of entire sanctification by appealing to the phrase that makes up 1 Thess 5:17, "pray without ceasing."[61]

> God's command to "pray without ceasing," is founded on the necessity we have of [God's] grace to preserve the life of God in the soul, which can no more subsist one moment without it, than the body can without air. Whether we think of, or speak to, God, whether we act or suffer for [God], all is prayer, when we have no other object than [God's] love, and the desire of pleasing [God].[62]

To be hallowed is to be in Christ what we were created to be; it is to be creatures in God's image and after God's likeness; it is to be human; it is to pray.

The English *pray* is an old word, the Middle English *preien* deriving from the Late Latin *precare,* "to entreat."[63] For centuries it was used of any personal entreaty, however far from the temple. To pray is to ask of an other earnestly, humbly, without demand. Prayer is supplication, a plea for grace. To pray is to place oneself at the mercy of an other. It is to seek the favor of this other and to *wait*. It is to voice one's concern and

60. Wesley, "On Working Out Our Own Salvation," 204 (II.1).

61. Wesley, *A Plain Account*, in *WJWJ*, 11:371–72, 401, 418, 442.

62. Ibid., 438.

63. *Oxford English Dictionary*, s.v. "pray."

to *listen for the other's reply*. It is to forsake one's rights, to *yield* to the other, and there to *abide*.

Prayer has no certain outcome. Since one makes no demand and claims no privilege, its end is from the perspective of the supplicant completely out of control. Therefore, the customary posture of prayer is kneeling with one's head bowed and one's neck exposed and vulnerable. One gives oneself to the possibility of a fatal blow from the other, over whom one has relinquished all rights. It is therefore no small wonder that our English word *precarious* has been derived from *precarius*, the adjective form of the Latin *precari* ("to pray").

Genesis 1:26–27 invites us to think of human being as called forth by the freedom of God. Human being is a vulnerability *coram deo*. It has vis-à-vis God no right or privilege, no ground upon which to stand and make a demand, no foundation upon which to build its case. Human being lives simply by the mercy of God, from moment to moment, and that since the first day that God breathed into Adam's nostrils. It is created to be vulnerable and to acknowledge its vulnerability—oddly, with thanksgiving. Thus, humans are created to pray. Let us for once be humble enough to admit that none of us is *homo sapiens*. Let us for once be humble enough to admit that we are created not as something in ourselves, but as something for God, that you are and I am *homo precarius*. "We do not live to ourselves, and we do not die to ourselves. If we live, we live to the Lord, and if we die, we die to the Lord; so then, whether we live or whether we die, we are the Lord's" (Rom 14:7–8). This is an uncertain way to be, no doubt; there is, nonetheless, a not insignificant blessed assurance to such a life of prayer. It is as if God, in going out to us, provides us with all that is needed to live freely from and to God's outgoing, in God's image and after God's likeness.

6

The Human Person as Intercessory Prayer[1]

WHAT FOLLOWS WAS ONCE two papers. They are now placed under a common title, barely separated, as if two subsections of the same continuous essay. They are not that, however. They remain very different, even as they are held together. The first is quite clearly a response to a position taken by Stanley Hauerwas. It was written to be spoken to those who had just heard Hauerwas's keynote address. Its style is accessible by non-specialists. It does not seriously engage the near or distant history of thought. It is in short a relatively light piece of nonacademic prose—though I hope not insubstantial. The second makes no direct reference to the work of Hauerwas. It was written to be heard, discussed, re-*read*, and pondered by specialists. It is a continuous engagement with both the near and the distant history of thought. It is, in short, a heavy piece of academic prose. However, both pieces were written for the same time and place, are situated in the same set of questions, come to the same conclusion, and could have been given the same title. I have considered rewriting them so that they might come together more peacefully; but it is perhaps better that they remain entangled as they were at first. If nothing else, let this be an experiment in intertextuality.

1. A paper delivered to tenth Oxford Institute of Methodist Theological Studies, Somerville College, Oxford University, 1997. An earlier version of the present essay was first published in Powell and Lodahl, eds., *Embodied Holiness*, 39–61.

1. Perfect Agape[2]

"Why perfection does not require a 'self.'"[3] An intriguing turn of phrase, especially for those children yet tracking campground mud across clean middle-class sanctuaries. Revival preachers indigenous to a different time and place once spoke unabashedly of such things. The way to be holy, the way to be perfect, they shouted (in no uncertain terms), is to "die-out to self." Even though this hyphenated word "die-out" remained overburdened with ambiguity, what a word it was! Had the evangelists who wrestled with us and the devil in those rings they called "tabernacles" not raised their voices, had they not spat out their hard consonants through sweaty faces and flailing arms, had they been more domesticated, this word would still have hit home and hit home hard, particularly where those already pummeled by identity crises lived. Some who contended there never made it out of the ring. Others who did, still limp. I am not sure into which group I fall, but I think I fall in one. That is why my ears perk up—with dread and with hope—when I read Hauerwas's subtitle.

And there is much in his essay that is worthy at least of hope. One finds here glimpses into an intriguing alternative to the *modern "self,"* that self most prominently delimited as Descartes's famous dualism that pits soul against body. Hauerwas's focus is on a "permeable" bodily life that embraces and holds together everything that Descartes holds apart.[4] This at least (let's call it) "quasi-postmodern" view finds us humans to be a lively sociality. We are bodily beings who concretely interact at work and at play, in vital health and in incapacitating sickness, in the exuberance of life and on the pathway to death. Unless it walls itself off by isolating defense mechanisms, bodily life occurs, Hauerwas suggests, as genuinely communicative.[5] The fragility of human being in time issues an invitation to us to tell stories, to tell them and retell them—stories ever open to revision, because ever open to the unforeseen. Indeed,

2. This is to be read in English as much as in Greek.

3. This is the subtitle of Hauerwas's address ("The Sanctified Body: Why Perfection Doesn't Require a 'Self'"), found in Powell and Lodahl, eds., *Embodied Holiness*, 19–38.

4. Hauerwas, "Sanctified Body," 24.

5. Ibid., 32.

truly humane stories must remain open, Hauerwas seems to say, because our lives together are finally at the mercy of a nearly "naturalistic" "necessity" beyond our control.[6] Our lives change and often change drastically. We are kept always in an uncertain "contingency" that gives rise to the narratives that mark the moments of—what in narrative form has become—our "journey." But none of this is for Hauerwas the stuff either of individualistic intellectualism or individualistic pietism. There are no insulated minds or spirits here. Life is lived out as the bodily interchange of permeable human lives.

It is shod in these ideas (many of them entering the argument implicitly via Dale Martin and Arthur Frank) that Hauerwas takes a few steps into a doctrine of holiness. Here his words get particularly interesting.

Holiness is understood, of course, as a bodily phenomenon. And since "body" is not an "individuality" but a sociality, it is not surprising that the body held out to us here is "the body of Christ," that is, the disciples of Christ, those who have (literally) entered into *his* permeable body. Holiness is "the work of the Holy Spirit building up the body of Christ."[7] And how does the Holy Spirit do that? By making us "a disciplined body," a "habituated body," a submissive body, a body that practices "the art of living" and thus learns "the art of dying," a body so "shaped . . . that the worship of God is unavoidable."[8] All of us human beings are the pattern of "what we do and do not do." We *are* "our habits." To enter into the body of Christ is to become *different*, because differently habituated. The real patterns of our real bodily lives change. Yet nobody changes in this way "without being forced to." It is here that "necessity" plays its part.[9]

Life jerks us around. We think all is going well and suddenly we have the ground cut out from under us by illness—and by and by find ourselves perilously suspended above the abyss of death, helpless to do anything. Here—if we've not learned it before—we discover "that we

6. Ibid., 36.
7. Ibid., 20.
8. Ibid, 36, 22.
9. Ibid., 36.

are fundamentally dependent beings."[10] Only thus out of control, led by God's grace ("which often is but another name for necessity"[11]), do we together learn in the communicative reciprocity of bodily prayer (stories?) that life and death are a journey before and into the eucharistic body of Christ. Thus we are sanctified. Jerked around—disciplined—by life together, we live with (and so tell stories to) one another and in word and deed are habituated precisely as our lives become a concrete journey that enters into the journey of Christ. The character thus habituated has a story quality. It is a kind of history, but only because story is a kind of history.

Thus Hauerwas lays out the outlines of what we might not unfairly call his doctrine of holiness. Though no revival preacher would confuse what is said in his essay with the "dying-out to self" that figures so prominently in the holiness preaching of misty past, what he says rings nonetheless true as an account of our lives together. Indeed, there is a remarkable honesty to his words. So much so in fact that it seems that one is rather duty bound to pause before writing more. What Hauerwas says here should fill the lungs of those who have come to imagine their lives to be disembodied monadic solitudes. His words are fresh and clean and oxygen rich. Much that we are compelled to ask, even when we cannot articulate an intelligible question, he has answered. And yet I believe we may think—we may question—a bit more.

At rather important places in Hauerwas's essay—and this is most unexpected—there appear, of all things, intimations of naturalism. Indeed, the word itself makes its appearance, as does its family member "necessity."[12] Admittedly, these words can be used in a wide variety of ways; but in what way do they contribute to what Hauerwas most wants to tell us? Do they not rather distract the reader from what is to be a postmodern reading of the human condition? Is it only a suspicious mind that disappointedly begins to wonder if perhaps *everything* that Hauerwas has said in this essay can be understood to be an account of the lives of folks who are *trapped* in an expanding universe, an expanding universe that makes itself felt not only at its cosmic edges, but also

10. Ibid.

11. Ibid., 37.

12. Ibid., 36, 37.

in the hospital rooms and marketplaces of our little planet? It is very helpful, it seems to me, to think of human life as a bodily sociality. It is very helpful, it seems to me, to see that bodily sociality as a storytelling sociality. But what in that is elucidated by the notions of "necessity" and "naturalism"?

I am also curious as to why movement into a holy life is described by Hauerwas as "forced."[13] Of course, classic Protestantism, with which Wesleyanism is at least connected, knows that human beings are so ruined by sin that they cannot make even the first step toward God unless God's grace is at work. However, certainly in the Wesleyan tradition God's grace is never an overpowering force. God approaches lost sinners as a loving parent and from time to time leads a very concrete person in a very concrete way *from* death *into* a life of holiness. And even here where God is most intimately and lovingly laboring there is the impossible possibility that one will not yield to God's grace, but will resist the Spirit to the end. Had Hauerwas said that holiness is impossible without the miracle of prevenient grace, I'd have no problem. And, of course, he could have used such words—in a certain way. However, grace is God, not a force. Is "the work of the Holy Spirit" understood in Hauerwas's essay to be very much like the blind necessity of a universe not quite at rest? I would think not. Yet why does it sound that way?

I am also uncertain about the way Hauerwas has chosen to connect the ironically healing effects of incapacitating illness with our realization that "we are fundamentally dependent beings."[14] Admittedly, we *are* dependent beings. Certainly, illness can make that as clear to us as anything. It seems also fair to suggest that illness can be instrumental in one's awakening to the mercy and holiness of God. However, long ago Rudolf Otto made clear that the business of holiness cannot be adequately elucidated by the notion of "dependence."[15] Although Otto has problems of his own, he is probably more on track when he suggests that before the holy, one is not *dependent* but, as Abraham says, "*dust and ashes*" (Gen 18:27). From such nothingness one does not learn that

---

13. Ibid., 36.

14. Ibid.

15. Otto, *Idea of the Holy*, 9–10.

"perfection is but another name for submission."[16] The hope of the cross (i.e., dust and ashes), the hope of the resurrection (i.e., the vitalizing work of the Holy Spirit), is that perfection is a liberation *from* deadly submission and *to* the newness of life.

Finally—and here I come closer to what is most dear to Hauerwas—I am not at all sure that a habituated life is a holy life, that "we are made perfect through our habits."[17] Of course, everything depends here on what is meant by "perfection." I am not sure that Hauerwas has told us. But let us say that perfection from his point of view is hard to come by. Let us say that it is a life taught *clear to the bone* by hard days and hard nights. Let us say that it is a pattern of remaining open to the uncertainty of each *new* day and night. Let us say that perfection for Hauerwas is a life lived with others; that it has achieved a community solidarity by learning the pattern of telling significant others the story of our journey together. Let us say that perfection for Hauerwas is a life that in bodily sociality has learned the pattern of creatively weaving into its old story the new unforeseen events that, when told, make that story no longer old, but as fresh as the wound it helps heal. Let us say that perfection for Hauerwas is a guarded life, one that has been taught the pattern of drawing a clear line around the community that defines it, one that encourages community discipline and community character and community identity, one that knows the difference between us and them, one that is clean. Is this a desirable mode of life? Oh, yes, no doubt often it is. Is this the kind of life that might be called "*evangelical perfection*"? Oh, I don't think so. For then the other, the outcast, the one not clean enough, the one defiled and defiling, the one without power, the one who will never be one of us, the one despised even by the noble peasant would be the object of concern. In other words, although the perfection Hauerwas describes may well be perfect friendship, it is not perfect *agape*. *Agape*—and here I must ask one to listen hard to what must remain counterintuitive—*agape* opens wounds, it doesn't heal them. It opens the walls of communities, it doesn't guard them. It tells a story that even the most far-reaching and flexible narrative cannot get its arms around. It lives not for us, but for them. It is not a perfection

16. Hauerwas, "Sanctified Body," 36.
17. Ibid.

that is hard to come by. It is a gift, even if a rare gift. It is not taught by hard times, but in spite of hard times, just as it is taught in spite of good times. It is an openness that prevails even when one can no longer cope with the chaos of another day, cannot say how the events of one's life are steps on a journey. *Agape* is perfection, holiness, because it is a kind of ek-stasis that unravels every communitarian fabric, every story, every virtue, every habit.

Does this mean that "*community*" is to be jettisoned in some lonely return to individualistic pietism? Is there no *story* of the holy life? Does virtue, does habit, have no complicity with perfection? No. Not this. There are indeed a community and a story and a habituation that are hallowed. However, this community is ecclesial, *gathered*—and *gathered by* what can never be lodged *in* that community—gathered by what will only disruptively dwell there. And so, the *story* of the community, however wordy it gets, however effectively it appropriates the events that befall it, must always come to silence—before an *ex*-propriating mystery that cannot be said. So, too, one's habits, as helpful as they are as a kind of collection of our worldly goods, are to be *offered*—in the freedom of the gift, the gift that is the Holy Spirit.

Thus "evangelical" perfection is a kenotic event that shifts the center of community, story, virtue, and habit from itself to the glory of the coming God. It is thus before *this God's unsettling absence* that we cry out, "Woe is me!" and "Here I am, Lord. Send me!" (Isaiah 6).

2. To Face Those Whom God Faces

2.1. The Modern Person

If it can be said that modernity has been a kind of presence moving on translucent wings, humming hypnotically about the enclosed board rooms and battlefields, the accounting offices and lecture halls, the stock exchanges and laboratories of our time, then it can also be said that modernity began to emerge from its chrysalis during the early moments of the Renaissance and first spread its wings in Descartes. The word "modern" says "just now,"[18] and its presence is perhaps best seen in its

18. "Ad. Late L. *modern-us* (6th c.), f. *modo* just now" ("Modern," in *Oxford*

preoccupation with the highly abstract notion of the self, that identity of consciousness and of will, that judge of perceptions and of truth.

In Descartes the self is asserted with particular force only after a methodic doubt has laid to rest everything upon which one might expect to be able to depend: authority, sense data, mathematics.[19] Indeed, the self breaks free precisely as it strives in a mortal struggle against a hypothetical, but no less malignant, being that wields against all belief a terrifying omnipotence. Alone before the possibility of infinite delusion, flirting with madness, the solitary, momentary, faceless ego prevails: it is *I* who stand as the single indubitable truth, the absolutely solid rock foundation of everything that might be judged to be true. Even if I were alone in the universe, even if every sight and sound were an illusion, even if $2+3\neq5$, *I* would yet be. I so forcefully assert myself as the thinker even of the most wildly erroneous thought that it is utterly impossible for this *I* not to be.[20]

It is on Descartes' terms that the word "person" comes to be defined, for example, by Leibniz as a monadic "self-consciousness and memory,"[21] by Locke as "a thinking intelligent being that can consider itself the same thinking thing in different times and places,"[22] and most importantly by Kant as an "identity," a "permanence," a "substantiality

---

English Dictionary).

19. Descartes, *Meditations on First Philosophy*, 13–16.

20. "Therefore, am *I* not at least something? But *I* have already denied that *I* have any senses and any body. Still, *I* hesitate; for what follows from that? Am *I* so tied to the body and to the senses that *I* cannot exist without them? But *I* have persuaded *myself* that there is nothing at all in the world: no heaven, no earth, no minds, no bodies. Is it not then true that *I* do not exist? But certainly *I* should exist, if *I* were to persuade *myself* of something. But there is a deceiver (*I* know not who he is) powerful and sly in the highest degree, who is always purposely deceiving *me*. Then there is no doubt that *I* exist, if he deceives *me*. And deceive *me* as he will, he can never bring it about that *I* am nothing so long as *I* shall think that *I* am something. Thus it must be granted that, after weighing everything carefully and sufficiently, one must come to the considered judgment that the statement 'I am, I exist' is necessarily true every time it is uttered by *me* or conceived in *my* mind." (ibid., 17 [24–25]; emphases added).

21. Leibniz, "On the Active Force of Body, On the Soul and on the Soul of Brutes (Letter to Wagner, 1710)," 507.

22. Locke, *Essay Concerning Human Understanding*, 315.

of soul,"²³ as one whose rational, autonomous nature constitutes it as a singular "end in itself."²⁴ By and large a person has come to be one who is responsible for its own actions, who executes its own purposes, who is punished or rewarded for its own deeds, who is thus the substantial owner of its own dignity.²⁵

Of course, not everyone has been entirely happy with the *scope* of Descartes' self-identical *cogito*. In fact, careful attempts have been made by very prominent modern thinkers to enlarge upon it so that it might include the manifold phenomena especially of sociality. Perhaps the most impressive and ambitious of these is Hegel's. Hegel's world is conflictual, one in which opposing entities—clashing, vying with one another for supremacy—make their way out of a virtual chaos. The person, the singular self, in Hegel is that unity that without such conflict remains an empty abstraction, but with it is enriched and matured.²⁶ Deep within every sleeping person is folded the potency of a spirit that has embraced its world and made it a part of itself. Indeed, the fully self-actualized person is one who by strife has found itself displaced in others and has won itself back again by appropriating them, by reconciling them to itself.²⁷ It is the person lost to find, gone to battle to return home, decentered to center, that becomes a self-identical unity once more. The *meaning of "person"* according to Hegel is enriched self-identity. In fact, the whole of universal history is finally for him the absolute return of the most extreme investment, an investment in which the Absolute Spirit, the ultimate self, sacrifices itself, consumes itself, that it might rise like a phoenix, but with greater freedom and strength and glory.²⁸ In the end Odysseus comes home more substantially and independently Odysseus than he would ever have been without the sacred and profane conquests of his odyssey.

23. Kant, *Critique of Pure Reason*, 341–44.
24. Kant, *Grounding for the Metaphysics of Morals*, 36 [428].
25. Danto, "Persons," 110–13; Lavely, "Personalism," 107–9.
26. Hegel, *Phenomenology of Spirit*, 113–14, 290–91.
27. Ibid., 356–58, 384–85.
28. Ibid., 11–12, 14.

2.2. Coming from the Outside

The ultimately substantial and independent subject of Descartes and Hegel is not as unquestionable as it appears, however. Despite claims to the contrary, the famous phrase *cogito ergo sum* and the more direct "I am" remain quite indeterminate. What is it that gives to these phrases their purported "immediate certainty"? Has "intuition" really shaken free from custom and habit and "got hold of its object purely and nakedly as 'the thing itself'"?[29] Indeed, there seems to be nothing to indicate that Descartes' formulations come to rest in and for themselves either as the simple unity at the heart of the *Meditations* or as the complex unity at the heart of the *Phenomenology*. Each moves rather as a tangle of strands of significance that trail off in every direction. Thus Nietzsche finds in the little term *cogito* an insuperable and insubstantial complexity that Descartes' meditations bypass in their haste to abide by "our grammatical custom that adds a doer to every deed."[30]

If the "I think" is not a singularity, then Descartes' solid rock foundation shatters and with it the modern spirit. An "I" become *essentially* complex is an "I" that has lost control; and an "I" that has lost control is no longer a modern person. Could it then be that there is no self at the center of its world, no substance or subject that in the face of disaster would remain or once again become self-identical, essentially the same, the inviolable owner of its properties? Perhaps it is rather the case that "the properties of a thing are effects of other 'things,'" perhaps "if one removes other 'things,' then a thing has no properties," that is, perhaps "there is no thing without other things." Perhaps "if I remove all relationships . . . of a thing, the thing does not remain over." Perhaps the whole world "is essentially a world of relationships" and thus a world with shifting centers, a world with no totalizing unity.[31] If so, then "the assumption of one single subject is perhaps unnecessary; perhaps it is just as permissible to assume a multiplicity of subjects, whose interaction and struggle is the basis of our thought and our consciousness in general." In that case one might hypothesize: not the subject as a unity,

29. Nietzsche, *Beyond Good and Evil*, 23.

30. Nietzsche, *Will to Power*, 268.

31. Ibid., 302, 306.

but the "subject as multiplicity," a nodal point of convergence of the lines of a network of relations, a motion of inevitable slippage to those others in whom it is intimately involved.[32]

Consider this: Let us say that a young woman has resolved to give something to a poor beggar on the street. However, she wants to give this time with an uncommon purity. This time she wants no adulation, no appreciation, no prospect of a return on an investment. She wants simply to give, as if her right hand did not know what her left hand were doing, as if she had lost herself, as if she were not in control. The more she calculates toward giving in this way, the more giving eludes her.[33] A gift *qua* gift unsettles a substantial subject. "One would even be tempted to say that [such] a subject as such never gives or receives a gift."[34] As long as one stands as the identity who gives, no gift occurs. As long as

---

32. Ibid., 270–71. Nietzsche's account of the relationality of the world weaves into its odd metaphysical aphorisms the deceptive phrase "the will to power." The phrase is perhaps best understood not as "the will to acquire power," but as "the will to expend power," e.g., artistically. However, there is much in Nietzsche that does not escape the grasp of the age he so frequently and so vigorously criticizes. For example, Nietzsche's metaphysical use of the notion of the "eternal recurrence of the same" may well be a survival of modern totalization. Although this notion does not function metaphysically (and may indeed function in a non-totalizing manner) in *Thus Spoke Zarathustra* (see e.g., 157–60, 215–21), it does at least at times in *The Will to Power* (see, e.g., 544–50). Nietzsche's writings get loose from their modern metaphysical entanglements (while remaining no less entangled) in the philosophical discourse of the late twentieth century, and in particular in the tradition of Martin Heidegger. Although what occurs late in the century is already to some degree taking place in Heidegger's *Being and Time*, it does not do so openly until Heidegger is read in earnest as an outsider in relation to "existentialism." The same may also be said of the writings of Kierkegaard.

33. "The moment the gift, however generous it be, is infected with the slightest hint of calculation, the moment it takes account of knowledge [*connaissance*] or recognition [*reconnaissance*], it falls within the ambit of an economy: it exchanges, in short it gives counterfeit money, since it gives in exchange for payment. Even if it gives 'true' money, the alteration of the gift into a form of calculation immediately destroys the value of the very thing that is given; it destroys it as if from the inside. The money may keep its value but it is no longer given as such. Once it is tied to remuneration [*merces*], it is counterfeit because it is mercenary and mercantile; even if it is real." Derrida, *Gift of Death*, 112.

34. Derrida, *Given Time*, 24, 40.

the other stands as the identity who receives, no gift occurs. Rather a transaction takes place. The gift becomes property.

Thus when a gift is truly given, giver and receiver are thrust back from one another just as they are held together. They are bathed in the *gift's* light, become *its* dependents.[35] The giver and receiver are not two independent entities who touch only via an item that passes from one right hand to another. There is rather something in the space *between* these two that prevents them from existing in themselves and for themselves, from taking control of the situation. There is something here that grants the fluctuating movement in which you and I meet, in which I hear your alien call. I am gifted by your call—by the otherness that sustains you, an otherness that gathers me and turns me to you.

It is the relationality of the gift that makes the giver everything she is by bringing her to a troubling acknowledgment of what she is not and never can be. She is a "who" not in herself, but in answer to the other's call. I am no personal identity. I am only *because* an other calls out to me and elicits the reply "here I am." The call of the other indeed "somehow precedes . . . [the giver's] identification with itself, for to this call I can *only* answer, have already answered, even if I think I am answering 'no.'"[36]

35. Cf. Heidegger, "Origin of the Work of Art," 143: "As necessarily as the artist is the origin of the work in a different way than the work is the origin of the artist, so it is equally certain that, in a still different way, art is the origin of both artist and work."

36. Derrida, "'Eating Well,' or the Calculation of the Subject," 261. The relationality of giver and other is the relationality of language, for Derrida. Language is the network of relations, the openness that grants the non-substantial "who" called forth in every non-economic gift. Relationality has priority over those related. Therefore, language has priority over those who speak and write. "Now if we refer, once again, to semiological difference, of what does Saussure, in particular, remind us? That 'language [which only consists of differences] is not a function of the speaking subject.' This implies that the subject (in its identity with itself, or eventually in its consciousness of its identity with itself, its self-consciousness) is inscribed in language, is a 'function' of language, becomes a *speaking* subject only by making its speech conform—even in so-called 'creation,' or in so-called 'transgression'—to the system of the rules of language as a system of differences, or at very least by conforming to the general law of *différance*, or by adhering to the principle of language which Saussure says is 'spoken language minus speech.' . . . It is the domination of beings that *différance* everywhere comes to solicit, in the sense that *sollicitare*, in old Latin, means to shake as a whole, to make tremble in entirety. Therefore, it is the determination of Being as presence or as

2.3. God *Vis-à-Vis*

Had the word "person" not accepted the feast-masters' invitation to occupy the honorific seat of "self as dignitary" at its celebration, the Nietzschean and Derridian critiques would perhaps not have threatened it. Indeed, "person" might have gone so far as to take its place in the ranks of their corps against the whole modern program. However, this was not to be. Modern thinkers saw in the term something that they could exploit, and their offer was too much to be refused. Of course, there was much to the person that would not fit at all. But the modern mind is nothing if not resourceful, and a term that might have been utterly unmarketable became profitable indeed. Thus it was that in the Age of Reason—an age in which knowledge was power, the power to harness untapped resources, the power to have and hold and be, the power to conquer, the power to identify, the power to reward and to punish—in this age "person" became a modern man.

Admittedly, already in the early sixth century Boethius had defined "person" in a way that recommended it to the children of Descartes. "A person," he said, "is an individual substance of a rational nature" (*persona est naturae rationabilis individua substanta*). However, this definition makes a significant turn from the trajectory of the word as one finds it in earlier (and much of later) Trinitarian discourse.

The Latin *persona* becomes a serious theological term for the first time in the writings of Tertullian. The word seems at first to have been equivalent to the English "mask" or "face," but also to a whole host of relations: those of the family, those that constitute friends or enemies, those at work in discourse. It is used by the Stoic Epictetus to indicate the modes of life given by providence: one is wise who lives one's *persona* as the divine playwright has written it. Even in Tertullian *persona* is not yet a technically precise theological term. He uses it often loosely

beingness that is interrogated by the thought of *différance*. . . . First consequence: *différance* is not a present being, however excellent, unique, principal, or transcendent. . . . This unnameable is the play which makes possible nominal effects . . . that are called names, the chains of substitutions of names in which for example, the nominal effect *différance* is itself *enmeshed*, carried off, reinscribed, just as a false entry or a false exit is still part of the game, a function of the system." Derrida, "*Différance*," 408, 409, 413–14, 419.

and he uses it in many ways; for example, in its older sense "of 'mask,' . . . [or] 'face,'" he uses it "in a quasi-dramatic sense, [as well as] in a sense equivalent to *homo* or *vir*."[37] Further, at the same time Tertullian was making theological use of *persona*, his contemporary Hippolytus was similarly using the Greek *prosōpon*.[38] *Prosōpon* seems also (and even more primarily) to have meant "face."[39] However, in Hippolytus it comes to signify, as *persona* does in Tertullian, the distinctiveness of the Son of God and of the Holy Spirit in relation to each other and in relation to God the Father.[40] Here the Greek and Latin terms begin to take on a profound significance. The words speak—as does the English "face"—of a distinctiveness, a uniqueness, which is simultaneously a relatedness. The Father and the Son and the Spirit are thought here as different, certainly. However, they are not different from each other in the way Aristotelian substances are.[41] These are three only as each faces the others and is faced by them. However, they are also one as they face each other.

Tertullian invented the word *trinitas* to get at the complexity and oddity of the notion that what is three *personae*, three *prosopa*, is also one. However, in order specifically to say "one," Tertullian chose the

37. Fortman, *Triune God*, 113.

38. Ibid. See also Kelly, *Early Christian Doctrines*, 110–15.

39. "F. πρός to + ψ, π- eye, face" ("Prosopalgia," *Oxford English Dictionary*).

40. In neither Hippolytus nor Tertullian, however, did the term involve "the idea of self-consciousness nowadays associated with 'person' and 'personal'" (Kelly, *Early Christian Doctrines*, 115).

41. Consider the following passage from Tertullian. He has just been discussing the Son's difference from and identity to the Father. He compares that difference and identity to a similar relation that obtains between oneself and one's thought: "Whatever you think, there is a word; whatever you conceive, there is reason. You must needs speak it in your mind; and while you are speaking, you admit speech as an interlocutor with you, involved in which there is this very reason, whereby, while in thought you are holding converse with your word, you are (by reciprocal action) producing thought by means of that converse with your word. Thus, in a certain sense, the word is a second *person* within you, through which in thinking you utter speech, and through which also, (by reciprocity of process,) in uttering speech you generate thought. The word is itself a different thing from yourself" (Tertullian, "Against Praxeas," 601 [5]).

Latin *substantia*.[42] The Trinity is one *substantia*, one solidarity, *as* it is three *personae*, three faces.

Among Greek-speaking theologians in the patristic era a similar move is made. The term *ousia* has been not uncommonly taken as equivalent to the Latin *substantia*. It, too, signifies concrete reality.[43] Therefore, it was not overly difficult for Greek theologians to acknowledge that the Trinitarian God is one *ousia*. Their difficulty came as they tried to find the words to say what they very much believed: that the Trinity is one because God is three. Although Hippolytus had already addressed this problem by his use of *prosopon*, the mainstream of Greek theology found that word to be a bit too weak, at least alone. The word was not simply rejected; indeed, one finds it in the Creed of Chalcedon. However, another moved alongside of it, and then took its place. In order to make clear that the three—Father, Son, and Spirit—are not mere labels that we have ignorantly pasted on the one homogeneous, monarchical God, but are genuinely real, they turned to the word *hypostasis*. God, the holy Trinity, they taught, is one *ousia* and three *hypostaseis*.

The irony is that *hypostasis* and *ousia* "were originally synonyms."[44] In fact, (*hypostasis* is a rather more natural equivalent of *substantia*.) Nevertheless the Greek formula distinguishes between the terms. This is not a denial of the relationality of the three. However, it is an affirmation of their reality. Whereas the Latin says emphatically that the Father and the Son and the Spirit are the *faces* of God, the Greek says emphatically that those faces are *real*.[45]

The radical nature of this idea may be seen to be at work in another Greek word that came to occupy the contentious center of the Arian controversy of the fourth century. The word is *homoousios*. What this word said to the defenders of the Creed of Nicea is that the incarnate one is truly and unequivocally God. What it is for Jesus Christ to be God is identical to what it is for the eternal Father to be God.[46] With the later Constantinopolitan declaration that the Holy Spirit is "worshiped

---

42. Kelly, *Early Christian Doctrines*, 114.

43. Ibid., 129.

44. Ibid.

45. Meyendorff, *Christ in Eastern Christian Thought*, 66.

46. Kelly, *Early Christian Doctrines*, 245.

and glorified together with the Father and the Son," the significance of the term widened. It comes now to be understood that whatever makes any one of the three God is identical to what makes any one of the others God. Indeed, to approach any one of the three is to approach the entirety of the Godhead.[47] The Father remains the wellspring of deity. The Son is deity "generated" or "begotten." The Spirit is deity "proceeding" or "spirating." However, each is fully God and there is no fourth, no generic deity, standing beyond these three as that of which they are expressions. There is no God but the one in three and three in one.

Further, this one is three and these three are one as the Father, the Son, and the Holy Spirit are mutually dependent. Although the Father is as such the source of deity, he is so only as the Son is generated and as the Spirit proceeds. Not only is there no Son or Spirit without the Father, there is no Father without the Son and the Spirit.[48] Though not to be confused with one another, they are also not to be ripped apart from one another.[49] Indeed, each is the entirety of deity precisely because it cannot be ripped apart from the others. To deal with the Son is always also to deal with the Father and the Spirit. One inevitably slips to the others in whom it is intimately involved.

Theologians of the West affirm the same dynamics of interdependence between the Trinitarian persons. It is Augustine who is

47. See, e.g., Augustine, *The Trinity*, 243–44 [8, preface].

48. See Gregory of Nyssa, *Against Eunomius*, 33–102 [2.2].

49. "Basil remarks, 'Everything that the Father is is seen in the Son, and everything that the Son is belongs to the Father. *The Son in His entirety abides in the Father, and in return possesses the Father in entirety in Himself.* Thus the hypostasis of the Son is, so to speak, the *form and presentation* by which the Father is known, and the Father's hypostasis is recognized in the form of the Son.' Here we have the doctrine of the co-inherence, or as it was later called 'perichoresis,' of the divine Persons. . . . [The] distinction of the Persons is grounded in Their origin and *mutual relations*. They are, we should observe, so many *ways* in which the one indivisible divine substance *distributes and presents Itself*, and hence They come to be termed 'modes of coming to be' (*tropoi parxeōs*). So Basil's friend Amphilochius of Iconium . . . suggests that the names Father, Son and Holy Spirit do not stand for essence or being ('God' does), but for '*a mode of existence or relation*' (*tropos parxeōs toun skreseōs*). . . . None of the Persons possesses a separate operation of His own, but one identical energy passes through all Three" (Kelly, *Early Christian Doctrines*, 264, 265–66, 267; emphasis added).

decisive here.[50] Although his starting point, unlike that of the Eastern Cappadocians, is the divine *substantia* rather than the divine *personae*, Augustine is nonetheless convinced that the unity of God is to be found only as the *personae* "severally indwell or coinhere with each other," just as "the distinction of the Persons . . . is grounded in Their mutual relations within the Godhead."[51] He clearly struggles with the idea. He concludes at last, in congruity on this point with the East, that a Trinitarian person *is* a real relation. "His own positive theory was the original and, for the history of Western Trinitarianism, highly important one that the Three are real or subsistent relations . . . (Father, Son and Spirit are thus relations in the sense that whatever each of Them is, He is in relation to one or both of the others."[52])

In Trinitarian discourse a person is thus not a self-identical subject; it is not a substance that *has* relations. Rather it *is* as such a relation; it is a reality *only as* a relation. A person is a face that is what it is only as it meets other faces. The Trinity is one concrete reality only as this *vis-à-vis.*[53] There is nothing, not even a divine reality, standing behind the faces that are the Trinity. Divine reality is the relationality of the faces that are the Father, the Son, and the Holy Spirit.

2.4. God Facing the World

Following the solidification of the orthodox doctrine of the Trinity, attention came to be given more and more to the problem of the relation between the divine and human natures of Christ. As it became

50. But also cf. Kelly's account of the position of Victorinus: "God is essentially in motion, and in fact His *esse* is equivalent to *moveri*. . . . Again and again he insists on the circumincession, or mutual indwelling, of the Persons (e.g., *omnes in alternis existentes*)" (270, 271).

51. Kelly, *Early Christian Doctrines*, 273, 274. For example, in Augustine: "Although, to tell the truth, it is difficult to see how one can speak of the Father alone or the Son alone, since the Father is with the Son, and the Son with the Father always and inseparably, not that both are the Father or both the Son, but because they are always mutually in one another and neither is alone" (Augustine, *The Trinity*, 209 [6.7]).

52. Kelly, *Early Christian Doctrines*, 274–75.

53. Cf.: "we do not call these three together one person" (Augustine, *The Trinity*, 236 [7.6]).

increasingly clear that Christ is both *fully* human and *fully* divine, and as language for the relation between those natures became more and more crucial, the terms that played so great a part in the history of the doctrine of the Trinity made themselves available once more.

The Creed of Chalcedon affirms that a solidly human reality and a solidly divine reality converge in the one Jesus Christ.[54] Yet what makes him one is the radical concurrence of his humanity (*homoousion*) with his deity (*homoousion tō patri*). These two natures are one precisely *in* the *prosōpon*, the *hypostasis*, of the divine Word, the person of the outgoing address of God. Human being is concretely here *as a divine relationality.* Leontius of Jerusalem in the sixth century is apparently the first to describe this concurrence as "enhypostatic," viz., that Jesus Christ is a human person only as he gives his life and destiny utterly in reply to the person of the divine Word.[55] He is a human person only as the concreteness of his undiluted human being moves *into* the outgoing movement of the second person of the Trinity.[56] That is, "person" is still in the first place the manner in which *God* moves, the way *God* faces. But the doctrine of the enhypostaton makes the human a person as well. In the incarnate second Adam the human is destined through

54. Meyendorff, *Christ in Eastern Christian Thought*, 29–46. The orthodox formulation in the middle of the Creed of Chalcedon (451) is this: "[We also teach] that we apprehend this one and only Christ—Son, Lord, only-begotten—in two natures; [and we do this] without confusing the two natures, without transmuting one nature into the other, without dividing them into two separate categories, without contrasting them according to area or function. The distinctiveness of each nature is not nullified by the union. Instead, the 'properties' of each nature are conserved and both natures concur in one 'person' and in one *hypostasis*. They are not divided or cut into two *prospoa*, but are together the one and only and only-begotten Logos of God, the Lord Jesus Christ" ("Definition of Chalcedon," 36).

55. Meyendorff, *Christ in Eastern Christian Thought*, 73–79; cf. 61–68.

56. "The hypostasis is not the product of nature: it is that in which nature exists, the very principle of its existence. Such a conception of hypostasis can be applied to Christology, since it implies the existence of a fully human existence, without any limitation, 'enhypostatized' in the Word, who is a divine hypostasis. This conception assumes that *God, as personal being, is not totally bound to his own nature; the hypostatic existence is flexible, 'open'*; it admits the possibility of divine acts outside of the nature (energies) and implies that God can personally and freely assume a fully human existence while remaining God, whose nature remains completely transcendent" (Meyendorff, *Christ in Eastern Christian Thought*, 77; emphasis added).

through to be a person, to face God without remainder and in so doing to face what God faces in his outgoing, to turn without remainder to those to whom God's face is turned.

2.5. Karl Barth

Perhaps the most influential treatment in our century both of the doctrine of the Trinity and of the person of Christ is to be found in the theology of Karl Barth. Barth's theology is a theology of revelation. It is definitely also a theology of the wholly other; but Barth speaks of this God only as he speaks of the apocalyptic event in which God is made known, in which God dramatically opens to what God is not. Indeed, everything Barth says emerges finally from that event in which two utterly alien realities—one creature, the other creator—become unconfusedly but also undividedly one.[57]

It is because of the exhaustively constitutive nature of God's self-revelation in Barth's theology that late in his career he could write of "the humanity of God."[58] The wholly other comes so close that one cannot speak of God in isolation from those to whom God comes. The place of God's coming is the history of the concrete human being, Jesus Christ. The unity of this history occurs as a movement of mutual self-giving, of mutual kenotic love.[59] It is the "yes" spoken by each to the other, the concrete and particular event of the absolute openness of the human Jesus to the God who is absolutely open to him. The history of Jesus Christ is the history in which there is no distinguishing what human being is about from what God is about.[60] Jesus Christ is human being corresponding (*entsprechend*) to God.[61] The history of Jesus reveals that both the truth of God and the truth of human being is an outgoing

57. Barth, *CD* I/2, 313: "Now the absoluteness of God strictly understood in this sense means that God has the freedom to be present with that which is not God, to communicate Himself and unite Himself with the other and the other with Himself, in a way which utterly surpasses all that can be effected in regard to reciprocal presence, communion and fellowship between other beings."

58. See Barth, *CD* III/2, 62; *CD* IV/1, 72, 519; and *Humanity of God*, 46.

59. Barth, *CD* IV/1, §59.1; and *CD* IV/2, §64.

60. Barth, *CD* III/2, 61–74, 161–77.

61. E.g., Barth, *CD* III/1, 197; *KD* III/1, 222.

movement of self-giving. They are not *entities* that go out, that love; they *are* the event of love.[62]

That God's self-revelation as the history of Jesus is for us, that it reaches out and gathers us to itself as our truth, is the work of the Holy Spirit, without whom nothing of God is revealed. The Father is the mystery that opens to human being (*der Offenbarer*), the Son is that openness as it penetrates the entirety of human being (*die Offenbarung*), but it is the Spirit that is the embrace of openness that gathers human being to itself (*die Offenbarsein*).[63] Spirit, Son, Father: none of these *is* without the others. Thus for Barth there is in God nothing that is static. God is the occurrent Trinity through and through, not a substance that occurs.[64] Thus in Christ the center of human being is outside itself in the outgoing Trinitarian movement of the Father to the Son by the Spirit, a movement that is simultaneously in the Spirit, through the Son, to the Father. To look to human being is to look to the shifting centers of the Trinity that open that being beyond itself.[65]

Further, the outgoing love of God occurs as the Son travels into "the far country," the region where human being plunges into the abyss of sin and death.[66] God's outgoing to the godless is thus God's self-humiliation, a humiliation that is never simply left behind.[67] As the Son returns home, exalting human being "in the closest proximity to God from the greatest distance," he is still the crucified one.[68] To be human is therefore to move down the path of the history of Jesus Christ, in the rhythm of the crucifixion and the resurrection, turned to the God who is love and with this God to the lost and abandoned.

62. Barth, *CD* IV/2, §68. See also *CD* III/2, 162: "It is obviously true of man in general that his being is not to be sought behind or apart from . . . [historical] movement, as if it were first something in itself which is then caught up in this movement. . . . Whatever his state may be, he is only *in* this state; it is not his being but only the attribute and modality of his being. His true being is his being in history grounded in the man Jesus, in which God wills to be for him and he may be for God."

63. Barth, *CD* I/1, 363; *KD* I/1, 383.

64. See the astonishing *CD* II/1, §28.

65. Barth, *CD* III/1, 69–71; IV/2, 49–50, 91–115.

66. Barth, *CD* IV/1, §59.1.

67. Barth, *CD* IV/1, 176–77; IV/2, 42–44, 352–60.

68. Barth, *CD* IV/2, 100.

2.6. Wolfhart Pannenberg

Barth's notions of the apocalyptic revelation of God, the centrality of the history of Jesus for the whole of theology, God's gracious embrace of creaturely being, the relational nature both of divine and of human life are affirmed in a rather different way by his former student Wolfhart Pannenberg. Pannenberg thinks both eschatologically and historically. History for him is not something added to reality. Reality is history, history is reality. There is no being except as it occurs in the irreversible forward march of time.[69] Each event is connected to each other event so that (the past is gathered and transformed by new occurrences) the way the opening words of a narrative are gathered and transformed as the story proceeds. Each event is a fragment of the whole that is to be, the whole that constitutes the ultimate future.[70] The eschaton is the final word, the determination of all being, the insuperable yes and no. Here reality takes place, becomes one, for the first time. There are no gaps, no deficiencies, no isolation, no enmity, no death. The eschaton is the event of the resurrection, emancipation, and solidarity of all the unrepeatable moments once discarded in the past. It is the undying event in which every unique phenomenon is affirmed. This is the event in which each is as it points to each and all. It is the fullness of creation.[71]

Pannenberg maintains that the eschaton is the event of God's rule, of God's deity. It is God by definition that speaks the final word, which is the reality that determines everything.[72] Indeed, one cannot speak of God with content without speaking of the eschaton: God has this future as God's mode of being.[73] The kingdom of God is the creative destiny of all reality.

The deity of Jesus Christ is for Pannenberg a matter of his relation to this coming kingdom. Certainly, this means in the first place that Jesus was raised from the dead, that he is in his resurrection the occur-

---

69. Pannenberg, *Faith and Reality*, 112.

70. Pannenberg, *Theology and the Kingdom of God*, 55–57, 58–64.

71. Pannenberg, *Systematic Theology*, 1:407–10, 438; 2:97–100, 139, 144–46, 160.

72. Pannenberg, *Basic Questions in Theology*, 1, 202.

73. Pannenberg reiterates his famous notion of the ontological priority of the future (*Kingdom*, 63) in his *magnum opus*, the *Systematic Theology* (see 2:100).

rence beforehand of what is to come.[74] However, it is also connected to the fact that(Jesus lived his life in utter abandonment to the coming kingdom) The kingdom of God occupies his time in a radical way. So important is it to Jesus that he proclaims that even now it determines what is worth doing, who is blessed, who is perfect, who is first, who is last. The coming kingdom is in this way even now immanent, even now a force, even now at work. Jesus' faithfulness to God is his faithfulness to the coming kingdom, and his faithfulness to the coming kingdom is his seeing everything he encounters as having its ultimate determination, its ultimate meaning, its ultimate being in the event in which God gathers all things together.[75] Thus my identity and your identity are to come, and when they come they will be inseparably united to each other, without confusion or division. Even now we are united to each other in anticipation of that day.[76]

2.7. God Is Agape

The Father, the Son, and the Holy Spirit *are* only as they entail each other, only as they turn to each other. Thus they are persons. The person of the Son goes out *from* and simultaneously goes out *to* the Father. As an other, the Son turns to the Father in love and *is* loved. The love of God is outgoing. Creaturely being, through and through dependent upon God's care, is penetrated and embraced and affirmed as the Son moves outward to it, and thus destines it for God's kingdom.

Jesus of Nazareth is a passionate turning to this outgoing, to this eternal Word of address, a responsive "here I am." All that he is as a human being is given to the outgoing of God, to the coming of the king-dom. Jesus is expropriated, but also glorified by it. He is simply given to the reign of God, to the love of God, to the coming of God. He is nothing but a face turned to God, a *vis-à-vis* that finally has only one visage. He is no substance, no self at the center of his world, no owner of his own properties; there is in him nothing standing beneath or behind. All that

74. Pannenberg, *Jesus—God and Man*, 67, 74–77, 129–35.

75. Pannenberg, *Systematic Theology*, 2:326–39; Pannenberg, *Jesus—God and Man*, 225–44.

76. Pannenberg, *Systematic Theology*, 2:454, 459.

has been given up. Thus before the face of God, he is a transparent human face. Thus he is a human person. Thus he is hallowed. There is one face, one *prosōpon*, one *hypostasis*, one *persona* here: the concurrence of what human being is and wills with what God is and wills. But, of course, *this* person is nothing but a relation to the Father and the Spirit.

Union according to *ousia* occurs in the gifting of mutual dependence of the persons of the Trinity. Union according to *hypostasis* occurs in the enhypostatic hallowing of Jesus of Nazareth to the eternal personal address of God. We, however, are gifted, hallowed, by the embrace of this union, an embrace that is even now eschatological.[77] In Christ our destiny is given to be God's kingdom. His yes to the lost, the poor, the suffering, the imprisoned, the condemned, the dying, the dead, the damned, is the eternal yes of God's coming rule. To be in Christ is to live from and toward what is to come, however fragmentarily. To be in Christ is to be a human person, however fragmentarily.

Life in Christ is shifted now to the life to come. We live in hope. The life to come is, however, no fixed, unbreathing state. It is a complex gathering of the shifting intersection-points of relations of giving. Yet this gathering lacks an intrinsic center. It is what it is as it in turn moves from itself in adoration to the one enhypostatized in the outgoing face of God, a face that is no self-identical substance, but God's eternal address, the second person of the Trinity, the one who *is* only as a relation of an other to the person of the Father and the person of the Holy Spirit. Thus the kingdom adores the Trinity to whom it has been liberated.

It is therefore our destiny to look beyond ourselves, to lay down our defenses, to lose control, to face God and in so doing to face those whom God faces. It is our destiny to pray, to pray as an abandonment to God's love that is itself by looking to others *whom* God loves.

It is because God loves with the complexity of what the Trinitarian persons entail that we, too, are persons, that we, too, go out to God and to one another. Therefore to pray to God is never a lonely act, not even in this broken world. It is always the one who is destined to be eschatological love, the one whose self is to be her neighbor, the one who is as she points to each and to all—it is always this one who prays. To be a

---

77. Panayiotis, *Deification in Christ*, 233.

human person is to be by God's gift a passionate act of communal prayer that says in one voice, "Here I am."

In the hearing of the gospel, in the regeneration of baptism, in the celebration of the Eucharist, in the act of mercy, in the quietness of meditation, in the ecstasy of joy, in the gift of justice, in the openness of faith, hope, and love, the kingdom has begun to arrive. Although it is only in the end that we will have become persons in the truest sense, insofar as we live concretely here and now from the end, persons have begun to arrive. It is thus not a complaint to say that "now we see in a mirror dimly," because our speech lives from the vital hope that "then we will see face to face."

7

(The) Church and (The) Culture
A Little Reflection on the *Assumptio Carnis*[1]

I

THE LITTLE ESSAY THAT follows is offered before the reader as an experiment in theology. That means that from beginning to end it traces a discourse—a *Proslogium*—of praise and gratitude. But the gratitude and praise that issue here are not finally offered to you, my fellow readers; for if you read me correctly, then you too will not read toward yourselves, but toward the One whom the attentive reader even now expects.[2] To put it a bit more simply, this essay is but an inscription of the truth: Jesus, the one Head of all things in heaven and on earth (Eph 1:10). Whether this discourse fares well or not has finally to do with the way it will come to join all those other things brought together under that one Head.

1. An earlier version of the present essay was first published in *Wesleyan Theological Journal* 24 (1989) 91–102.

2. Anselm, "An Address," 72–73 (I): "Teach me to seek thee, and when I seek thee show thyself to me, for I cannot seek thee unless thou teach me, or find thee unless thou show me thyself. Let me seek thee in my desire, let me desire thee in my seeking. Let me find thee by loving thee, let me love thee when I find thee." See also Barth, *Anselm: Fides Quaerens Intellectum.*

II

The life that human beings live is not given to them beforehand. Their options, of course, are limited by the environments into which they stumble as well as by the organic structures with which they struggle. But what their lives come to be is not exhaustively preprogrammed, for example, instinctually.[3] And so humans begin as quite uncertain about where they are going. Further, when they choose a way to go, they have to take themselves there. If there are no alternative routes and they do not choose to go elsewhere and there are things in the way, then they have to move them. If those things are too heavy for the muscles in their arms and legs, then they must invent tools to move them. If the weather turns bad, they must clothe themselves and make shelters. To minimize conflict and to maximize the efficiency of a family or larger group, rules must be made. And all of this takes language, perhaps the most impressive of all human inventions. In other words, humans make their own way, and the way that they make is called culture.[4]

Culture is an artificial world only partially determined by geography and climate and vegetation and the migration patterns of animals. Culture is a world shaped to a surprising degree by human hands and

---

3. See Pannenberg, *Anthropology in Theological Perspective*, 27–42.

4. This is of course not to say that God is uninvolved in human life. God is the Creator of all (*die alles bestimmende Wirklichkeit*, to use the phrase Pannenberg picked up from Bultmann). But God creates in human cultural activity always as humans create, i.e., human creativity reflects God's creativity. T. S. Eliot, "Choruses from 'The Rock,'" in *The Complete Poems and Plays*, 111 (IX): "The soul of Man must quicken to creation. / Out of the formless stone, when the artist united himself with stone, / Spring always new forms of life, from the soul of man that is joined to the soul of stone; / Out of the meaningless practical shapes of all that is living or lifeless / Joined with the artist's eye, new life, new form, new colour. / Out of the sea of sound the life of music, / Out of the slimy mud of words, out of the sleet and hail of verbal imprecisions, / Approximate thoughts and feelings, words that have taken the place of thoughts and feelings, / There spring the perfect order of speech, and the beauty of incantation. / LORD, shall we not bring these gifts to Your service? / Shall we not bring to Your service all our powers / For life, for dignity, grace and order, / And intellectual pleasures of the senses? / The LORD who created must wish us to create / And employ our creation again in His service / Which is already His service in creating." This is illustrated in Adam's naming of the animals in the garden (without a name book): "and whatever the man called every living creature, that was its name" (Gen 2:19b).

ideas. It is a world of tin plates and huts and paths and clans and villages. It is a world of alliances and national laws and city governments and police forces and sales tax; a world of etiquette and customs and honors and classes and races and languages; a world of definite work and a world of indefinite play.

III

Culture then is the way humans live their lives. And since the Christian life is also quite obviously a human life, it is very easy to conclude that the church is *in toto* a species, perhaps even the best or purest species, within the comprehensive genus "culture," that is, it is very easy to conclude that the church is purely cultural. But where such a very easy conclusion wants to take us and whether or not we should make the journey are not immediately settled. Consider two of the ways this easy conclusion approaches its goal.

On the one hand, the church might be taken as an assembly within the last remaining fortress of a land invaded by an evil people, a people who have corrupted the laws and customs that only *we* have purely preserved; we might believe that the church is huddled within an ark awaiting the rain, while the perverters of that true culture which only we carry seal their own doom by their foolish obsession with the passing pleasures of today. On the other hand, the church might be taken as the assembly that provides the example for those around it; we might believe that it shows people what they are to be and perhaps to some extent are already, but which along with the church they can only now fully be; we might believe that it is the best and the truest and the most beautiful, even by the standards of those who observe it from outside (but never really outside) its wide, open doors. On the one hand, then, the church is regarded as a sphere of culture diametrically opposed to another sphere of culture (the world). On the other hand, the church is regarded as a kind of institutional reminder within (a) culture of how we all really ought to live, a kind of purified essence of the larger, less-than-perfect cultural world. Here are two different positions that are essentially the same: they both affirm emphatically that the church is purely cultural.[5] Since the church claims that Jesus Christ is its reason for being, the adequacy of these views or any view can be evaluated with depth only if one attends to *his* meaning. But the tools of hermeneutics provide escape routes, if one but looks. The Christ can be understood,

5. What I am discussing in this paragraph and more indirectly in the next are the first two "types" of H. Richard Niebuhr's classic *Christ and Culture*. But unlike Niebuhr, who sharply contrasts what he calls "Christ against culture" and "the Christ of culture," I am saying that they are variants of the same position. For "Christ against culture," see Tertullian, *The Prescription Against Heretics*, 246 (7). For "the Christ of culture," see von Harnack's attacks against Karl Barth in *The Beginnings of Dialectical Theology*, 165–66, 171–74, 186–87 (see esp. question 10 on 166); and Cobb, *Liberal Christianity at the Crossroads*, esp. 11–16. It also seems clear that Niebuhr's types three and four, "Christ above culture" (exemplified by Thomas Aquinas) and "Christ and culture in paradox" (Luther), fall under the same heading. The added grace that brings holiness, according to Thomas, is the fulfillment of culture and in no sense contrasts with the good, the true, and the beautiful of even fallen humanity. What distinguishes this position is that the supernatural adds a certain complexity; but the whole is subsumed under the same ahistorical, Aristotelian (Platonic) *archai*. See Aquinas, *Summa Contra Gentiles, II: Providence, part II*, 223–25 (147), 230–33 (150). The position of Luther, "Christ and culture in paradox," begins by contrasting Christ and culture (even more extremely than Tertullian does). But for the sake of guarding against chaos and the destruction it would bring, Luther strongly advocates Christian involvement in worldly affairs. This involvement is not to transform the world; Luther is much too pessimistic to expect that. Rather, the Christian is involved in worldly (sinful) society to keep things from getting any more overtly evil than they already are. One should live one's life where God puts one, expecting no great improvement on the outside, but internally trusting in God, loving one's neighbor, and enjoying the peace that God sheds abroad in one's heart. See Luther, "Secular Authority"; Althaus, *Ethics of Martin Luther*; Niebuhr's excellent discussion in ch. 5 of *Christ and Culture*; and Webber, *Secular Saint*, 113–27. The fifth position is called "Christ the transformer of culture." This position at least begins to "historicize": it can contain ahistorical elements, as it does in Augustine, who makes the *archai* of reality eternal, i.e., changeless. But even Augustine breaks out of the static view of at least the created order and expects novelty. See Augustine, *City of God*, 1054–55, 1062–64 (XXII, 13–14, 20); and Löwith, *Meaning in History*, 160–73, esp. 163–64. If this position can free itself from Platonic dualism and an equally static Aristotelian schema of potentiality-actuality, and if it can give itself to genuine novelty (including *die Weltoffenheit*), then it would be rather close to what is argued below. To the extent that it gives itself to genuine novelty, it not only frees itself from subsumption under the genus "culture," but it provides a basis for evaluating culture, and accounting for it. The reader might also want to consult Geoffrey Wainwright's discussion of the church and culture in his *Doxology*, 357–98; see in particular 386–87 for a proposed sixth type, "the pluralistic type," which may in fact be a variant of the second type, "the Christ of culture."

analogously to the understanding of the church just presented, as the completion of what we all should be, as the One who possesses perfection, as the One who is humanity fulfilled, as the One who has arrived. Then, depending on how bad the rest of us are taken to be, either he is the One who is sharply contrasted with those of us (probably most of us) who remain under the curse of sin—the corrupt, the diseased, the spiritually dead—or he is the One who is an example to the rest of us of what we can become, perhaps by valiant effort. Grace is perhaps needed more in the one case than in the other, but again Jesus Christ functions the same way in both: as a kind of flesh-and-blood platonic form, the complete One whom we are to imitate from a distance: *imitatio Christi*. Of course, if one wishes to be Chalcedonian, one can quite easily explain that his being fulfilled humanity is what constitutes his full deity.

IV

And yet is this what is to be said of Jesus Christ? Does the New Testament go to so much trouble to explain his humble birth, his homelessness, his rejection by the people of his nation and by his closest followers, his being arrested by the officials of a foreign occupying power, and his humiliating crucifixion—does it do all this in order to explain his *fullness*? Is it out of his fullness that he sweats drops of blood at Gethsemane? Is it out of his fullness that he prays, "*Eloi, Eloi, lama Sabachthani?*"

The whole of the life of Jesus Christ is not a fullness;[6] it is an emptying in which he does not assert himself, but rather asserts the

6. This is written with the recognition that the Old and New Testaments give a very prominent place to the idea of being filled with the Spirit, and I do not have any desire to challenge Scripture. How could I write such a thing, therefore? Well, because being filled with the Spirit is not like filling a flour sack with flour. It is not being completed or finished (cf. John 19:30). It is movement. One might note that Hans Walter Wolff defines the *nepeš* that Adam becomes when God breathes into him (Gen 2:7) as "neediness," which is free to hope in and to praise Yahweh, and thus not as a completeness that is in itself well situated with Yahweh. See Wolff, *Anthropology of the Old Testament*, 10–25; see also 59–60. Notice also Paul's sarcasm (in 1 Cor 4:8–13) to the Corinthians who believe they have arrived: "Already you are filled! . . . [But] we have become, and are now, as the refuse of the world, the offscouring of all things" (vv. 8a, 13b). Of course, the most obvious text for this argument is Philippians 2. In other words, being filled with the Spirit is, when compared to other kinds of filling,

other.[7] And yet his relationship to culture is not simple. Just as culture-Christianity stops far short of Jesus Christ, so also does a Christianity that keeps him detached from culture. Since he asserts the other, one can never see him as either unrelated to human life as a kind of docetic phantom, or related to it simply as the destroying agent of divine wrath. In Christ, human life is neither simply pulled up by the roots and cast into the fire, nor allowed to be as it is. In him, life is *aufgehoben*—the old is ended, but in such a way that it becomes new.

Among the old ideas that become new in Jesus Christ are two that already speak of novelty, or that at least point at it. The first is the idea that something comes to be only as a series of events is established and bound together in continuity by God.[8] The second is the idea that something comes to be only from beyond itself, from beyond what it has been; that what it comes to be is given to it in discontinuity with the past, that is, out of nowhere; and this too by God.[9] The wandering

an emptying.

7. The word *assert* means literally "to join to." But its etymology becomes immediately even more interesting. It means "to put one's hand on the head of a slave, either to set him free or claim him for servitude, *hence*, to set free, protect, defend." *Oxford English Dictionary*, s.v. "assert." In light of the cross and resurrection one might change the "either-or" to a "both-and."

8. There is an excellent discussion of this idea in von Rad's *Old Testament Theology*, 2:105–12. Among other things, von Rad writes the following: Israel "did not stop short at basing her existence on a single historical event: she went on to specify a whole series of them, and it was this series of events as a whole which called the people of Israel into being" (105). "At the same time, the whole . . . was itself very much more than the sum of all its various parts" (106). "Jahwism too experienced Jahweh as a power who established fixed orders, but with a difference. In the other religions the deities exercised their functions and received their worship *within* these orders—they in fact embodied the orders on which the cosmos and the state rested—whereas for the faith of Israel Jahweh was *outside* of these. He was their creator and guarantor; but he could not be identified with them" (111–12).

9. This, of course, is the other side of the first idea. Von Rad's discussion of this is perhaps even more important (see ibid., 115–18). Again some selections: The notion of the eschatological in the Old Testament is that there is a historical "break which goes so deep that the new state beyond it cannot be understood as a continuation of what went before. It is as if Israel and all her religious assets are thrown back to the point of *vacuum*, a vacuum which the prophets must first create by preaching judgment and sweeping away all false security, and then fill with their message of the new thing" (115; emphasis added). "The prophetic teaching is only eschatological

people of Israel move beyond their dwelling, their camp is broken, their settlement is interrupted. It is this interruption[10] that is the breaking in of the new, the occurrence of the unprecedented, the movement into the open. The new is in its first movement the nihilation of the old, the denial of whatever is given, even of potentiality, because it is the radically other. But these people remain those who dwelt here, who settled, for the novel embraces the old. But in so doing it at the same time makes it new. This is the historicizing of reality that takes place as God acts.

In Jesus Christ the historicizing of reality becomes both more comprehensive and more nihilating. There is no level of human reality excluded by him.[11] Not only does he show love and compassion toward both the powerful and the powerless during his public ministry (speaking with authority to the former, weeping with the latter), but he, the Christ, God the Son, through whom all things were made, joins thieves on Golgotha and is accursed. Jesus Christ therefore embraces all the living.[12] And yet as his hands stretch out to embrace, he dies. Now this death is not merely bodily; it is not only that the building that housed his immaterial soul has perished. He is dead; his life is gone; he has ceased to be. Therefore his embrace takes in the living and the dead, and among the dead whom he embraces are to be numbered those who died

---

when the prophets expelled Israel from the safety of the old saving actions and suddenly shifted the basis of salvation to a future action of God . . . ; it is reduced to the extremely revolutionary fact that the prophets saw Jahweh approaching Israel with a new action which made the old saving institutions increasingly invalid since from then on life or death for Israel was determined by this future event" (118). Cf. this from Wolff, *Anthropology of the Old Testament*, 88–89: "Now, for the first time, the concept of the 'future' can also consequently be formed in Hebrew: *habbā' ōt*, what is to come. . . . Future events themselves move first in the direction of man; only the person who has heard the promise turns expectantly towards the things that have up to then lain invisibly behind him. Now the future is defined as 'what is new' . . . ."

10. See Jüngel, "Truth of Life," 231–36.

11. If one understands that human reality embraces nonhuman reality, then in him is gathered together everything. Von Rad, *Genesis*, 60: "Thus man's creation has a retroactive significance for all nonhuman creatures; it gives them a relation to God." Cf. Karl Barth, *CD* III/1, 184: "The being created in this [divine] image is [human being]. The rest of creation has this character of a copy or image only insofar as it has found its conclusion and climax in the creation and existence of [human being]."

12. Cf. the recapitulation theory of Irenaeus.

accursed. This descent, this humiliation, this emptying "unto death, even death on the cross," is itself embraced by God the Father, embraced and exalted above all things (Philippians 2).[13]

Here indeed God turns to the world, and the world is redeemed, but—and this is crucially important—not simply as it is. Jesus Christ is indeed the resurrected One. But his resurrection takes place only with his crucifixion. Further, his resurrected body is not simply a repetition of the body that reclined at the Last Supper. It is that body certainly. Otherwise Jesus Christ would not have been raised. But the resurrected body is that body transformed, not resuscitated. It is the old, certainly; but the old has become new.[14] The redemption of the world therefore takes place only as it moves with Jesus Christ beyond what it is, only as it ceases to grasp at the status it wishes to possess and reaches rather for the other, only as it embraces the humiliated and shares in that humiliation, that is, only as it is nihilated, only as it comes to be a servant, only as it gives itself up to the other,[15] only as it joins Jesus Christ on the cross. The resurrection that follows cannot be guaranteed, since it comes from the outside, that is, it is resurrection *ex nihilo*. And yet in Jesus Christ everyone is resurrected, that is, in him the old human life

13. Perhaps the most eloquent theological explication of this is Moltmann's *The Crucified God*. See also Moltmann's essay "The Crucified God and Apathetic Man." Cf. the following from Bornkamm, "On Understanding the Christ Hymn": The way of Christ "bursts all bounds of earth and yet precisely in so doing opens the horizon by which alone there can be real life in faith" (112). Further "the 'form of a servant' is not a role he plays, but the very nature that he assumes. But then it is surprising that humanity and servanthood here are identified so directly" (115). Christ's "subsequent exaltation as Lord is founded only in his obedience even to death" (116). "The Lordship of Christ means the complete and full turning of God to the world. The exaltation of the humiliated One is God's victory over the world" (118). "But this means at the same time that humiliation and obedience are now henceforth the kingly way of faith, the seal of the liberated, the pledge of coming redemption. Therefore, the congregation already now joins in the hidden praise of the world and makes it manifest—vicariously for the world for whom the truth of God is not yet open: 'Jesus Christ is Lord—to the glory of God the Father'" (12).

14. See Pannenberg, *Jesus—God and Man*, 74–81, 86–88, 98–100.

15. "The transcendence that living is, and that cannot be satisfactorily expressed in life itself as survival (a surpassing of life), is rather the pressing demand of an *other* life, the life of the *other*. From this life everything comes, and turned to it, we cannot turn back." Blanchot, *Writing of the Disaster*, 105.

is made incomparably new. Thus culture enters into this discourse explicitly once again.

V

The light of the cross and resurrection shines back on culture. Culture happens as people take a world that in itself is just there and make it something else. They take a stone and make it into an axehead. They take seed and turn it into a crop. They take trees and turn them into shelters, tables, carvings. They take grunts and clicks and whistles and turn them into language. The products of culture, however, immediately become part of the world that in itself is just there. They then await further cultural activity, further change. Insofar as this activity is done non-possessively, that is, done toward the other, doxologically, awaiting God's yes or no, it reflects the light of the cross and resurrection, it shines as history. But of course, axes can become weapons; shelters, tables, and carvings can become possessions; language can become slander. Such a perverted culture is in itself opaque. And yet even opacity does not overcome the cross and resurrection (see John 1:5).[16] Indeed, the cross and resurrection are themselves the overcoming of opacity (Matt 4:16), but only as the opaque is emptied, and that happens only with time.

It is in Jesus Christ that human life becomes the church.[17] It is not essential that there be many or few human lives gathered together. It is not essential that the gathering manifest one sociological structure rather than another. It is essential only that human life be in Jesus Christ, and that means that it pass through his death and resurrection. And yet where there is the church there is also to be found a whole world that is not gathered together in Jesus Christ. The church is not the Kingdom of God. It is not the absolute, universal embodiment of God's rule over God's creation. The church therefore must struggle; it can never stop, it will not arrive, until the reality that it only anticipates has been estab-

16. "Apparently, the key mark of Jesus in the image/form of God is that he did not grasp after equality with God but became obedient. God is the one who does not grasp. And human persons in his image are those who do not grasp. Grasping power cannot create. Grasping power cannot enhance creation . . . grasping brings death." Brueggeman, *Genesis*, 34.

17. Schmidt, "Ekklesia," 509, 512.

lished by its Lord and Savior.[18] Of course, the hostile world that is not gathered together in Jesus Christ has been broken by him.[19] But in a sense the breaking is still to be done. Already and not yet.

The people gathered together in Jesus Christ continue to be related to the institutions of this world. The difference between these people and those who are not gathered is that the former have been granted freedom.[20] They are to be subject to rulers, but only insofar as that subjection can be lived out in that freedom that arises in subjection to the true Lord (Romans 13); wages are to be earned, but only insofar as doing so makes clear that the gospel is "free of charge" (1 Cor 9:1–18); taxes are to be paid, but only insofar as those taxes are "things that are God's" (Mark 12:13–17); customs are to be observed, but only insofar as that leads toward liberating others to the freedom in Jesus Christ (1 Cor 8:1–13; 10:14—11:1). Unfortunately, there are institutions that cannot be preserved in a kingdom of love. The church is about the conversion of these institutions, but conversion takes time. Therefore, it is inevitable that followers of the crucified Lord will be required to suffer. But the hope that such unconverted systems cannot finally stand in the

18. Ibid., 522, 534.

19. Bornkamm, "Christ and the World in the Early Christian Message," 21–22: "Into this world over which as it were the gigantic shadow of guilty [humanity] lies, and which has marked the vanity of its coming and going by this guilt, even to the sighing of the creation; into this world, which has become the sphere of power of the forces which, though exalted on the throne by [humanity itself], reproach [humanity] in [its] imprisonment in guilt; into this world, which I am myself, God has sent [God's] Son in the form of sinful flesh, in the form marked and disfigured by sin—made sin for us. . . . What makes the world this world, what makes [humanity] this [human being] is borne and conquered by Christ. On the cross which the world sets up for him and on which he dies, the world itself finds its end."

20. "What characterizes and differentiates believers is just that in their ties and obligations to the world they stand as the children of freedom, no longer as the enslaved who seek life in it, but as those in Christ, liberated by Christ by his dying and rising and transplanted into the lordship of his love. As those at home with a heavenly citizenship, they recognize the time and know that the night is retreating and the morning approaches." Ibid., 24. "A thing can be purely secular only to [one] who thinks of it in this way. As nothing is charisma in itself, so nothing is secular in itself. For, in the time of the Eschaton, this sphere of the 'in itself,' this demilitarized zone, this 'indifference' exists no longer." Käsemann, "Ministry and Community in the New Testament," 72.

presence of the one who raised that Lord from the dead weakens their oppressive hold and places one in a position to do a redemptive work (1 Pet 2:11—3:9; 4:7–11; Eph 5:21–33; 1 Cor 11:2–16).

Therefore those people who are gathered together in Christ, that is, the church, will inevitably undertake the task of transforming the cultures in which they move, whether they know it or not. They will inevitably see not only that the world as it is now given is the focus of God's profoundly redemptive resolve, but also that the world as it is now given is passing away and is far from ultimate.

The course to be taken in this transformative enterprise must follow the lead of what emerges in the cross and resurrection of Jesus Christ. What emerges there is (1) the nihilation of everything that is, and (2) the embrace of everything that is. What emerges is redemptive love in the midst of absolute loss.

The church therefore is to stand with everyone—not only or primarily with the best or most deserving, not with the majority, not with one sex or race, but with all; and in particular the church is to stand with those who stand closest to the cross: the neglected, the poor, the homeless, the deprived, the outcast, the sinner, the forsaken. The church therefore is to make clear that the crucified and resurrected One is Lord, to walk with everyone to the cross, to hang there with everyone, to rise with everyone to newness of life. The church therefore is to make clear that individuals and institutions are never acceptable merely as they are in themselves, and that they can never make themselves acceptable. This is to say that acceptability has everything to do with the One who is beyond.

Therefore the church's stance toward the institutions of the culture in which it moves must in the first place be critical. The self-deification to which institutions (including religious institutions) are inclined must be unmasked. No institution is complete in itself; nor is it in a position to guarantee its own survival; nor does it have its reason for being in itself. The Lordship of Jesus Christ means that every institution must come to be what it is not yet, that God alone grants reality (and that from the outside), that every reality has its reason for being only in the other.[21]

21. "To be converted is to know and experience the fact that, contrary to the laws

Racism or sexism is to be condemned, for they exempt one race or sex from the cross and bar another from the resurrection. The church is to condemn systems that imprison persons in social or economic classes and that perpetuate poverty, disease, ignorance, isolation, and despair, for they deny the hope that is in Jesus Christ. The church is to condemn the expenditure of resources for the production of weapons that for the sake of national self-preservation threaten to destroy all life on earth, for such expenditure reverses and thus perverts what emerges in the life of Christ—the revelation that life is to be poured out, given away for the other, and never for oneself.

On the other hand, the church is to support even non-Christian institutions that help clarify the cross and resurrection of Jesus Christ. It will join hands with organizations that pursue the same general goals as it does, recognizing that those organizations have different reasons for acting. The church therefore would find much with which to agree in peace movements, civil rights movements, economic reform movements, educational institutions, and institutions that seek physiological, psychological, or social welfare.[22] It will of course take wisdom and deliberation to decide how to distinguish between institutions that are relative allies and those that are not, and every such alliance cannot be uncritical. But to make clear that Jesus Christ is Lord requires that we not let the given order be.

The church is enfleshed in culture; and yet it is the church only as it lives according to the Spirit. It cannot therefore simply be taken as a species of the genus "culture." And yet every move it makes is to make clear that not only is this world passing away but it is the focus of God's profoundly serious redemptive resolve. The life of love carries the church into the miseries and hopes of real flesh-and-blood human beings. It is not for the sake of some ideology that the church cannot confine itself to an inner, private sphere; it is rather because Jesus Christ has awakened mercy and compassion in our midst, because our Lord poured out his

---

of physics, we can stand straight, according to the Gospel, only when our center of gravity is outside ourselves." Gutiérrez, *Theology of Liberation*, 205.

22. See Moltmann, *Crucified God*, 330–35.

life for those who are lost and forsaken and impoverished, because no servant is above his/her master.[23]

23. Paul Tillich has developed one of the most impressive theologies of culture in this century. Central to his view is his distinction between "autonomy," "heteronomy," and "theonomy." "Autonomy asserts that [humanity] as the bearer of universal reason is the source and measure of culture and religion—that [humanity] is [its] own law. Heteronomy asserts that [humanity], being unable to act according to universal reason, must be subjected to a law, strange and superior to [it]. Theonomy asserts that the superior law is, at the same time, the innermost law of [humanity itself], rooted in the divine ground which is [humanity's] own ground: the law of life transcends [humanity], although it is, at the same time, [humanity's] own." Tillich, "Religion and Secular Culture," 56–57. Tillich is saying that there is something fundamentally wrong with autonomy and heteronomy. The first fails to recognize that the truth of human life cannot be taken directly from the conditioned things around us, not even from ourselves. The second fails to recognize that the truth of human life emerges out of the depths of human life itself, out of the unconditioned richness in which even fallen human life is rooted, and therefore it fails to see that the truth always brings integrity, wholeness, health to human life. These two are destructive, demonic. The third, theonomy, sees that "religion is the substance of culture and culture the form of religion" (57). It sees that no matter how mysterious and frightening the truth may seem, it is always also fascinating, the truth with which we were connected all along, the truth that was there all along. It has not come out of nowhere, it does not disturb closure, it vibrates up from below, where it was vibrating all along, in the eternal now. Theonomy means healing, integrity, wholeness. The ground in which we are rooted, from which our life emerges, is of course God.

I find that I cannot accept this view, and for the following reasons. First, it is a delusion to maintain that an open relationship with God will bring health, completeness, wholeness. In fact, in light of the cross (which remains the cross even on Easter), it seems that an open relationship with God is just that: open, as in "open wound." Tillich can talk about novelty, and he does so in terms of cultural activity. See idem, *Systematic Theology*, 1:181–82. But because there is an *analogia entis* between us and God, i.e., because what we are and can become are both our possession as potentiality and in unbroken (even if twisted) continuity with God, there is only the relatively new, the new that was "latent" before it became "manifest." See idem, *Systematic Theology*, 3:220; cf. 94–98; see also idem, *Courage to Be*, 89, 155–90. Thus Tillich can write: "The human heart seeks the infinite because that is where the finite wants to rest [!]. In the infinite it sees its own fulfillment." Idem, *Dynamics of Faith*, 13. In turning to God one re-turns to the essential, the original, the old (see esp. his discussion of the fall in *Systematic Theology*, 2:29–44 and passim). Further, the fulfillment that Tillich's theology of culture longs for is, as far as I can see, incompatible with the notion that faith, hope, and love are self-effacing, self-emptying, self-denying. Thus Tillich sees faith as "centeredness," and as "self-affirmation." Idem, *Dynamics of Faith*, 4–8; *Courage to Be*, 172. Barth's alternative seems far superior at this point. See, e.g., Barth, "Rudolf Bultmann: An Attempt to Understand Him," esp. 86–88.

8

"Whom Shall I Send?"
Toward a Theology of Nature[1]

We live in a scientific civilization.... Behind our manipulation of nature ... there exists a certain way of seeing the world, a peculiar perspective which molds nature into a specific form.... Somewhere in [the] dim ages [of the distant past] human beings began to think symbolically. Their thoughts about nature were pure inventions of their human minds.... This was truly a momentous change; science since then has been one or another variation in the means of representing nature, both in thought and in action.... If this unique blend of imposing our symbols upon nature and transforming what we perceive accordingly is the hallmark of homo sapiens, we can thus assert that science has been around from the very beginning of the species.[2]

—M. ANTHONY ALIOTO

Culture is the "artificial, secondary environment" which [the human being] superimposes on the natural. It comprises language, habits, ideas, beliefs, customs, social organization, inherited artifacts, technical processes, and values. This "social heritage," this "reality sui generis," which the New Testament writers

1. A paper originally presented to eleventh Oxford Institute of Methodist Theological Studies, Christ Church College, Oxford University, 2002.

2. Alioto, *History of Western Science*, 1, 3.

frequently had in mind when they spoke of "the world," which is represented in many forms but to which Christians like other [human beings] are inevitably subject, is what we mean when we speak of culture.[3]

—H. RICHARD NIEBUHR

I

THERE IS LITTLE THAT comes easier to us than fixing a line of demarcation between nature and culture. The things lying outside us—though there first—are now simply there for us, we think; we have the means and the motive and the opportunity to manipulate them, to transform them, to tame them, to harness them, to exploit them, to make them ours, to adopt them, to give them our name. Knowledge, we say, is power. Thus what are naturally trees and stones become a house; what is naturally a river becomes a generator of electricity; what is naturally blind impulse becomes eloquence, competition, human resource management. We who are different from nature sink our hands—our freedom, our rationality, our creativity—into nature, and behold a new creation: "culture."[4] Nature is waiting over there, culture is over here with us.

We who are inclined to be Christian have little to add. God created nature, we say; we have created culture. Nature is good; culture is infected with the defects that plague our lives. Of course, God created

---

3. Niebuhr, *Christ and Culture*, 32.

4. Hepburn, "Nature, Philosophical Ideas of," 5:454: "In a particular philosophical context the sense in which nature is being used can be brought out most clearly by insisting upon the question 'What is nature (or the natural) being contrasted with in this context?' In one group of cases the natural is contrasted with the artificial or conventional. This contrast requires some conception of how the object or organism would behave by reason of its immanent causality alone, the causal factors that are peculiar to that type of thing and make it whatever it is—a stone, a fish, or a [human being]. The artificial and conventional are seen as interferences, modifying by an alien causality the characteristic patterns of behavior . . . In some contexts [the human being] is contrasted with nature. . . . To set [the human being] against nature is to emphasize [her] distinctiveness—[her] rationality, creativity, and freedom. But it may also support an unwarranted and distorting anthropocentricity."

us as well. Indeed, we were created in the image of God and with a cultural mandate to make good things of the good things God made. Unfortunately, we fell—we violated the plan of God—and suffered the consequences. Corrupt, perverse, our work upon nature now is but an ugly caricature of what it otherwise had been. That is what we say.

II

Though this is hardly a new way of thinking, it is a rather modern one. Long ago in the morning of Western civilization there was no such neat division between nature and culture. Nature, *physis*, embraced everything without exception, including the ways of the earth's *rational* animals.[5] Thus Homer and Hesiod, Parmenides and Heraclitus, Plato and Aristotle all agreed: there is no way to separate meaning from reality, form from being, culture from nature. "The decisive question was not why something existed, but how it could exist meaningfully, that is, in orderly form. Real being begins with intelligible form, with a multiplicity rendered harmonious through unity."[6] Even the gods were integrally connected with all else within the whole. And so, such integrity suggested definiteness to the Greeks. The cosmos is circumscribed by its own inherence.[7] Here everything is. There can simply not be any out-

5. Dupré, *Passage to Modernity*, 15: "In Greek myths as well as in early philosophy, *physis* appears simultaneously as a primordial, formative event and as the all-inclusive, informed reality that results from this event. *To be* consists in partaking in an aboriginal act of expression. Nothing precedes that expression. As ontological ultimate it provides the definitive answer to the question how things came about."

6. Ibid., 22

7. Ibid., 21. For this reason, the cosmos is not infinite, but limited. Thus the standard translation of the idiosyncratic Parmenides speaks in its own way for the intellectual heritage within and for which Parmenides never stops speaking: "Indeed, there is not anything at all apart from being, because Fate has bound it together so as to be whole and immovable. . . . Since there has to be limit, Being is complete on every side, like the mass of a well-rounded sphere, equally balanced in every direction from the center. Clearly it cannot be greater in any direction than in any other, inasmuch as there is no not-being to prevent it from reaching out equally, nor is it the nature of Being to be more here and less there. The All in inviolable. Since it is equal to itself in all directions, it must be homogeneous within the limits." Parmenides, "Fragments," 98 [8:34–41, 8:42–49].

side; certainly not an outside from which a human being might fashion or refashion its own wares.

All of this, however, changed. The first sign of trouble came with this tradition's encounter with Christianity and in particular the Hebrew and Christian conception of a transcendent Creator, one "who remained outside the cosmos."[8]

> An all-inclusive concept of *kosmos* such as the Greeks knew did and could not exist in Israel. The whole of creation manifested Yahweh's power and presence, but it never attained the kind of self-sufficient unity that the Greek *kosmos* possessed. Moreover, the later Christian idea of a world created "from nothing" [*ex nihilo*] and hence devoid of intrinsic necessity would have conflicted with the divine character of Greek nature.[9]

Indeed, the danger of this encounter was great. As Christianity rose to prominence, it could well have rejected the ideas that were so endemic to the ancient Hellenistic world. But that was not to be. Whether due to an inevitable pagan seepage, or to the surrender of an eschatology that had previously made it homeless in this world, or to an outgoing hospitality written into its liturgy, creeds, and Scriptures, Christianity found a way to reconcile apparently irreconcilable Hebrew and Hellenistic ideas. Of course, Christians could not say with pagans that the universe is inherently divine, but they did come to maintain that it has upon it the fingerprints left by the creator-God.[10] None of nature is simply to be explained in itself, of course; a transcendent God made it all that it is. Yet nature, for these Christian metaphysicians, has come from God and so, it is said, God must be re-presented in it. It is the human *physis*—the image of God—that is this re-presentation most completely.[11]

And so, though perhaps marking a significant deviation from the church's earlier trajectory, Christian intellectuals gradually appropriated

8. Dupré, *Passage to Modernity*, 3; cf. 22, 29, 126–27.

9. Ibid., 29–30.

10. This is not to say that the notion that there is evidence of God's creative work is a coherently Christian position.

11. Dupré, *Passage to Modernity*, 30–31.

pagan synthetic thinking. However, it was a difficult history. The new Christian metaphysics had much behind it in the ancient Greeks, and in particular in the ancient Greek ideas of form and nature, but its forward march was less certain; it had to endure "some severe crises." Indeed, "How could a cosmic symbolism prefigured in and centered around one individual—the Christ—conform to the universal Greek idea of form? Moreover, if God had definitively revealed himself in the 'man of sorrows,' how could one continue to regard the splendor of the universe as the image of a God who had appeared 'in the form of a slave'?"[12] Therefore, one finds moves made throughout the church that emphasize the difference between the things of this world and the things of God.[13]

Though Christian metaphysics persistently advanced, employing as it does the notions of form and nature,[14] a dramatic change occurred,

12. Ibid., 30.

13. In the East a remarkable simplification of icons downplays the relevance of "natural beauty" to the coming of God's ineffably mysterious glory. The iconoclastic controversy bears witness as well to the East's recognition of the otherness of God in relation to the cosmos. However, iconoclasts were not the only ones who wished to emphasize God's transcendence. The church's defense of icons stresses the openness of the icon to the mystery of God that will forever be other than the icon itself. See Meyendorff, *Christ in Eastern Christian Thought*, 173–92. Further, at the same time in the West an increasingly radical doctrine of sin highlights the godlessness of the human being apart from grace. In other words, precisely as Greek and Roman synthetic thinking moves to center stage in Christian thought, there is a growing and contrary realization of the deep gulf that stands between pagan and Christian notions of the world (Dupré, *Passage to Modernity*, 31–33).

14. For example, the idea that the Christ of the Gospel narratives was an oddity and beyond this world's comprehension was countered forcefully and ambitiously. He, too, became an example of a metaphysical order, secondary to a cosmic system. Thus: "toward the end of the eleventh century . . . a fresh awareness of the Incarnation as a cosmically transforming event suddenly dawned upon the entire civilization and spawned a new trust in nature . . . and for the first time a genuine Christian naturalism emerged" (Dupré, *Passage to Modernity*, 33). That is, the saving event to which the church testifies comes to be regarded not as an outside that is born elusively inside the world, but as the true immanent center of the world. With this kind of God who is human comes a profound valuation of human being as such and a concomitant new confidence in the human subject. Indeed, this may well be the moment in history when the subject, that center of self-consciousness so important to all of modern thought and life, is invented. "The human microcosmos resides at the center of the macrocosmos, thus giving physical nature its definitive meaning"—giving meaning

a change opening a new and uncertain era. And it occurs with a singularity that signals its own peculiarity. The unassuming revolutionary is Francis of Assisi. His revolutionary act is his gazing nakedly upon the *particularity* of the human Jesus. Yet he was an ambiguous revolutionary. Initially, the image of his rapt attention to Jesus mixed well with the growing sense of the connection between the human microcosm and the macrocosm in which it resides. Parallel to the revelatory specificity of Jesus, item after natural item was understood in its direct particularity as a symbol of the great meaning of the whole. Nothing was simply a brute fact. Everything was bursting with interpretable symbolism.[15] However, it is the second way that Francis came to be heard that was of the greatest moment and that had the most destabilizing effect on late medieval synthetic thinking—thinking that thought first to the universal and only on the universal's terms to the particular. Francis pointed differently.[16]

> His devotion to Jesus of Nazareth, the individual, opened a new perspective on the unique particularity of the person. Francis upset an intellectual tradition which he hardly understood and which he certainly had no intention of challenging. If the Image of all images is an individual, then the primary significance of individual form no longer consists in disclosing a universal reality beyond itself. Indeed, the universal itself ultimately refers to the singular.[17]

---

as one does before a passage in a book, say, a passage in the Holy Bible (ibid., 34–35): "'Some people read books in order to find God. Yet there is a great book, the very appearance of created things. Look above you; look below you! Note it; read it! God, whom you wish to find, never wrote that book with ink. Instead, [God] set before your eyes the things [God] had made.' Thus wrote Augustine. The metaphor was resumed in the twelfth century and resulted in Alain de Lille's well-known verse: Omnis mundi creatura / Quasi liber et scriptura" (ibid., 102).

15. Ibid., 36–38. So thoroughly was the entire world addressed in this way, even ancient pagan texts were understood to speak implicitly of God. One might say that it was simply taken for granted that all "truth" is God's truth.

16. See Dupré's discussion of the great import given to the particular human being in Christian thought from the very beginning. *Passage to Modernity*, 94–97; cf. 148.

17. Ibid., 38.

It is William of Ockham who brings Francis' piety to massive philosophical fruition. According to Ockham, Plato, Aristotle, and the long tradition of medieval thought through even Duns Scotus have failed the individual. They are still assuming that nature (i.e., each entity before us) carries within itself literally the power and patterns of being understood, that entities are woven together out of the very fibers of a universal, overarching meaning. Understanding an entity is thus actualizing those powers and patterns, bringing nature's inherent meaning to light, making nature's own intelligibility come to resonate with the knower's intelligence, stepping from the particular to the form it exemplifies. It is this that Ockham rejects, and his rejection brings with it the dawning of the modern world.[18]

The impact of nominalism is terrific upon the high medieval onto-theological synthesis. There is here no longer any form inherent in the natural world. Form, meaning, resides in the human mind, the human mind alone. What is more, there is no longer any inherent continuity between the natural world and God, for it had been the world's form that had linked it to the divine.[19]

Where the implications of Ockham's arguments are most felt, form continues to play an important role, but it does so only in relation to a formless nature, a nature stripped of its own meaning. The human mind is now the home of that. Form can make an impact upon nature now only by being ex-pressed out of the independent human mind toward nature through speech and writing and art and technology.[20] The mind in fact comes to occupy the place once held not only by Greek nature, but also by God.

---

18. Dupré, *Passage to Modernity*, 39: "Ockham no longer takes such a built-in harmony between mind and nature for granted, which subjects God's ways of creation to human norms. Even the assumption that in knowledge the mind shares a universal form with the real . . . is abandoned. . . . [Universals] exist neither in an independent realm outside the mind as Plato was believed to have held, nor even inside the singular reality as Aristotle had taught."

19. Ibid., 40–41.

20. See Dupré's second chapter for an explication of the struggle that continued after Ockham's time between his strong nominalist position and a lingering naturalism.

> When theology ceased to guarantee that meaning and value would be given with the world, it fell upon the mind to define or invent them. Such a move inevitably resulted in a separation between a meaning-giving mental subject and a physically given but meaning-dependent world. This was the option actually chosen by modern philosophy and science.[21]

Thus in the seventeenth century one finds the division between the meaning that the mind might bestow and the nature that might receive it reaching clarity in terms of human power. When Francis Bacon defines knowledge as power, he bears witness to a will to exploit. There is no knowledge for the sake of knowledge, no knowledge for the sake of the virtue of the human soul and community. The quest for that kind of "idle knowing" was the original sin, Bacon believes. To say that knowledge is power is to commit oneself to the early vocation of the Adam and Eve of the Garden, namely, the vocation "to dominate nature." Nature has no native telos. Human beings have been charged with imposing one upon it.[22]

> When the motive of knowledge becomes practical, the epistemic process tends to become restricted by the boundaries of what is conducive to productive action. Method acquires a meaning it never had before. . . . With Bacon and most seventeenth-century philosophers, method turns into a screen imposed upon the subject matter that restricts the investigation to what will most effectively and most speedily yield reliable results. . . . [Thus the idea of science to which the seventeenth century gave birth] gave rise to a characteristically modern belief in the unlimited human ability to conquer nature by rational methods combined with an unshakable confidence in a state of universal happiness that would follow from this conquest.[23]

21. Ibid., 58; cf. 63–64.
22. Ibid., 71–72.
23. Ibid., 73–74.

To say that nature has no telos is not to say that nothing is going on in nature. It is only that nature moves by the force of external pressure, namely, efficient causation, moving mechanistically toward no goal of its own, that is, simply moving because it has been pushed. To impose meaning on what is otherwise a blind flood of force is to harness it, to control it, to make it our servant. That is the *raison d'être* of modern technology. Implicated in that program is a vision of a machine-like universe, a closed system, one that has decisively and utterly broken for the first time from the metaphysics of the Greeks.[24]

A meaning-imposing being divorced from nature and yet bent upon controlling it is a consciousness thrown toward what it is not, a subject trained upon an object. The mind is so constituted that it can reflect within itself the objects it encounters, as a mirror might. It does so by arranging its own ideas so that the world outside the mind is represented truthfully.[25] It is Descartes who most clearly shows how important it is to the modern mind to gain mastery over modern nature. The procedure of Descartes turns finally upon the certainty of the subject, the *res cogitans*, the "I." Indeed, Descartes is so dependent upon the subject that it is fair to say that his is a new ontotheology, a metaphysics resting upon an unshakable solid-rock foundation, upon an ultimate reality, the substantial self.[26] Everything knowable finds its place in this

24. Dupré, *Passage to Modernity*, 74–76.

25. Ibid., 79–80. This is, of course, difficult, and one of the tasks facing seventeenth- and eighteenth-century philosophy is determining how one might know for sure that the world outside is as our minds have taken it to be.

26. "All ideas—including the idea of God—have their formal basis in the mind, which envisions all beings as *cogitata*. At least in that sense the self forms the foundation for the idea of God, and without that foundation the second ontological one, laid by God's causal activity, would play no role in the soul's reflection. God has to be proven, and to be proven on the basis of the prior certainty of the self. The thinking self, then, remains the ground—though not the cause—of the idea of God" (ibid., 117–18). Dupré comes to this from Marion's work in Descartes. This is in fact Marion's conclusion. One should not (and Marion does not) discount the role played by the idea of God in Descartes' meditations. The idea of the infinite could have provided a disruption of Descartes' new ontology (as it does, e.g., in Levinas and in Marion), but in the end even God here remains a component in a meditative move of self-mastery. See Dupré, *Passage to Modernity*, 87; Descartes, *Meditations on First Philosophy*, "Meditation III"; Levinas, *Of God Who Comes to Mind*, 62–65; Marion, *God Without Being*, 202 and passim in addition to his numerous treatises specifically

"I," an "I" that may have limitations of knowledge, but that has absolutely no limitations of (formal) will.[27]

With the stripping of form/meaning from nature came the removal of God from involvement in the natural world in any terms other than those of efficient causation. God is thought to be a center of power—not unlike the human subject—who created the world of nature from a position above the natural, that is, as an extrinsic reality. Of course, since God remains the (supernatural) creator of *nature*, intelligent crea-

---

on Descartes. Descartes: "But there is a deceiver (I know not who he is) powerful and sly to the highest degree, who is always purposely deceiving me. Then there is no doubt that I exist, if he deceives me. And deceive me as he will, he can never bring it about that I am nothing so long as I shall think that I am something. Thus . . . the statement 'I am, I exist' is necessarily true every time it is uttered by me or conceived in my mind" (Descartes, *Meditations*, 17 [Meditation II: 25]). Descartes may not here know who this "deceiver" is, but it is clear not only from the first two meditations, but also from the third, that this hypothesized being is omnipotent, one with unlimited power. (See, e.g., Descartes, *Meditations*, 24 [Meditation III: 36]).

27. Once Descartes establishes the existence of God (and concomitantly the non-existence of the omnipotent deceiver) he examines the power of the subject to err and is led to consider the will, the power of judgment that so often oversteps the boundaries of knowing: "I cannot complain that I have received from God an insufficiently ample and imperfect will, or free choice, because I observe that it is limited by no boundaries. And it seems eminently worth noting that nothing else in me is so perfect or so great that I do not understand how they can be even more perfect or greater . . . to the extent that the will is principally the basis for my understanding that I bear an image and likeness of God. . . . [T]aken formally, will precisely as such, it does not seem greater [even in God] . . . " (Descartes, *Meditations*, 37 [Meditation IV: 56–57]). This is not to say that Descartes has no metaphysics of objective reality. He does. Indeed, it is a metaphysics founded upon a transcendent God. Here Descartes understands that without God even the thinking substance could not be said to be. God is here the guarantor of all reality; but God is this, according to Descartes, only as the supreme efficient cause. So comprehensively does Descartes think of God as efficient cause that he speaks of God as the one self-cause, the *causa sui*, the one who could not have a cause outside of itself. This peculiar term, which Descartes coins, underlines the extent to which he thinks of God's movement of power in causal terms (Dupré, *Passage to Modernity*, 87–88). Descartes thus exemplifies here too the modern break with the ancients: "While Greek philosophy of the classical age had defined being in terms of form and its dependence primarily (though never exclusively) in terms of participation, modern thought conceived of nature as a causal interaction of forces and of transcendence as a supremely powerful divine will which created and ruled all things by means of efficient causality" (ibid., 88).

tures can find evidence of God's work (i.e., God's efficient causation) by studying the world (as one might find evidence of a watchmaker's work by studying a watch).[28] Such "natural theology," however, is little more than a polite tip of the hat in the direction of a departing old acquaintance. In fact, the supernatural became an emptier and emptier category. Nature came to be understood to be so radically independent that it was thought now (not only by Spinoza) to exist simply in itself. "As the concept of nature lost its transcendent orientation, the assumptions on which natural theology came to be based contained the seeds of late-modern atheism."[29]

And so, here we stand: nature is an empty object technologically controlled and imposingly named by an isolated and empty—though power-hungry—subject; God is relegated to supernatural irrelevance; all that exists is pressed together in a closed system of efficient causation. This is the legacy of the modern age. And no one likes it.

III

The poverty of a natural theology that is captivated by modern nature does not foreclose the prospect of a theology of nature with a difference. "Nature" need not be abandoned by theology; but it must be approached in a very new way, to be rethought from the beginning. The history that we've considered begins with the ancient Greeks. Perhaps thinking *physis* once again, but not entirely in the same way this time, might provide new direction. The boldest and most inviting rethinking of the Greeks in general and of *physis* in particular may well be Martin Heidegger's.

Heidegger's resolve to think the meaning of being (*Sein*) has a notoriously devotional tenor. Thus he speaks of such thinking as "meditative," as "an openness to the mystery," as a kind of "thanking," as a "calling."[30] Furthermore he approaches the task of thinking being as a pilgrimage to a distant, forgotten place that lies buried under centuries

28. Dupré, *Passage to Modernity*, 178–79.

29. Ibid., 181.

30. See Heidegger, *Discourse on Thinking*, 54–57; *What Is Called Thinking?*, 138–47 and passim.

of systematic neglect. Insight into the meaning of being, he says, came with the dawning of Western thought; but with the rise of metaphysical thinking, especially in Plato and his heirs (and his heirs are the whole of the history of metaphysics), that original insight came to be disregarded. The task of thinking that original insight and thinking it beyond its first moments, however, is no romantic dismissal of all that has transpired since then. Heidegger is not leaping across over two millennia of history to get back to some golden age. Rather he is thinking through that history, thinking through it to think what remains buried in it.[31] And if he is right that this original insight is buried in the very thought of the Western world, it remains buried in your thought and in mine and in his. To think it would thus be a destructuring move that would unsettle our greatest confidences, our greatest rational securities, our firmest foundations.[32]

Again, nature has come to be understood as the object of plotting calculation and technological control. We stand over-against it and press our plans upon it as if it were nothing but available raw material, present at hand, awaiting our exploitation. The earliest Greeks, Heidegger says, saw all of this quite differently.[33] There is no cold calculation, no detachment from the complexities of life in the world, life on the earth. For the Greeks, *physis* concerns what is happening, a happening in which we are

31. Heidegger calls this *Destruktion*, or "destructuring." See Heidegger, *Being and Time*, 22. Cf. also Polt, *Heidegger*, 130: "Our understanding of Being is restricted to a particular meaning that has been established *historically*. Whether we know it or not, we move within certain tracks that were first laid down in the beginning of Greek philosophy."

32. It is not the purpose of the following exposition of Heidegger to lay out his position in any detail, but rather to lay out his account of certain early Greek texts. It is, however, Heidegger's quest for being that leads him in every inquiry. Thus Heidegger does not idealize the Greeks. His work looks to what remains covered over—even if suggested—in their most "primordial" texts.

33. "But now let us . . . attempt to regain the unimpaired strength of language and words; for words and language are not wrappings in which things are packed for the commerce of those who write and speak. It is in words and language that things first come into being and are. For this reason the misuse of language in idle talk, in slogans and phrases, destroys our authentic relations to things." Heidegger, *Introduction to Metaphysics*, 13–14. Heidegger does not simply rest his position on what he finds to be said by the Greeks. However, it is precisely what he finds to be said by the Greeks that is of interest in this essay.

involved, about which we are concerned. It is all about coming and going, labor and growth, life and death. Using his idiosyncratic and highly
metaphorical prose, Heidegger says that for the Greeks, *physis* "denotes
self-blossoming emergence (e.g., the blossoming of a rose), opening up,
unfolding, that which manifests itself in such unfolding and perseveres
and endures in it; in short, the realm of things that emerge and linger on.
According to the dictionary *phyein* means to grow or make to grow."[34]
Such an emergence and lingering is the occurrence of "being itself." To
say that something *is* is to say that it emerges and lingers. And so, *physis*
is an "opening up and inward-jutting-beyond-itself [*in-sich-aus-sich-
hinausstehen*]." Again, "Being as a whole reveals itself as *physis*, 'nature,'
which here does not yet mean a particular sphere of beings but rather
beings as such as a whole, specifically in the sense of upsurgent presence
[*aufgehendes Anwesen*]."[35]

The painfully difficult thing about understanding what Heidegger
is saying here is that, since he is asking us to think "nature" otherwise
than as we have come to think it, we must begin by stepping through
and beyond our most comfortable conceptions in order to learn not only
to think new ideas, but to think them in a new way.

Physis for the early Greeks, Heidegger says, is an ontological term.
It speaks of being. However, it does not speak of being abstractly. If
anything, our difficulty thinking what he understands the Greeks to
have thought is that we are the ones who want to think abstractly; they

34. Ibid., 14. Dupré objects to this etymology (*Passage to Modernity*, 256 n. 2).
However, in this case Heidegger's word study is not idiosyncratic at all. See, e.g.,
Claiborne, *Roots of English*, 69 (I quote this whole passage because of the numerous connections it makes with Heidegger's texts): "BHEU-, [Germanic] BE or exist, also dwell, grow; [Latin] FUTURE [meaning] 'what is to be.' The 'dwell' sense
begot [Germanic] BUILD (a dwelling), BOOTH (a temporary building), HUSBAND
('dweller in the house'), and NEIGHBOR (someone dwelling near). A BOWER was
originally a dwelling, and a servant (in the dwelling) was in BONDAGE (the word's
sexual sense is very recent). More remote [Germanic] descendants are BOUND
for ('growing toward') a place and—possibly—BEAM, from a word [meaning] tree
(? 'growing thing'). The same root sense [became] [Greek] *physis*, growth, nature,
which [became] PHYSICS—originally, the study of the natural world—whence the
idiomatic PHYSICAL." Dupré's alternative does not contradict Heidegger, but rather
distracts from the dynamics of his position.

35. Heidegger, "On the Essence of Truth," 126.

do not. We imagine that they look at all the manipulable items in their world and abstract from them a hyper-universal category, "being." He says no, this is not what the Greeks are doing. When they come to think *physis*—as being—they do not put themselves in the kind of privileged outside position required to engage in abstraction. *Physis* is a concurrence of all events; not as if each were lost in a kind of uniformity, but as if each occurrence happened in such a way that each other occurrence—and emphatically the human being who is open to them—were entailed.

> Hence *physis* originally encompassed heaven as well as
> earth, the stone as well as the plant, the animal as well as
> [the human], and it encompassed human history as a work
> of [humans] and the gods; and ultimately and first of all,
> it meant the gods themselves as subordinated to destiny.[36]

Heidegger is saying that for the Greeks *physis* is not just some static, heavy settling-into-place, some "inert duration." As a specific way of attending to being, the word *physis* combines both what we ordinarily think of as "being" with what we ordinarily think of as "becoming."[37] There is certainly something particular here, for *physis* has everything to do with what it means for an entity to be and thus to "stand"; but it stands in "the process of a-rising," as a kind of "emerging," an emerging of what is otherwise hidden. Further, that emerging does not occur except in its connection with every occurrence that similarly comes to stand. Thus *physis*—being—is a specific happening of the totality of occurrences.[38]

36. Heidegger, *Introduction to Metaphysics*, 14.

37. Ibid., 114–15: "In the initial disclosure of the being of the [happening of being], it was therefore necessary to oppose becoming as well as appearance to being. On the other hand, becoming as 'emerging' belongs to *physis*. If we take them both in the Greek sense—becoming as coming-into-presence and going-out of it; being as emerging, appearing presence; nonbeing as absence—then the reciprocal relation between emerging and declining is appearing, being itself. Just as becoming is the appearance of being, so appearance as appearing is a becoming of being."

38. Ibid., 14–16.

In this way the Greeks think being as a kind of presence (*ousia*, *parousia*)³⁹—that is, what emerges and stands is precisely what is present.⁴⁰ Furthermore, what is present is what has emerged and come to stand from *concealment*. Thus a happening of being, an entity, is what is revealed, not as something subsequent to be-ing, but precisely *as* be-ing. There is here no binary opposition between the real and the ideal or the objective and the subjective. A happening of being is an emergence of what comes to stand, an emergence from concealment, an emergence that appears and is present.⁴¹ This movement out into presence is truth, *aletheia*, unconcealment.

> Since the [happening of being] as such *is*, it places itself in and stands in *unconcealment, aletheia*. We translate, and at the same time thoughtlessly misinterpret, this word as "truth." . . . For the Greek essence of truth is possible only in one with the Greek essence of being as *physis*. On the strength of the unique and essential relationship between *physis* and *aletheia* the Greeks would have said: . . . The power that manifests itself stands in unconcealment. In showing itself, the unconcealed as such comes to stand. Truth as un-concealment is not an appendage to being.⁴²

39. Ibid., 61: "*ousia*, or more fully *parousia*. . . . For *parousia* we have in German a corresponding term—*An-wesen* [presence], which also designates an estate or homestead, standing in itself or self-enclosed. . . . [*Physis*] means the emerging and arising, the spontaneous unfolding that lingers. In this power rest and motion are opened out of original unity. This power is the overpowering presence that is not yet mastered [*bewältig*] in thought, wherein that which is present manifests itself as [a happening of being]."

40. Thus for Heidegger the Greeks neglect the hiddenness, the concealment, that plays with every manifestation of being. See Foltz, *Inhabiting the Earth*, 56–57.

41. Heidegger, *Introduction to Metaphysics*, 101–2. Heidegger's discussion of "appearance" is relevant to this essay, but treating it would take us too far. It is important at least to note here, however, that it is in appearance, an appearance that always accompanies an occurrence of being, that one can be led to simple oppositions, say, between what something seems to be and what something really is. See ibid., 159, 98–115.

42. Ibid., 102.

Physis and *aletheia*, emergent standing and unconcealment, "nature" and "truth" concur.

Of course, such *aletheia* does not come easily. *Physis* is not simply available to the casual observer. To think the truth of being requires one to give oneself in a certain way "to being as it opens around [one]," to give oneself to the entities here and there not as items that one might indifferently take or leave, but as happenings of being. If one does so, if one lets emergent standing and unconcealment concur, one comes to be oneself a kind of site of the revelation of being, what Heidegger calls *Dasein*.[43] *Dasein* is there, then, as the togetherness of the totality of the happenings of being as it all concurs in the *specific* happening of being that *Dasein* thus thinks.[44] That kind of "togetherness" is, again, no blending, no dissolution of differences. It is rather "a gathering of conflict and unrest, . . . the belonging-together of antagonisms."[45] Thus it is quite hard for a human to let the truth of being happen as it happens; so much that is so varied happens in such thought, there is so much to let go of.[46] But according to the Greeks, that is the human calling, Heidegger says; so much so that the human being "belongs to this appearing. . . . And since apprehension—accepting apprehension of what shows itself—belongs to such appearing, it may be presumed that this is precisely what determines the essence of being-human."[47]

43. Ibid., 110.

44. This is the concurrence of *physis* and *logos*, according to Heidegger: "*Logos* is the steady gathering, the intrinsic togetherness of the [happening of being], i.e., being. Therefore in [Heraclitus'] Fragment 1 *kata ton logon* means the same as *kata physin*. *Physis* and *logos* are the same. *Logos* characterizes being in a new and yet old respect: that which is, which stands straight and distinct in itself, is at the same time gathered togetherness in itself and by itself, and maintains itself in such togetherness. *Eon*, beingness, is essentially *xynon*, collected presence; *xynon* does not mean the 'universal' but that which in itself collects all things and holds them together. . . . [Thus] not a universal, not something that hovers over all and touches none, but the original unifying unity of what tends apart" (ibid., 130–31).

45. Ibid., 134, 138. Heidegger is citing Heraclitus in particular.

46. Cf. Heidegger, *Discourse on Thinking*, 54–57.

47. Heidegger, *Introduction to Metaphysics*, 139–40. He adds (141): "Apprehension is not a function that [the human being] has as an attribute, but rather the other way around: apprehension is the happening that has [the human being]."

However, Heidegger understands that "accepting apprehension" is something that must be wrested away from the ordinary. It never comes simply as a matter of course. Human life is "strange" in this way; it finds its destiny only in violence:

> But [the human] is the strangest of all, . . . because [the human] departs from [its] customary, familiar limits, because [it] is the violent one, who, tending toward the strange in the sense of the overpowering, surpasses the limit of the familiar [*das Heimische*]. . . . But woven into one with this violent excursion [*Aufbruch*] upon the overpowering sea is the never-resting incursion [*Einbruch*] into the indestructible power of the earth. Here the earth is the highest of the gods. Violently, with acts of power [*gewalt-tätig*] [the human] disturbs the tranquility of growth, the nurturing and maturing of the goddess who lives without effort. Here the overpowering reigns not in self-consuming wildness but without effort and fatigue; from out of the superior tranquility of great riches, it produces and bestows the inexhaustible treasure that surpasses all zeal. Into this power bursts the violent one; year after year [it] breaks it open with his plows and drives the effortless earth into [its] restless endeavor. Sea and earth, departure and upheaval are joined . . .[48]

This is the way human beings are called to be. They break out and break up, capture and subjugate, and so open up the happening of being, for example, "*as* sea, *as* earth, *as* animal."[49]

> The strangest ([the human]) is what it is because, fundamentally, it cultivates and guards the familiar, only in order to break out of it and to let what overpowers it break in. Being itself hurls [the human] into this breaking-away, which drives [it] beyond [itself] to venture forth toward

48. Ibid., 151, 154. It is tempting to leave the translator's masculine language as it is; it somehow in this case works.

49. Ibid., 157.

being, to accomplish being, to stabilize it in the work, and
so hold open the [happening of being] as a whole.[50]

What constitutes knowledge for the Greeks, Heidegger says, is thus
to be understood as a violent movement of power that is a certain kind
of ontological work: they call it *technê*. The Greeks also speak of *art* and
the work of art as *technê*, "because art is what most immediately brings
being (i.e. the appearing that stands there in itself) to stand, stabilizes it
in something present (the work)." What makes something a work of art
has little to do with a representation of some objective state of affairs or
some expression of the artist's ideas or feelings. A work of art is a work
of art only because

> it brings about the phenomenon in which the emerging
> power, *physis*, comes to shine [*scheinen*]. It is through the
> work of art as [the being of the happening of being] that
> everything else that appears and is to be found is first con-
> firmed and made accessible, explicable, and understand-
> able as being or not being.[51]

50. Ibid., 163.

51. Heidegger, *Introduction to Metaphysics*, 159. Heidegger's point here may be
illustrated by perhaps his most eloquent passage, one in which he speaks of what is
revealed to thoughtful attention in one of Van Gogh's paintings of peasant shoes: "We
shall choose a well-known painting by Van Gogh, who painted such shoes several
times. But what is there to see here? Everyone knows what shoes consist of. If they are
not wooden or bast shoes, there will be leather soles and uppers, joined together by
thread and nails. Such gear serves to clothe the feet. Depending on the use to which
the shoes are to be put, whether for work in the field or for dancing, matter and form
will differ.

"Such statements, no doubt correct, only explicate what we already know. The
equipmental quality of equipment consists in its usefulness. But what about this usefulness itself? . . . The peasant woman wears her shoes in the field. Only here are they
what they are. They are all the more genuinely so, the less the peasant woman thinks
about the shoes while she is at work, or looks at them at all, or is even aware of them.
She stands and walks in them. That is how shoes actually serve. It is in this process
of the use of equipment that we must actually encounter the character of equipment.

"As long as we only imagine a pair of shoes in general, or simply look at the empty,
unused shoes as they merely stand there in the picture, we shall never discover what
the equipmental being of the equipment in truth is. From Van Gogh's painting we
cannot even tell where these shoes stand. There is nothing surrounding this pair of
peasant shoes in or to which they might belong—only an undefined space. There are

But it is also important to understand that art (even in its visual, auditory, and tactile forms) is essentially poetry, the art of language.[52] Even when one sculpts, one speaks, not representationally or expressively, but as a receptive act of violence. *Technê* is the work that yields itself in speech to the happening of being and does so with the violence that makes human being homeless, strange, at the same time that it brings human being into the midst of the totality of the happenings of being, as a kind of convergence point, a kind of "between," where being is tended.

> The violence of poetic speech, of thinking projection, of building configuration, of the action that creates states is not a function of faculties that [the human] has, but a taming and ordering of powers by virtue of which the [happening of being] opens up as such when [the human] moves into it. This disclosure of the [happening of being]

not even clods of soil from the field or the field-path sticking to them, which would at least hint at their use. A pair of peasant shoes and nothing more. And yet.

"From the dark opening of the worn insides of the shoes the toilsome tread of the worker stares forth. In the stiffly rugged heaviness of the shoes there is the accumulated tenacity of her slow trudge through the far-spreading and ever-uniform furrows of the field swept by a raw wind. On the leather lie the dampness and richness of the soil. Under the soles stretches the loneliness of the field-path as evening falls. In the shoes vibrates the silent call of the earth, its quiet gift of the ripening grain and its unexplained self-refusal in the fallow desolation of the wintry field. The equipment is pervaded by uncomplaining worry as to the certainty of bread, the wordless joy of having once more withstood want, the trembling before the impending childbed and shivering at the surrounding menace of death. This equipment belongs to the *earth*, and it is protected in the *world* of the peasant woman. From out of this protected belonging the equipment itself rises to its resting-within-itself.

"But perhaps it is only in the picture that we notice all this about the shoes. The peasant woman, on the other hand, simply wears them. If only this simple wearing were so simple. When she takes off her shoes late in the evening, in deep but healthy fatigue, and reaches out for them in the still dim dawn, or passes them by on the day of rest, she knows all this without noticing or reflecting. . . . By virtue of this reliability the peasant woman is made privy to the silent call of the earth; by virtue of the reliability of the equipment she is sure of her world. World and earth exist for her, and for those who are with her in her mode of being, only thus—in the equipment. We say 'only' and therewith fall into error; for the reliability of the equipment first gives to the simple world its security and assures to the earth the freedom of its steady thrust." See Heidegger, "Origin of the Work of Art," 158–60.

52. Heidegger, *Introduction to Metaphysics*, 185.

is the power that [the human] must master in order to become [itself] amid the [happening of being], i.e. in order
to be historical.[53]

The history from Greek *physis* to modern *nature*, Heidegger
thinks, is a decline of the very destiny of human being. What was once
the glory of an intense engagement that is simultaneously a kind of letting go of control and an openness to mystery, has become—by way of
a thoughtless, forgetful, rote memory of words on pages—a scrambling
after "correctness," "accuracy," and the logic of logistics. In the Greeks'
physis there is a fellowship of the occurrences of being. In modern nature there are only isolated, exploitable objects.

III

There is no direct entry from Heidegger's account of *physis* to a theology
of nature that moves with the currents of Christian tradition. Though
the word stands prominently in early trinitary and christological thinking, it is not specifically the *physis* of the ancient Greeks. By the fourth
and fifth centuries, God was understood by the church to be quite different from the network of relations that is Greek being. Talk of *physis*
here could simply not have the interest of the Greeks at heart. Certainly,
all of what the Greeks have agonized their way to know is entailed here,
is conscripted, is advocated, but effacively toward the advent of what
remained unknown to them.

It is in particular in relation to the christological controversies of
the fourth and fifth centuries and their relative resolution in the Council
of Chalcedon (451) that "nature" (*physis*) enters seriously into the vo-
cabulary of the church.[54] The Creed of Chalcedon maintains first that

53. Ibid., 157. This "violence" should not, however, be understood as a human
assault against nature. Rather human "violence" is but one of the ways that the strife
that is the happening of *physis* erupts. See McNeill, "Porosity," passim; Heidegger,
"Origin of the Work of Art," 41–47; Heidegger, "Language," 200–205.

54. The Definition of Chalcedon: "Following, then, the holy fathers, we unite in
teaching all [men and women] to confess the one and only Son, our Lord Jesus Christ.
This selfsame one is perfect [*teleion*] both in deity [*theotēti*] and also in human-ness
[*anthrōpotēti*]; this selfsame one is also actually [*alēthōs*] God and actually [human],

"our Lord Jesus Christ" is identical in deity to God "the Father" and at the same time is identical in human-ness to human being.[55] This confusing combination becomes even more so when the creed in the closing words of its first paragraph speaks of Mary as *theotokos* not in respect of her son's *deity*, but "in respect of his human-ness"!)

As the second paragraph begins, the phrases of the first, *homoousion tō patri* and *homoousion hēmin*, give themselves now to the phrase "two natures [*duo physesin*]"—Christ, it is said here, is the concurrence of the nature of God and the nature of the human. Neither of these two natures is dissolved into the other or divided from and taken as separable from the other. They happen together. Though different, they stand in relation to each other, that is, without indifference: God occurs here; the human occurs here; God and the human *concur* here. There are, then, *two*: the happening that is human and the happening that is God. But it is also said that there is *one*: the *prosōpon*, the *hypostasis*, the "person": "the one and only and only-begotten Logos of God, the Lord Jesus Christ."

---

with a rational soul [*psychēs logikēs*] and a body. He is of the same reality as [the Father] [*homoousion tō patri*] as far as his deity is concerned and of the same reality as we are ourselves [*homoousion hēmin*] as far as his human-ness is concerned; thus like us in all respects, sin only excepted. Before time began [*pro aiōnōn*] he was begotten of the Father, in respect of his deity, and now in these 'last days,' for us and on behalf of our salvation, this selfsame one was born of Mary the virgin, who is God-bearer [*theotokos*] in respect of his human-ness [*anthrōpotēta*].

"[We also teach] that we apprehend [*gnōridzomenon*] this one and only Christ—Son, Lord, only-begotten—in two natures [*duo physesin*]; [and we do this] without confusing the two natures [*asunkutōs*], without transmuting one nature into the other [*atreptōs*], without dividing them into two separate categories [*adiairetōs*], without contrasting them according to area or function [*achōristōs*]. The distinctiveness of each nature is not nullified by the union. Instead, the 'properties' [*idiotētos*] of each nature are conserved and both natures concur [*suntrechousēs*] in one 'person' [*prosōpon*] and in one *hypostasis*. They are not divided or cut into two *prosōpa*, but are together the one and only and only-begotten Logos of God, the Lord Jesus Christ. Thus have the prophets of old testified; thus the Lord Jesus Christ himself taught us; thus the Symbol of the Fathers [N] has handed down [*paradedōke*] to us." The Definition of Chalcedon (451), in Leith, ed., *Creeds of the Churches*, 35–36.

55. This "identity" (rather than, say, "similarity") is indicated not only by the use of the prefix *homo-*, but also by the use of variations of the words *teleios* ("perfect") and *alēthōs* ("true," "actual," "unconcealed") in the paragraph as well as the tenor of the creed as a whole.

Prosōpon is a highly relational term. It is the Greek equivalent of the Latin *persona*.[56] It means "mask" or "face," the area around the eyes.[57] It is the word for the *way* one stands in relation to others, as when one's face is turned toward or away. Yet the word also speaks of what is peculiar, what is unique, as unique as is a face. *Hypostasis*, literally "standing under" (as the Latin *substantia*), is a word that suggests reality, being. It is in fact often used precisely in this sense. Thus without denying relationality, *hypostasis* stresses reality—just as *prosōpon*, without denying reality, stresses relationality.[58] To say that "the one and only and only-begotten Logos of God, the Lord Jesus Christ" is this *prosōpon*, this *hypostasis*, does not yet resolve the question of what Chalcedon is saying, but it does clearly proclaim that the particular place that we find the concurrence of the *physis* of God and the *physis* of the human is in this one "real relation." And yet, who is this one? What or whom does this word *prosōpon*, this word *hypostasis*, announce?

It is on the basis of certain documents closely associated with the Creed of Chalcedon that some answer to those questions begins to come to light. Cyril of Alexandria and Pope Leo I stand at the center of the controversy that gave rise to the Council. Two of Cyril's letters and one of Leo's were in fact published with the creed. What the creed says is said (at least in part) in them, but differently.[59] The incarnation, Cyril says, was not the transformation of the eternal Logos of God into a human being. The nature of the Logos remained the nature of God. The nature of Jesus of Nazareth remained the nature of the human. Yet, "while the natures which were brought together into a true unity were different, there is nevertheless, because of the unspeakable and unutterable convergence into unity, one Christ and one Son out of the two." The initiative, Cyril says, is with the Logos: what takes place as unity here is not a balanced accord of the divine on the one side and the human on

56. Neither *prosōpon* nor *persona* is to be thought as involving "the idea of self-consciousness nowadays associated with 'person' and 'personal'" (Kelly, *Early Christian Doctrines*, 115).

57. "F. pros to + ops, psp- eye, face" (*Oxford English Dictionary*, s.v. Prosopalgia).

58. See Keen, "*Homo Precarius*," 52–57, for a more extensive treatment of the implications of these terms.

59. Norris, ed., *Christological Controversy*, 26–31.

the other, but a "taking up of . . . humanity into God," as the Quicunque Vult says.[60] Cyril put it this way: "The Logos united to [itself], in his *hypostasis*, flesh enlivened by a rational soul, and in this way became a human being"; or more emphatically, the Logos "united human reality hypostatically to [itself]."[61] Leo says this:

> Since, therefore, the characteristic properties of both na-
> tures and substances are kept intact and come together in
> one person, lowliness is taken on by majesty, weakness by
> power, mortality by eternity, and the nature which cannot
> be harmed is united to the nature which suffers. . . . The
> impassible God does not disdain existence as a passible
> human being, and the immortal does not disdain to sub-
> mit . . . to the laws of death.[62]

For Leo as well as for Cyril, and thus for Chalcedon, it is because of the outgoing movement *of the eternal Logos of God*, spoken, begotten, eternally of the Father, moving out into and assuming all the vulnerability and mortality of the human "flesh," that two natures—what happens as God and what happens as the human—happen together. Not only everything that is God, but truly also everything that is human occur here. However, there is one *prosōpon*, one *hypostasis*. And so, it is in this sense that "the catholic church lives and grows by the faith that in Christ Jesus there is neither humanity apart from real divinity nor divinity apart from real humanity."[63] The *physis* that is God and the *physis* that is human become one event as the face of God turns decisively to the world.

60. The Athanasian Creed, in Leith, ed., *Creeds of the Church*, 706.

61. Cyril of Alexandria, "Cyril of Alexandria's Second Letter to Nestorius," in Norris, ed., *Christological Controversy*, 133. Cf. "Cyril's Letter to John of Antioch," in ibid., 143.

62. Leo I, "Pope Leo I's Letter to Flavian of Constantinople," in Norris, ed., *Christological Controversy*, 148, 149.

63. Ibid., 154.

IV[64]

There yet remains some ambiguity even with this more nuanced reading of Chalcedon. It is not entirely clear where to situate the one "person" with which the creed is concerned. It is quite possible, however, to think it in trinitary terms very precisely as the person of the outgoing, eternal Son of God. This is exactly what is affirmed by Leontius of Jerusalem.[65] His formal position in brief is that Jesus has no independent human *hypostasis*. Although there is nothing in particular lacking in his human being, that is, he is in no way other than as human, all that he is as human is given to the movement of God that performs the incarnation. That is, whatever might have been his own human "person" is in fact a transparency to the outgoing eternal Logos. To look at him is indeed to see a human being, but a human being that is nothing but a capacity filled with God's love. Jesus Christ is thus to be said to be one *hypostasis*, that of the Logos, but one as human nature is yielded to the nature of God. Two natures (ours and God's), one *hypostasis* (the Logos).

What does this mean?

The event that is the human being, Jesus, is an event of the absolute self-abandonment of the whole of the relationality of this human being to the event of God. The event of God, however, is an event in which the eternal Logos of God faces—goes out to—the world. In Jesus the human faces the irruption of God into the world and, moving out into God's coming, gives itself up to all that is happening here *as* God. In this way Jesus' human *hypostasis* is abandoned, it is nothing but an "en-"—an "into"—in relation to God's *hypostasis*, the incoming Logos.[66] There are

64. The brief sections that follow need (even more than the sections that precede them) to be much more fully developed and much more carefully nuanced. Limitations of space and time kept that from happening here. However, I am convinced that the "over-reading" (one might say "misreading") of Wesley and Leontius that is found here can be shown to be invited by the texts themselves, even though it may not simply be exegeted from them.

65. Leontius wrote sometime in the first half of the sixth century. He and the position he comes to define are often confused with Leontius of Byzantium and his work, for obvious reasons (among them that the latter uses identical obscure terminology, but in a quite different way). See Meyendorff, *Christ in Eastern Christian Thought*, 61–68, 72–82; and Grillmeier, *Christ in Christian Tradition*, 2:271–75.

66. Grillmeier, *Christ in Christian Tradition*, 2:291–94.

two "natures" here—the happening of the human and the happening of God—but finally only one set of relationships, those of God's incarnation for the very life of the world.[67]

Furthermore for Leontius a *hypostasis* (a "person") is not a "product" of a *physis*, but that *in* which a *physis* occurs.[68] Christ's two natures concur finally in and as the one *hypostasis* of the Logos, and as they concur, they are not closed spheres, but open movements. The human nature of Jesus Christ, which lacks nothing that is human, is no blockage to the nature of the radically other God as it goes forth in the *hypostasis* of the Logos. God is bound neither by what is proper to human, nor to divine nature. In the *hypostasis* of the Logos God is open to what God is not; the *hypostasis* of the Logos "admits the possibility of divine acts outside of the [divine] nature," the possibility that "God can personally and freely assume a fully human existence while remaining God, whose nature remains completely transcendent."[69] But the human *hypostasis* of Jesus Christ, as it is assumed by the Logos, is also open beyond itself to all that is human. The human *hypostasis* of Jesus Christ (now the *hypostasis* of the Logos) is not his own (*idikē*), it is rather a fellowship (*koinē*) with everything human.[70] Thus as the *physis* of God—precisely in the *hypostasis* of the Logos—moves out and receptively opens to the *physis* of the human—as the *hypostasis* of Jesus Christ in which that *physis* occurs—each receives the other: the human *hypostasis* as capacious, the *hypostasis* of God as kenotic. The *hypostasis* of God here fills, becomes, what we are (without ceasing to be what it is) and thus the *hypostasis* of the human is filled by, becomes, what God is (without ceasing to be what it is). The human *hypostasis* is in this way not its own. It is, of course, there utterly for God. But it is also utterly for other human beings. It is deified by the irruption of the Logos, whose hypostasis takes on all that is weak and broken and wounded and suffering in human

67. Cf. Wesche, "Defense of Chalcedon in the Sixth Century," 63.

68. Meyendorff, *Christ in Eastern Christian Thought*, 77; Wesche, "Defense of Chalcedon in the Sixth Century," 51, 55.

69. Meyendorff, *Christ in Eastern Christian Thought*, 77.

70. Ibid., 74.

life—without losing the impassibility of the divine nature beyond which the Logos has opened.[71]

V

It is quite possible to think the Chalcedonian-Leontian tradition in the light of Heidegger's account of ancient Greek thought; but not without some precarious navigation. In the one event that is the history, the *prosōpon*, the *hypostasis* of Jesus Christ there comes to stand all that occurs—all that comes and goes, labors and grows, lives and dies; all that rises out of itself, thrusts forth from itself; all that comes to presence, all that is unconcealed; all that is and becomes; all that is involving, engaging. This is the event in which being happens, in which *physis* happens, in which nature happens, in which the totality of the happenings of being come into play. Thus the one occurrent entity, Jesus Christ, is itself and the site of the occurrence of every other. However, this is to be said of every entity, according to Heidegger; and though every entity is unique, its uniqueness is not that of the Jesus Christ of Chalcedon. Furthermore, this account only directs attention clearly to one of Christ's natures, and Chalcedon maintains that there are two. Given that one can think human nature in these terms, how is it possible to think the nature of God this way without subsuming God within a comprehensive network of relations that would deny God's transcendence? But it must also be asked how it is possible to think God's transcendence without making it an abstraction that never comes to stand before the world?

VI

It is the theology of John Wesley that leads in the direction of an answer to these questions. Wesley is as acutely interested in the deification, the sanctification, of life—and particularly human life—as is Leontius. What breaks forth in Wesley, however, is a radical understanding both that God is love and that the sanctification of the creature is love—lov-

71. Ibid., 78–79; Grillmeier, "Defense of Chalcedon in the Sixth Century," 277, 291.

ing as God loves. The world was created to be holy; above all, human life was created to be holy.[72] For a creature to be holy, according to Wesley, is for it to partake of the divine nature, but to do so without losing anything that occurs as its creaturely—for example, human—nature; that is, it is to be what it is as not-God and concurrently a capacity for filling by God.[73] It is Jesus Christ that is the embodiment of this holiness: his life shines with the glory of God.[74] What happens here is a double movement[75]—a movement to God, to whom he prays, and a movement to his neighbor, with and for whom he lives and dies.[76] Jesus Christ is in this way the salvation of the world, the one in whom the world is hallowed, the one whom the world follows to and in whom the world enters into the holy God:

> For Christ does not give life to the soul separate from, but
> in and with, Himself. Hence His words are equally true of
> all [human beings], in whatsoever state of grace they are:
> "As the branch cannot bear fruit of itself, except it abide in
> the vine; no more can ye, except ye abide in me: without"
> (or separate from) "me ye can do nothing."[77]

Yet for Wesley to say this is not to compromise God's transcendence. God and world remain radically different precisely as God and world concur in Jesus Christ. What occurs here cannot be thought simply as arising from and lodged in the midst of the world. The concurrence of God and world arises from what is not the world—what in concurring with the world dislodges it. It is in fact only because the God who comes as Jesus Christ is and remains radically other that this concurrence is an event of love. God goes to what God is not, speaks a

72. Wesley, "The General Deliverance," in *WJW*, 2:445–50 (III.1–12); idem, "God's Love to Fallen Man," in *WJW*, 2:423–35 passim; idem, "The New Creation" [1785], in *WJW*, 2:500–510 passim.

73. Wesley, *A Plain Account*, in *WJWJ*, 11:441.

74. Wesley, "The End of Christ's Coming," in *WJW*, 2:477–84 (II.1–III.6).

75. Kierkegaard, *Fear and Trembling*, 34–36.

76. Keen, "*Homo Precarius*," 140–47.

77. Wesley, *A Plain Account*, in *WJWJ*, 11:39; cf. also Wesley, "Spiritual Worship," 90–95 (I.1–10).

"yes" to it, "is" a "yes" to it. Thus this transcendent one, this holy one, is for what is not God nothing but love.[78] At the same time this love works love, it is not indifferent to its other as it affirms it,[79] it calls its other to itself, to a loving "yes" that pours itself out to this God as this God has poured itself out to it. In this way God's other is hallowed, it is filled with the God who moves non-indifferently out into it, out into what is not and cannot be God.[80]

However, since this God is nothing but love, for what is not God to be hallowed is for it to be filled with love, a love that orients all that happens as this event in the world first to God, the love that fills it, *and* second orients it in and with this God to the world that this God—this love—loves. This is the event that is the history of Jesus, and it is the event repeated—though differently—in us.[81]

Of course, being loved by and at once loving one who is radically other is a very unique love. It has the flavor of an assurance built upon nothing under our control, a confidence, a conviction in what remains imperceptible. It is a love that is a faith that is, say, a *hypostasis* cast forth into a future that yet comes.[82] Thus this love is also a hope in what cannot arise out of what is and has been, that can only come to it. Thus this love is a prayer, a receptivity, that calls out to what cannot be commanded.[83] Everything one is calls out, is abandoned, is sacrificed to this

78. See Wesley, *A Plain Account*, in *WJWJ* 11:441; idem, "God's Love to Fallen Man," passim. It might be helpful to note that both of these references support the point I am making rather indirectly—but I think especially effectively. In the first the holy creature is described as having made herself "void" before God. In the second the sermon as a whole speaks of the importance of distance from God (in this case in sin) in order for the intensity of one's relationship with God to be perfected. Neither of these passages is making a specifically metaphysical point. However, that is even better; and the apparently merely rhetorical quality they exhibit may well be a move from the domain of modern nature to something more responsive to the otherness of God.

79. One might say in the phrase of Kierkegaard that God "loves forth love" (Kierkegaard, *Fear and Trembling*, 217).

80. Wesley, "The Marks of the New Birth," in *WJW*, 1:425–27 (III.1–5).

81. Wesley, *A Plain Account*, in *WJWJ*, 11:417–18, 436–37, 442–43, 444–45.

82. Cf. Wesley, "The Scripture Way of Salvation," in *WJW*, 2:160–62 (II.1–4).

83. Wesley, *A Plain Account*, in *WJW* (Jackson), 11:437–38.

other—but with the freedom and ecstasy of one gifted by the grace of the freest of loves. Thus this love is joy. And since this love is free and hopeful and trusting and receptive and joyful, it is life. To love this God who is love is to turn to all that this God loves—to turn to all that occurs—and love it, love it to life, love it to the love, the movement, the coming, that we might say God "is."[84]

VII

The natures of Christ declared at Chalcedon, explicated by Leontius, and implicitly clarified by Wesley invite entry into a theology of nature. The challenge in writing such a theology is not the explication of Christ's human nature and thus of nature whenever it occurs. The challenge is in the explication of divine nature in any sense. The question remains how it is that one can speak of the nature of God without subsuming God under the dynamics of the world, that is, without losing God's transcendence. Wesley's understanding of God's love suggests an answer.

In the one occurrence of Jesus, being—the coming to stand of all occurrence—juts forth from itself, as the growth and lingering of presence. However, all that occurs here—all relations, all connections, all that is entailed between heaven and earth, between mortals and immortals, all that is brought forth into unconcealedness, all that is wrested away from and with the elusive strife that contends in and through everything, the whole totality of occurrences—is abandoned to the one who loves without reserve, who thus sends it all back, to be repeated with a difference, with glory, hallowed. Thus in Jesus Christ the nature that as it occurs in him is human nature goes out freely, lovingly to the outside of nature and is freely, lovingly sent back—dispossessed, expropriated, but no less to be what it is. Thus it *is* very much nature happening here as the human event, Jesus Christ; but this nature is not his. It belongs to the outgoing love of God, the God who is not to be found in the midst of being except as otherwise than being, as an outside that has broken inside without ceasing to be outside.[85] The nature as it is in itself

---

84. Wesley, "On Zeal," in *WJW*, 3:312–15 (II.1–11), 320–21 (III.11–12).

85. See Levinas and in particular his work *Otherwise than Being, or, Beyond*

becomes the nature of God and so is sanctified. But love's possession is un-possessive, and what is given to and received by love is concurrently given back. But to give oneself to love, and by love to be oneself given is to be gifted by love, to be hallowed. One is oneself as this self-denial, thus not *in* oneself—but only in God, only in the love that loves without coming to stand as an event of being. Jesus Christ is the event in which simultaneously human nature is abandoned to what eludes nature *and* given as human nature from this other. There are then two "natures" here: (1) the nature that is the human event itself and (2) that nature, that event, as it is gifted by God, nature's other. Two natures happen here precisely as the love of God breaks into and disrupts all that happens. It is because *nature gifted* is gifted by *love* that it remains *itself* even as it is gifted, hallowed, "othered." One nature is lost, a second nature is found, but this second nature is the first nature—only with a difference. The difference is the *hypostasis* of God's Logos (of love) going out into the world.

However, the human nature that is hallowed in Jesus Christ is not an isolated in-dividuality, an atom. All occurrences of being are entailed here. In one sense for this life to be hallowed is for the totality of being to be hallowed. But life is to be lived and remains at every step a task that has not yet been performed. The task of Jesus Christ is at once to give to God the whole of what emerges as any presence—as nature—and in God to give that nature *to* nature, that is, to love it and thereby to love forth love there. Again, nature remains what it is, but with an unheard-of difference. In the cross and resurrection of Jesus Christ this task is performed *ad infinitum*—uniquely so—and it is in it that the whole of his life and the whole of every event of nature is to be situated.

What was and is and is to come as Jesus Christ remains the destiny and task of nature. Nature, by definition, is what it is. Yet the history of Jesus Christ declares that nature can indeed be not only what it is—but also "what it is" no longer in itself, but in an other, an otherwise than

---

Essence. But also see *Totality and Infinity*, 301–2 and passim, as well as *Of God Who Comes to Mind*, 55–78; and along a similar line Marion, *God Without Being*, 53–107 and passim.

nature, that is, in a love that calls it outside into love and in love outside itself into nature itself: thus to lose itself and find itself.[86]

86. What the position of this paper means, e.g., for a conversation between a theologian and a scientist is yet to be determined and should no doubt not be worked out ahead of time, but wait for such a conversation to begin. Some suggestions of how Heidegger's position might give rise to an environmental ethics is worked out by Foltz in his *Inhabiting the Earth*. This is not yet a theological word and is not even implicitly so. However, it at least clears the ground for serious theological thought. As for the doctrine of creation and redemption, these, too, need to be rethought from the beginning without a presumptive acceptance of the notions chained to modern meta-physics and technology. The apocalyptic image of the coming reign and rule of God, the image front and center in the preaching, ministry, and life of Jesus in the New Testament gospels, is perhaps where helpful discussion could be carried forward. The reign and rule of God are God's insuperable, infinitely de-totalizing irruption into the spatially and temporally unrestricted totality of occurrence. It is here that "nature" as it is hallowed by God in Christ can be said to entail every event without abstraction, i.e., with exhaustive concreteness.

Part III Teaching Holiness

9

The Just Shall Live by God's Faithfulness[1]

I

Hɪ! Iᴛ's ɢᴏᴏᴅ ᴛᴏ see you. It is a very big room, of course, and there are lots of us here. Sometimes it's hard to talk when there are lots of people crammed together in a big room. But who knows what might happen here today in this big space and in this little time. Please pray for me. And I will pray for you, too.

My task is to describe for you what the word *justice* signifies. That may not seem like much of a task. *Justice* is a very ordinary word, after all. We use it freely, with ease. There are justices of the peace, halls of justice, the Justice League, poetic justice, criminal justice, the Chief Justice of the Supreme Court. There is the hope of "liberty and justice for all," and so many more ordinary phrases using this word! It would seem that nobody would need a chapel address devoted to saying what this word signifies. But maybe we do. Maybe there is a way to think of justice that not only differs from the ordinary way we use the word, but that might in fact set us to work *doing justice—doing justice* perhaps as we *love mercy* and *walk humbly* with a very particular *God*.

1. Chapel address delivered on January 28, 2009, at Azusa Pacific University, Azusa, CA.

Ordinarily, we think of justice as a kind of balance. Justice, as the word is ordinarily used, says "you get what you deserve," your "fair share," "what you're owed." And so, if you have been unjust—for example, if you have taken more than you have coming—you will need to make up for it. The image here is of a stable and secure space—a quiet room, let's say, in a walled city guarded by a well-equipped standing army, a place where no wind blows. On the hard, thick, smooth floor of that room is a heavy table, let us say, resting on thick legs, its surface perfectly flat. Resting securely on the table—perhaps bolted to it—is a pair of scales, perfectly calibrated. On these scales we are weighed. If what we have taken, if what we have done, if what we have become is not more or less than is our fair share, then we are deemed just. If not, then something has to be done to get even—to balance the scales. That is the ordinary way of imagining justice. And so, it is not uncommon to find in or near a courthouse a bronze statue of a woman, blindfolded (to keep her personal biases in check), holding a pair of scales aloft. Justice is balance, we think.

But let us say that we don't live in a safe and secure city, a city with thick walls and a well-equipped standing army. Let's say that we have no quiet room where the wind does not blow. Let's say instead that we are nomads, wanderers, who sleep under the sky in tents. Let us say that we are in a strange land, that we do not know our way, that we cannot go back to the place from which we've come, that we must go on. This image, this scenario, is different than the one we usually imagine. Here on this journey we don't need *scales*. We need a *guide*. We need *direction*. We need a *promise*. We need *someone*, someone to say, "*Come*, follow me!"

II

The most honored of all ceremonies in ancient Israel was the Passover. It was the ceremony that told those ancient Hebrews who they were. As they performed it, they remembered what it was like to be enslaved in a strange land, in Egypt. They told stories of how God had heard their cries and had sent Moses to declare to Pharaoh the word of God, "Let my people go!" They told stories of how in the wilderness God sent a cloud for them to follow during the day and a flame in the sky for them to follow at night. And during the Passover, as they celebrated the journey of their ancestors, they dressed in their ancestors' traveling clothes, walking sticks in their hands, walking shoes on their feet, and the time that separated them from their ancestors melted away. In this ceremony they journeyed with them. "My father was a wandering Aramean!" they declared. "When we were slaves in Egypt!" they declared. To be a Jew was to be a nomad, a wanderer, traveling across a strange land out into *promise*. Justice here is *traveling* aright. Justice here is traveling *aright*. It is moving out into the promised future. It is following the elusive way of God, letting God lead, saying "yes" to the path God cuts, saying "yes" to what God determines is a good route, saying "no" to what God determines is a bad route. Justice is where God is going. We are just if we go there, too. Justice here is *traveling aright*.

And so, God gives these wandering Arameans the law. God says by the law, "*Travel* this way!" And all is well as long as the law does not become something in itself, as if a road sign became more important than the place the road sign points you to. And so, we find the prophets deriding those who become proud of the fact that they had mastered the road sign. The prophets say, "Lift your eyes from the road sign to the God who goes before you!" They say, "God's promises went out to our ancestors, to us when we were slaves in Egypt!" They say, "God is a God of people like we were when we were slaves: the oppressed—strangers, orphans, widows, the poor! God goes to them! Go with God!"

But, of course, our world is not a world that attends to the oppressed, to strangers, orphans, widows, and the poor. It is a world that defers to the powerful, to property owners, to the well connected, to those who can pull their own weight, to the rich. And certainly God loves them, too. It's just that God loves them on the way to the oppressed, to strangers, orphans, widows, and the poor. To put down roots with the "haves" of this world is to fail to travel down the path that God cuts to the poor. To be just is to go with God to them. Or so we hear from the prophets.

When times came to be especially tough, when the whole powerful world seemed to press down on God's people to crush the life out of them, when the heirs of Alexander the Great and then the Romans seemed to take away every escape route, the Jews of the ancient world did not give up hope. Their very particular God, the God who created them and the whole world, the sovereign God, the God of justice, would not forsake God's people, they insisted, but would break into this closed world and shatter the heavy weight piled onto their backs. From the outside, it was maintained, from the outside of the powers of this world, God would come to *reign* with justice, lifting the lowly and humbling the mighty.

The phrase "the kingdom of God," or perhaps better, "the reign of God," emerges out of this hope, this hope that is tempted from every side to despair, this hope that says an angry "No!" to despair. When the powers of this world work to keep God out, "Run!" these ancient apocalyptic Hebrews said, "Run to the coming of God's reign!" It is precisely those who run to the coming of God's reign who by definition are just.

III

When Jesus made his appearance in ancient Palestine, in the cities of Bethlehem and Nazareth and Jerusalem and Bethany and Capernaum and Caesarea Philippi and the spaces in between, he went about with this phrase, "the kingdom of God," "the reign of God," on his lips. He was to that extent, at least, an apocalyptic prophet. Indeed, he was consumed by that phrase, "the reign of God." It was all he ever talked about, and he talked about it with such passion and such confidence that it must have been almost comical to hear him coming, this man soaked in "the reign of God." "Here comes 'the reign of God,'" folks likely would say as he approached. And it was not only on his lips. It was on his hands, hands that touched and healed the sick and raised the dead. It was in his belly and blood, the belly and blood that received the food that the oppressed—the strangers, orphans, widows, poor, and unclean people of this world—fed him. And what he declared with his lips and hands and belly and blood, with all he said and did, was that "the reign of God is coming—run, run with me to meet it!" And as it turned out, it was just this adventure of going out to meet the coming of God that constituted justice in all that Jesus entailed. Justice here is journeying out into the coming of the God whose ways are not our ways, whose loves are not our loves, whose mercies are not our mercies, whose grace is not our grace.

Jesus is so abandoned to the coming of God that he comes to be inseparable from it. Everything he is and does is an adventure out into the coming of God. He goes where God's reign goes. God's reign goes where he goes. So, if while reading the Gospels you ever wonder where it is that God's reign is breaking out, just watch where *Jesus* is going.

And where do we find Jesus going? He goes to the poor. He goes to the sick. He goes to the outcasts of society, the powerless, the unclean, the despised; he goes to women and Roman collaborators and terrorists and common laborers and children and foreigners—the subalterns, the mulattos, the mestizos, the Samaritans, beggars—and he says to them all: "Run out into the coming of God! Run out into the coming of God and all that you are, all that you do will be *just!*" "The *just* shall live by faith," Paul tells us—and Jesus demonstrates (Cf. Hab 2:4; Rom 1:17; and Gal 3:11). "Come unto me all you who labor and are heavily burdened, for as I have come to you, God has come to you to reign" (Cf. Matt 11:28).

Certainly, Jesus goes as well to those who are well heeled, to various holders of political power in his ancient land, some of them Romans, most of them Jews. And he says to them the same thing he says to all: "Follow me to the coming of God's reign!" And then he goes to the poor, the forgotten, the lonely, the broken, the unclean, the renegade. It is a rarity among the rich and powerful that such a one might come to go with Jesus. That is likely because to go with him where he goes means to enter into solidarity with the people he goes to, to enter into solidarity with them the way he did—and that would mean a loss of all that makes one rich and powerful. The rich young ruler came to know that. That's why he went away sorrowful. And yet even the rich and powerful need not despair, for with God all things are possible. Even the rich and powerful might learn to go with Jesus to where God goes. Francis of Assisi did. Further, traveling with Jesus to the oppressed is not some condescending beneficence, as if the oppressed needed me. Indeed, Jesus calls the oppressed—in even greater numbers—to travel with him *to* the oppressed. It is to poor people above all that Jesus says:

"If any want to become my followers, let them deny themselves and take up their cross and follow me."

But Jesus' story goes farther than this. In fact, all of his travels in ancient Palestine were a kind of prelude to his final journey, the one that makes up what we call Holy Week. If it was audacious for him to claim that God's reign was breaking out as he ate supper with harlots and bandits, or as he touched a corpse, the implication of his last week is outrageous. His travels then took him from the Garden of Gethsemane to the high priest's house, to Herod, to Pilate, to the whipping post, to the Via Dolorosa, to Golgotha, and to a slow, agonizing, publicly humiliating execution in solidarity with thieves, insurgents, terrorists. If where Jesus goes God goes to reign, then "the kingdom of God," "the reign of God" breaks out on the bloody hill outside the gates of Jerusalem that dark Friday. Jesus' slow death was his call even there to those accursed with him: "Come unto me!" his weak voice says to those thieves. And one of them, Luke tells us, says, "Yes!"

When Jesus breathes his last, is taken down from the cross, is washed and entombed, and a day and a half later is resurrected by the Spirit of the one he calls "Father," a spotlight comes to shine on all his life's journeys. Indeed, where he went, the reign of God broke out—in the most unlikely of places. It is he who is the "*just* one of God." It is from his story most of all that we come to learn what the word *justice* signifies.

IV

And what do we learn from his story concerning justice? Well, we learn that justice has *nothing* to do with getting even. We learn that it has *nothing* to do with receiving what you are due. We learn that it has *nothing* to do with getting and holding and keeping. We learn that justice has *everything* to do with going where God goes. We learn that it is a traveling word. We learn that justice is a journey on which travelers hold loosely to what they once thought were obviously "good" and "evil" in our world, for on this journey they have learned that it might in fact be to the "evil" that God most directly travels—to those, say, who make their beds in hell. We learn that justice is traveling to and with the oppressed—to strangers, orphans, widows, the poor, and the unclean—and it means *that* whether or not one is oneself oppressed. We learn that to travel to the oppressed is to come to live with them, to pray with them, to work with them, to die with them—for of such is the reign of God. We learn that justice is all about the life of God, the life breathed into us by God, the life by which women and men work their fields, raise their babies, cook their meals, laugh, cry, and sing—and by which in all things they give thanks, rejoice without restraint, and pray without ceasing to the Sovereign and Giver of Life.

Justice does not mean that the lowly of this world get lifted up to "our level," whatever that might mean. The American Dream is in the end a nightmare of acquisition, isolation, violence, and fear. To work to move the poor into the American middle class has nothing to do with the justice of the story of Jesus. But for us—for you and for me—to remain captivated by the American middle class is for us, too, to have forsaken the justice of the story of Jesus. It is in that story that we learn what it means to be saved by grace through faith, what it means that by the grace of God the faithful are made just. In that story we learn that those saved by grace have nothing to fear. They are liberated from fear not only of hell, but also of economic ruin, of humiliation, of the loss of power and status. We become *just by grace through faith* because it is by *faith* that we follow Jesus to the arrival of God's gracious reign where life seems most certainly to be crashing and burning.

It is of justice that Paul speaks when he says: "For I am convinced that neither death, nor life, nor angels, nor rulers, nor things present, nor things to come, nor powers, nor height, nor depth, nor anything else in all creation, will be able to separate us from the love of God in Christ Jesus our Lord" (Rom 8:38–39). That is a call to give your life away. To follow Jesus is to follow him where the powers of this world did their worst. When God raised him from the dead, God declared to all creation that those who move in Christ are set free to be free, for they have nothing to lose or to win. You are set free to be free to live danger-ously. You are set free to be free to stare the Beast of injustice in the eye and not blink. You will not know what to do when you follow Jesus to the oppressed of this world—no matter how well trained you are in the tactics of economic development. That's okay; for God has gone ahead of you and you are following. And besides, to fixate on tactics is to confuse the road sign with the journey it is pointing you to. That is not to say that you are to leap into the belly of the Beast without first looking. Learn all you can, remember all you can, but do so in order to give away all you have—even if in the end you let go of all you've learned.

Justice is to be done precisely as we love mercy and humbly follow the God who breaks into this world where Jesus entangles the lives of others in his own life. If you want to be just,)"Let the same mind be in you that was in Christ Jesus, who, though he was, like Adam, in the image of God, he did not regard likeness with God as something to be grasped, but emptied himself, taking the form of a slave, washing feet, serving, caring for others, being born like Adam, you, and me in human likeness. And being found like us in human form, he humbled himself and became obedient to the coming of the reign of God—to the point of death—even death on a cross."

Make no mistake, this world of ours does not treat the just kindly. God goes where life is threatened, where life is taken. The just go with God. And if you want to be "like Jesus," and like Jesus to be just, remember that there is only one answer to the question, what would Jesus do? He would die. He would die where the powers of this world fight to keep out the grace of God. He would die where mercy is thought to stand in contrast to justice. He would die where the least of us die—not because dying is noble or desirable or superhuman (it is not!), not because the least of us are the best people (they are not!), but in order with God to keep the dying from dying alone, and to declare to them that the reign of God is coming, and it is coming for them.

10

"I Am the Lord and There Is No Other"

The Allure of "Faith Integration"[1]

I

HI. IT'S A GOOD thing for me to be here. I get happy when I'm on this campus. What a great place to go to school! And what great human beings have found their way here—while *you* are here! In fact, some of my favorite people in the entire world hang out here. I'd best not begin naming them—that typically ends badly, as the annual Academy Awards ceremony illustrates so well. But I would like to say that I am really glad that Eric Severson is here—for you. He is good and smart and brave and wise and funny; and I dare say—though it will take me some time to clarify what such a turn of phrase might signify—that he is "a holy man." I hope you know him and have found ways of drawing close to him. Your President, Corlis McGee, is also a friend of mine. We were junior professors together at Trevecca Nazarene College long, long ago—meeting first there sometime between the theatrical release of *The Empire Strikes Back* and *Return of the Jedi*. She, too, is good and smart and brave and wise and funny; and I dare say—though it will take me some time to clarify what such a turn of phrase might signify—that she

---

1. The first of two Gould Holiness Lectures delivered March 31–April 3, 2009, at Eastern Nazarene College, Quincy, Massachusetts.

is "a holy woman." I hope you know her and have found ways of drawing close to her.

There is something at least a little awkward about chapels like this one. "The Gould Holiness Lectures"—that's a heavy label to put on a couple of chapel talks. I mean, there's hardly anything less cool than "holiness." (Can you imagine the pickup line: "Hey, baby, you entirely sanctified?") Furthermore, here I am standing behind this box, a stranger to most of you. I can't think of any good reason why you should trust anything I have to say. I guess it's a good thing for me, stranger that I am, Holiness Lecturer that I am, that it *is* chapel—and thus obligatory. Were attendance at this event optional, I'm not sure we could fill many chairs. And I also need to *warn* you about *me*. I don't know how to make things easy. What I say is always too complicated, too subtle, too heavy, too much, too passionate—even if it is passion of the smoldering, rather than explosive, kind. Further, I'm not *myself* a very holy person. I dare say—though it will take me some time to clarify what such a turn of phrase might signify—that I am the worst of sinners. So, please pray for me. I promise that I will pray for you.

II

The title of this Gould Lecture is: "I Am the Lord and There Is No Other: The Allure of 'Faith Integration.'" There are two parts to this title, each separated from the other by a semi-colon. The first part, "I Am the Lord and There Is No Other," is a phrase lifted out of Isaiah 45. Isaiah 45 is one of the most extreme and excessive declarations of the sovereignty of God to be found in holy writ. In it is at play the logic of the ancient Hebrew understanding of God as creator of Israel and of the cosmos. In it is at play the logic of God's holiness—articulated in the face of a whole world of competing deities.

The second part of the title, "The Allure of 'Faith Integration,'" speaks to a vision, sometimes called "the integration of faith and learning," that has become a favorite on all the college campuses I have been a part of for the past three decades. It is a favorite of the Council of Christian Colleges and Universities, a distinguished organization of which both Eastern Nazarene College and Azusa Pacific University are members. It is because I suspect that the notion of "the integration of faith and learning" is familiar to you and perhaps also one of *your* favorites that I bring it up already in my first public lecture at ENC. If it is not, please forgive me. In any case, in order not to be too sneaky, I will announce right here and now that I'm pretty sure the first half of the title of this lecture stands in judgment against its second half.

Isaiah 45 is quite a chapter. The setting is the Babylonian captivity of the children of Israel. The Babylonians have conquered Israel, have devastated the promised land, have mown down all its cities and its temple, and have hauled off to Babylon as slaves those not left dead or dying on smoking battlefields or beside tents or under toppled city walls. Yahweh—the God of Abraham, Isaac, and Jacob, the God of David and Hezekiah, the God of Moses and Elijah—Yahweh, the champion of Israel, has been from all appearances defeated by the gods of Mesopotamia. Powerless before those whom Babylonian generals and priests served, Yahweh has been knocked down and out—or so it seemed. And certainly the *descendents* of the Hebrew men and women who had fought for the promised land were tempted, when that land fell, to forsake the faith that had carried their mothers and fathers, to throw in with the gods whose superiority was made evident by the hard facts of imperial might.

It is in the light of this bloody, devastating defeat that Isaiah 45 speaks. And its explosive word is that Yahweh—the God of Abraham, Isaac, and Jacob, the God of the exodus—is a holy God, poised even now to act—to save the Hebrew children. Yahweh is not to be *confused with* any other god, not to be *counted alongside* any other god, not to be *sublimated* and *universalized* as a vague "divine essence" variously manifested as one or another god in a religious world. Rather Yahweh is *one particular God*—in *distinction from* every other god. Yahweh is *that one particular God* who has come to be made manifest among *one particular people*, the lowly Jews—once enslaved by and powerless before the Egyptians, now enslaved by and powerless before the Babylonians. This one particular God, Yahweh, stands out, Isaiah 45 declares, with such earth-shakingly impossible and unnamable power that before this one particular God all other gods, all other claimants to divine status, are unmasked as imposters, as fakes, as wooden or stone or imaginary or conceptual products of that flesh which before Yahweh is grass: "The grass withers, the flower fades, when the breath of the Lord blows upon it" (Isa 40:7). And in case anyone doubted the Lord—and, of course, Jews and Babylonians doubted the Lord in that time of Jewish social, political, and economic devastation and Babylonian prosperity—the Lord was sending, of all people, an unbelieving Persian king to save the Lord's children. Before this pagan king the Lord would cut a path and throw aside every obstacle, the Lord would "level the mountains, . . . break in pieces the doors of bronze and cut through the bars of iron" (Isa 45:2). And so, Isaiah 45 announces to the captive Jews:

> Assemble yourselves and come together, draw near, you survivors of the nations! They have no knowledge—those who carry about their wooden idols, and keep on praying to a god that cannot save. . . . There is no other god besides me, a righteous God and a Savior; there is no one besides me. Turn to me and be saved, all the ends of the earth! For I am God, and there is no other. By myself I have sworn, from my mouth has gone forth in righteousness a word that shall not return: 'To me every knee shall bow, every tongue shall swear.' Only in the Lord, it shall be said of me, are righteousness and strength. (Isa 45:20, 21–24)

For a body of people to be holy, Isaiah is saying, is for it to understand that there is no other god besides Yahweh; for a body of people to be holy, Isaiah is saying, is for it to understand *this* in its bones, with its backs and arms and bellies, with its babies and sisters and brothers, with its forebears and descendents, with the fruit of its labor and the work of its hands, with every mouthful of food and every day of sweat, pain, laughter, and delight. For a body of people to be holy, Isaiah is saying, is for it to turn to this one particular God and *there* be saved, to find in Yahweh alone all righteousness, all justice, and strength—to live out into the coming of this wild, particular God—and to do so both with abandon and with hope. It is Yahweh who comes. It is out into the coming of Yahweh that a holy people are to run. In that encounter is the liberation that pulsates with the rhythm of a future that no replicated experimentation, no extrapolated regularity, no market forecasts, no church growth projections, no strategies for effective evangelism, no calculus of investment and return can begin to understand. In the encounter between the coming holy God and the liberated holy people is the life that will not rest easily with the gods of this world.

III

It was a slow day
And the sun was beating
On the soldiers by the side of the road
There was a bright light
A shattering of shop windows
The bomb in the baby carriage
Was wired to the radio

It was a dry wind
And it swept across the desert
And it curled into the circle of birth
And the dead sand
Falling on the children
The mothers and the fathers
And the automatic earth

It's a turn-around jump shot
It's everybody jump start
It's every generation throws a hero up the pop charts
Medicine is magical and magical is art
The Boy in the Bubble
And the baby with the baboon heart

And I believe
These are the days of lasers in the jungle
Lasers in the jungle somewhere
Staccato signals of constant information
A loose affiliation of millionaires
And billionaires and baby
These are the days of miracle and wonder
This is the long distance call
The way the camera follows us in slo-mo
The way we look to us all
The way we look to a distant constellation
That's dying in a corner of the sky
These are the days of miracle and wonder
And don't cry baby, don't cry
Don't cry[2]

These are indeed the days of miracle and wonder, and it is above all we academics who take credit for it. We remember the dark days before the dawning of the European university. We remember the days of superstition and inelegant rhetoric, of uncertain national boundaries, of inadequate defenses against flood, famine, disease, and marauding gangs of barbarians. And then we recite bright tales of how a rebirth of culture occurred as the profound and beautiful Greek and Latin texts of antiquity were rediscovered: the writings of Aristotle, Plato, the Stoics, and the Skeptics, of philosophers, physicians, and poets. We recite bright tales of how light began to dawn on Europe, of how explorers reached out to find that there was a whole new world to be used for the "good" of European centers of newly emerging economic and military power—what would in a few centuries mature into the modern nation-state. We recite bright tales of how the forces of nature were harnessed by technology and its twin, "science," the two joined at the chest, sharing the same heart. We recite bright tales of how civilization was carried to the whole world from Europe—to what we call "Latin America"—was carried to the land to Latin America's north, whose indigenous people

2. Paul Simon, "Boy in the Bubble."

also yielded to progress, was carried from Europe and America to the rest of the world. And when we've finished our bright tales, we all agree that what is needed at places like ENC and APU is the wedding of the "learning" that gave rise to these miracles and wonders with the "faith" of our churchy fathers and mothers, the "faith" of our own hearts.

What we don't as often remember is that as the modern nation-state marked out its boundaries by the coercive power of standing armies, and promoted its identity through the enforcement of a common language and culture for the people who lived and died within its borders, it learned to compete with its neighboring nation-states and to increase its coercive strength through the boundary-enlarging technology, science, and economics of colonialism. And "learning" has been hard at work in the wars and boardrooms that launched a thousand thousand slave ships to make those colonies the kinds of resources that would keep the glow of Enlightenment bright. It is no surprise that the most civilized nation-state in the world was the one that designed and implemented the Holocaust and that the same technology and science in the hands of an enemy of that nation-state would turn energy of a previously unimagined degree to *its* benefit in Hiroshima and Nagasaki—both nation-states knowing how to draw upon the theological and philosophical wisdom of the Western world to explain why and how these were noble and necessary deeds.

This is a darker story than the one we normally tell. We prefer the happier story. In fact, we academics (among others) tell that happier story to ourselves day in and day out, protesting perhaps too much—methinks—in the face of our critics, as if we could not bear the thought that what we academics call "learning," what we academics have labored so hard to achieve, may not always and everywhere be life affirming. We churchy academics especially like to think that the "learning" with whom we have been married is a real *breadwinner*, not a thief who would *steal* bread from the children of the poor.

And yet, perhaps there is grace for us, too—even if it is the grace of conversion, of repentance, of *metanoia*—grace, that is, to admit that there may well be a preferable future for colleges like ENC and APU, a future, for example, preferable to "the integration of faith and learning."

It seems to me that the sooner we admit that a preferable—a different—future might be beckoning us, the sooner we can get on with it.

IV

And what might that something different be? We are so used to the notion of "faith integration" that it may perhaps be difficult for us to begin to imagine it, though I think that it is in imagining it that places like ENC and APU come to be faithful to their calling as socially just and righteous bodies. The "something different" I have in mind here . . . is what may be termed . . . "holiness." Really! Something different from the integration of faith and learning may be a mode of thought and practice that runs out to meet the coming of Yahweh, the Yahweh who in creating Israel from the chaos of Babylonian captivity creates the whole cosmos (and not the other way around). Something different from the integration of faith and learning may be the mode of thought and practice that will not secure the future on the foundation of a solid past from which reliable extrapolations may be drawn, because the God it runs to meet is a God who needs no foundation in any past, however solid it may seem to be. This God is the God before whom not even the mightiest empire can stand. This God is the God who liberates those who are captive to what is to every unbelieving mind a brute fact. Something different from the integration of faith and learning may be a mode of thought and practice that is open and hospitable, that takes in what the Western world calls "wisdom" and "civilization," but does so not only or chiefly with appreciation, but also and above all with the crisis of judgment (remembering that the very wisdom that makes our lives safer built and still builds slave ships.)

Frankly, when I hear the phrase "the integration of faith and learning," I think of the response of the leaders of the Black Power movement of the late 1960s and early 1970s to previous calls for "*racial* integration." The leaders of the Black Power movement knew very well that "*racial* integration" on the lips of the Establishment was code for a new and more subtle pattern of submission to a European/American world, that it signified "we want you to give up everything about you that is distinctive and become what we tell you that you are to be." What I would like to see in colleges like ENC and APU is a holiness that is not afraid of calling classy academics—like me!—to account, that is not afraid of disputing the most revered of ideologies of Western civilization—not for the sake of some *newly* fashionable ideology, perhaps one with the prefix "post," but for the sake of a possibility that nothing that *is* or *has been* could ever produce.

"Holiness" is what the rich young ruler was asked to abandon his life for. He was asked to give up what he grasped so tightly and to run out into the coming of God—precisely by following Jesus to Golgotha. I suspect that when academics like me walk up to Jesus and ask, "Good Teacher, what must I do to inherit eternal life?" Jesus' reply will be quite similar. He will say, "Take all your intellectual capital and let it go, keep nothing, not even the benefits you receive by letting it go; and come follow me to the cross!" It is my prayer that when I hear his words—the worst of sinners though I am—I will not go away grieving because I have many intellectual possessions. It is my prayer that when I hear his words—the worst of sinners though I am—I will turn my face toward the earth-shakingly impossible and unnamable power of the coming Yahweh who liberated the Jews from Babylonian captivity and raised Jesus Christ from the dead, and that there, with all of you, I and we will with all that is in us expend ourselves—heart, soul, mind, and strength—in a thanksgiving that will not be harnessed to the bone-crushing engines that drive Western civilization.

11

"My Lord and My God"
The Allure of "Excellence"[1]

I

HI! THANKS FOR COMING back. And thanks for treating me so well while I've been here. I take your hospitality seriously. I promise you that I will work hard to keep our time together this morning from being wasted. Of course, making good on that promise may be harder than you'd think. Occasions such as this one typically set up addresses—to waste time. I do understand that I am addressing *you*, flesh-and-blood human beings, human beings who are alive at this particular *time*. And most of you and I don't know each other well at all. So, you'll have to do a lot of guessing about the subtext and pretext of my words, and I'll have to do a lot of guessing about the post-text of my words, the way my words will be heard and remembered by you. And, of course, when you are asked to listen *closely* to an address that is too complicated, too subtle, too heavy, too much, too passionate—even if it is passion of the smoldering, rather than explosive, kind—everything gets even harder. But you have invited me and I do not take your hospitality lightly. So, pray for me. I will pray for you.

1. The second of two Gould Holiness Lectures delivered March 31–April 3, 2009, at Eastern Nazarene College, Quincy, MA.

II

The title of this Gould Lecture is: "My Lord and My God: The Allure of 'Excellence.'" Once again, there are two parts to this title, each separated from the other by a single punctuation mark. The first part, "My Lord and My God," is a phrase lifted out of John 20. John 20 is one of the most extreme and excessive declarations of the sovereignty of God to be found in holy writ. In it is at play a further radicalization of the logic of the ancient Hebrew understanding of God as creator of Israel and of the cosmos. In it is at play a further radicalization of the logic of God's holiness—articulated in the face of a world of competing principalities and powers.

The second part of the title, "The Allure of 'Excellence,'" speaks to a vision that has become a favorite on all the college campuses I have been a part of for the past three decades. It is a favorite of the Council of Christian Colleges and Universities, a distinguished organization of which both Eastern Nazarene College (ENC) and Azusa Pacific University are members. It is because I suspect that the notion of "excellence" is familiar to you, and perhaps also one of *your* favorites, that I bring it up in my second public lecture here at ENC. If it is not, please forgive me. In any case, in order not to be too sneaky, I will announce right here and now that I'm pretty sure the first half of the title of this lecture stands in judgment against its second half.

John 20 is quite a chapter. It is set in the shadow of the crucifixion of Jesus. The Romans and certain upright Jews (who on this occasion have chosen to collaborate with the Romans) have just lynched Jesus, have devastated him, have mown his body down, have pierced and bled him dry, and have dumped his bloody corpse and sealed it in a cold, hard, dark pit. Jesus—in whom had believed Andrew and Peter; Nathanael and Philip; Mary, Martha, and Lazarus; the woman at the Samaritan well and the woman who anointed his feet; the lame, the blind, and the hungry—Jesus, "the Holy One of God," has been crushed by the principalities and powers that torment the weak and poor of this world. Jesus, who would be the Messiah, has been abandoned on a barren hill, and by all appearances has been forsaken above all by the one he adoringly called "Father," the one against whom no empire could prevail. Powerless before the inclusive deadly force of Rome and the exclusive deadly purity of Jerusalem, the body of Jesus has been arrested and humiliated, mocked and executed, broken open and drained of life. And certainly this lowly Nazarene's *disciples*, the ones who had followed him as if he were a pillar of cloud by day and a pillar of fire by night, were tempted, when their Lord fell, to forsake the faith that had carried them from their old jobs and homes out into the vision of a new world. Certainly, they were tempted to throw their lot in with the old order whose superiority was made evident by the hard facts of imperial might and ritual purity. And indeed, they yielded to that temptation and once more took up their old jobs.

It is in the light of this bloody, devastating defeat that John 20 speaks. And what it speaks is the explosive word that Yahweh—the God of Abraham, Isaac, and Jacob, the God of the exodus—is a holy God, a God who is not to be judged by the standards of propriety and consistency, but who, precisely as holy, precisely as this one wildly particular God, chooses what is low and despised in the world, things that are not, to reduce to nothing things that are (1 Cor 1:28). The explosive word of John 20 is that this holy God cannot be quarantined, cannot be kept out by the demands of an abstract justice or righteousness or purity or power. The word of John 20 is that the Father, whom Jesus adored, had indeed been with him all the way to his bloody end, and that Jesus had indeed been obedient to his Father to the point of death, even death on a cross (Phil 2:8). Only because Jesus had not forsaken his Father—even when he was thereby led into the deepest darkness—does his Father not forsake him. Thus, Easter Sunday declares that the Father of Jesus Christ is on this new first day—and thus on all other days—not to be *confused with* any other power, not to be *counted alongside* any other power, not to be *sublimated* and *universalized* as a vague "power" variously manifested as one or another power in a social, political, and economic world of domination. Rather Yahweh is *one particular God in distinction from all other gods*. Yahweh is *that one particular God* who has come to be made manifest *as one particular Jew*, the lowly Jesus, enslaved, slaughtered, and forsaken—and thus the *friend of* the enslaved, the slaughtered, and the forsaken. This one particular God, the Father of Jesus Christ, stands out—so John 20 declares—with such earth-shakingly impossible and unnamable power that before this one particular God, all other claimants to power are unmasked as imposters, as fakes, as imaginary or conceptual products of that flesh which before Yahweh is grass. And though everyone doubted that this God was the Father of Jesus in that time of Jesus' devastation and the prosperity of those who had pursued him to death, his Father had, of all things, raised *him*, crucified and forsaken, *from the dead*—with a life so abundant that not even death itself could stand up to it.

This is the context out of which John 20 speaks, which provides the significance of the first half of the title of this address. The words "My Lord and my God!" are spoken by Thomas a week after the Father raised Jesus from the dead. Jesus had already appeared to the other disciples, but not yet to Thomas. Thomas had heard the disciples' accounts of the appearance of the resurrected Jesus, but as an intelligent man—as a person who knew what the resurrection of one *crucified* would entail—he did not believe them. And so, he said to them, "Unless I see the mark of the nails in his hands, and put my finger in the mark of the nails, and my hand in his side, I will not believe" (v. 25). When finally he saw the resurrected body, Jesus, and was invited to do as he had demanded, all his defenses melted away; no proof was any longer required—not because he now had it, but because no proof could bear the one he encountered in that room. His words, "My Lord and my God!" are not a kind of conclusion—say of inductive or deductive reasoning—but a new beginning. His words make a doxology, an irruptive praise that, not built on empirical data, opens from the body of Jesus standing before him, opening as Jesus' wounds do, opening out into a God so holy, so unqualifiedly, uniquely, singularly, particularly loving, that nothing—not even death and damnation—could separate us from this holy God, whom we now understand *is* love. What it means for God to have embraced the crucified Jesus and for Jesus to remain crucified even in his resurrection life is that God is holy precisely as the God who rushes to the poor, the sick, the dying, the dead, the damned—and bathes them with God's own holy life.

Thus for a body of people to be holy, John is saying, is for it to understand that there is no other God besides the Father of the crucified Jesus; for a body of people to be holy, John is saying, is for it to understand *this* in its bones, with its backs and arms and bellies, with its babies and sisters and brothers, with its forebears and descendents, with the fruit of its labor and the work of its hands, with every mouthful of food and every day of sweat, pain, laughter, and delight. For a body of people to be holy, John is saying, is for it to turn to this one particular God and *there* be saved, to find in the Father of the crucified Jesus alone all righteousness, all justice, and strength—to live out into the coming of this wild, particular God, and to do so both with abandon and with hope. It is the Father of the crucified Jesus who comes. And it is out into the coming of the Father of the crucified Jesus that a holy people are to run. In that encounter is the liberation that pulsates with the rhythm of a future that no replicated experimentation, no extrapolated regularity, no market forecasts, no church growth projections, no strategies for effective evangelism, no calculus of investment and return can begin to understand. In the encounter between the coming Holy Father of the crucified Jesus and the liberated holy people is the life that will not rest easily with the powers of this world; it is rather the life that will live and die with those whom the powers of this world despises.

III

It's a turn-around jump shot
It's everybody jump start
It's every generation throws a hero up the pop charts
Medicine is magical and magical is art
The Boy in the Bubble
And the baby with the baboon heart

And I believe
These are the days of lasers in the jungle
Lasers in the jungle somewhere
Staccato signals of constant information
A loose affiliation of millionaires
And billionaires and baby

These are the days of miracle and wonder

This is the long distance call

The way the camera follows us in slo-mo

The way we look to us all

The way we look to a distant constellation

That's dying in a corner of the sky

These are the days of miracle and wonder

And don't cry baby, don't cry

Don't cry[2]

These are indeed the days of miracle and wonder, and it is above all we academics who take credit for it. We are the ones who have practiced the art of excellence—and without excellence where would our world be? Without excellence there would be no miracles or wonders (or so we think). And, of course, everybody agrees that it is excellence that we are to pursue. "Excellence" is shouted loudly and persistently from every street corner, from every monitor, every official, every newsflash, every lesson and transcript. "Excellence" is "success" and "accomplishment" and "power" and "resourcefulness." It is assumed that in every chapel, even, we have been called together to honor excellence (or so it would seem). And though there may be a "God-honoring excellence," it may also be worth our time to pray for discernment so that not just any god will be honored during those long days and nights when we strive to reach higher and higher. In fact, we may want to ask ourselves what kind of god would ask us even to begin to reach higher and higher.

But perhaps we should not talk this way. Even beginning to ask those little (implicit) questions may fail to pay proper respect to academe, no doubt the most respectable of respectable institutions. Excellence is, in fact, among the most time-honored virtues of academe. Of course it is. What higher virtue could there be than excellence? By what rule could we even measure something higher than excellence, which it is reasonable to take as virtue itself? And so, of course, we will honor excellence at this Gould Holiness Lecture. Of course! Everything, everything, everything is to be hauled before the high court of excel-

2. Paul Simon, "The Boy in the Bubble."

lence—and judged! And we are hauled before that court day in and day out to be asked, "How have you measured up?" And parents and professors and registrars and admissions officers and personnel officers and search committees and advancement committees and rank committees will size us up to determine according to respectable standards whether or not we have measured up. And we will think, "Of course, they *must* do so. How else could the institutions of this world be guaranteed effectiveness?" And it all does make such good sense.

And yet consider once more the words of Thomas before the resurrected crucified body of Jesus: "My Lord and my God!" It is *here*, perhaps especially, that we may be given to hear *another* voice—other than the loud voice that shouts at us wherever we turn—here, perhaps, we may be given to hear another than the voice of power and fear. Here, perhaps, we may be given to hear instead a still, small voice.

It is, indeed, of a *gift* that Thomas speaks: a gift that yields good work, certainly, but a gift that isn't *achieved* by work of any kind; a gift that is so freely given that we can find nothing in it to be proud of, to brag about. It is of a gift that Thomas speaks: a gift that, when freely received, gets us off of ourselves and the excellence we strain to achieve. *That* gift, the gift of God, the gift of the resurrected body of the crucified Jesus, is received only with the gratitude of praise, the gratitude of an abandon and a hope that will not confuse our *achievements, effectiveness,* or *excellence* with *resurrection.* And resurrection here is not some *heavenly* return on an *earthly* investment. Insofar as *we* taste resurrection—even if it is much more of a foretaste—we have tasted it precisely by having been made alive with Christ, by having been woven into Christ's *body,* by having been given the task of living and dying together with him—as he lived and died.

In the body of Christ—the body that in being cut by spikes, whips, thorns, and a spear, opens to us—in the body of Christ we have been given the gift of freedom from the games of power and fear, of winning and losing. As we are baptized into the body of Christ, we die and are raised with him. We are thrown down and kicked into the ditch with him; we breathe our last with him on his rough-hewn cross. We are enlivened and lifted up with him; we are anointed with the very breath that saturated his lifeless body as he lay motionless in a borrowed tomb—the very breath of God that hauled him out of the pit and set him on two strong legs on the hard ground. As we eat and drink the bread and the wine of the Eucharist, we are fed on the broken body and shed blood of Christ and the resurrection by which that broken body and shed blood are glorified. From and in *this* body of Christ we have learned in our bones that we have nothing either to lose or gain. When a body of people has learned *that* in their bones, there is no telling what they might do. And make no mistake, those who know *that* in their bones *will do something*; and what they do may well bring down mighty empires and lift up the poor, who themselves have been thrown down and kicked into the ditch. Those who know in their bones that in Christ there is nothing either to lose or gain *will do something*—though they may do it so patiently and slowly that no film crew will be able to pick it up, so patiently and slowly that only in the long-suffering time of God will their work come to shine with the glory of the face of the risen Christ.

This is the second of two Gould Holiness Lectures. You and I—all of us gathered in this big room—have been called together, even if the "reason" we'd give for our being here is that it is required. We are here now, but we know that after we leave this big room, we will be stepping again into a world in which being baptized into and nourished by the body of Christ counts for less than nothing. You and I know that this is a world of winning and losing, and down deep we know to our shame that we have yielded to it and that our default setting has come to be *its* imagination. You and I also know that to have our stories written into the story of Jesus will not produce success in this world, because we know that to be written into the story of Jesus is to be written into the story of crucifixion. But, if we listen hard, we may also learn that being crucified *in this story* is not bad news. To be crucified in this story is to bear witness with our bodies to the body of the Christ whom the Father's long arms raised up and seated in heavenly places. To be crucified in this story is for us to be raised up with him—the one forever bearing the wounds of the cross, "for by grace you have been saved through faith, and this is not your own doing; it is the gift of God—not the result of works, so that no one may boast" (Phil 2:6–8).

This is the second of two Gould Holiness Lectures. You and I, all of us gathered in this big room, have been called together—called together by the whisper of a lover who reminds us that this day is not yet done, and that a new day is coming. The God of Jesus and Thomas, the God who with tender mercy embraces the Jesus who did not strike back when struck, the God who in this Jesus loves those to whom everyone, everyone, everyone says, "No!," the God who fills the heavens with this broken Jesus, who fills the future with this broken man—this Jesus whose body has opened to take in everyone, everyone, everyone—the God and Father of our Lord Jesus Christ *speaks*. And what *this* Father of *this* Son says to you and to me is, "Yes!" Live, live, live out into that "Yes!" Live out into the call of *that* holiness.

12

The Root from Which They Spring[1]

I HAVE BEEN A university educator for over a quarter of a century. My area of expertise is theology. Theology is, if it is anything at all, a way of paying attention to God. Simply put, professors of theology profess God. That is why good people send their children off to college to study with theologians, with people like me. And I—professor that I am—do profess God overtly, loudly, passionately. What is so embarrassing, though, is that I have such a hard time saying what it is that God means. You would think that someone laboring in this field for so long would have at least that much nailed down! Yet I must confess that I do not.

The Life Which I Now Live in the Flesh

The problem is not that I am a closet infidel, hiding behind some plastic mask of public piety (like a candidate running for office). I try very hard to be honest and open, particularly where I am most professional. That is, my comprehension failure is no secret. In fact, I would think nothing would be more evident, as I go on and on in class, than that I *strain* just to get that black hole of a little three-letter word out. But, of course, my

1. A Presidential Address given to the forty-first annual meeting of the Wesleyan Theological Society, Nazarene Theological Seminary, Kansas City, MO, March 4, 2006. An earlier version of the present essay was first published in *Wesleyan Theological Journal* 42 (2007) 148–59.

task as a professor of theology is not *just* to get that one word out; I am to throw out a whole galaxy of words and ideas and images and practices and passions that are agitated by and drawn into that black hole.

Of course, on the other hand, speaking of God in this way is misspeaking, hopelessly so. To say "God" is surely not to say a compressed and compressing density, that heaviest, darkest phenomenon of orthodox physics. And, though there are speculative physicists and writers of science fiction who think of a black hole as a portal to another, distant point in space-time—and it might not be out of the question to think of one as an exit portal to some altogether different *configuration* of space-time, some new cosmos even—I have for a long time now been unable to speak of God as a way out of this earthy world. Speaking of God seems rather to be a way into it, even if from the outside.

There, I have already said too much. My social/historical/political location is showing. Yet there is nothing surprising about that. Every college sophomore knows that God is tradition specific. One opens the dictionary to the *G* tab and there one finds a meandering account of the roots of the little English word, roots that draw nutrients from deep inside pagan soil, where perhaps the ordinary usage of God is more happily at home. Provocative phrases about sacrifice and invocation appear in the midst of its history, their subjects and objects mingle, and in it all there is no outbreak into anything particularly transcendent (though transcendence appears as a universal within this system). Everything swims in the warm immanent amniotic fluid of human consciousness. God as such is held fast, protected from aphasia, and assigned the task to speak well in accordance with the language that houses it. Thus, God says something that is generally true, able to be heard everywhere and by all: a grand linguistic phenomenon, an absolute truth, the chief exemplification of all metaphysical principles, no doubt.

And yet, I read in another big book that when the very particular Job sits on the ash heap, alone, aching, burning, and with every new upset tempted to curse God and die, he turns his two wide eyes to the mystery of the open sky and, with a passion that rips apart the fabric of space-time and its God, cries, "Violence!" (Job 19:7)—and, as if encountering something new on the far side of the sun, prophesies, "I know my redeemer lives" (Job 19:25; cf. Eccl 1:9). And I read that with him—in a maelstrom so fierce that even Job's immeasurable suffering seems a shadow cast from what is for him yet to come—Emmanuel, hanging, dying, gasping for air, opens his throat and cries, "My God, my God, why have you forsaken me?" (Matt 27:46); and when "the curtain of the temple [is] torn in two," Jesus—as if encountering something new on the far side of death and damnation—Jesus, "crying with a loud voice, [prophesies], 'Father, into your hands I commend my spirit'" (Luke 23:45b–46).[2] It strikes me that there is uttered in these narratives a word that no sequence of letters, however small or large, can contain. And I strain to say this new word when I stand before a classroom full of the children of good people. I strain to say it in such a way that no good person could ever say or hear it. And likely, were I just able to find a really good counselor, I'd put this obsession behind me and get on with my life.

The question for me, then, is, Why, why do I see and hear this way? Most of my colleagues these past decades have seen and heard differently. They seem much calmer about it all, speaking as they do of the good, the true, and the beautiful and of how God fits so well into a system of values, goals, and ideals, that is, a world view, how the story of Job and of Jesus and of God is a story that resolves questions, not complicates and ruptures them. They have told me that it is all about absolutes and universals—and all I seem ever to see and hear are contextualized particulars, the life stories of people with *particular* faces and voices, of a God with a *particularly elusive* face and voice. Of course, it may just be that I have been beguiled by Protestant nominalism, that I have fallen prey to that most modern of all perversions, postmodernism, that I am a child of my age. Indeed, I suppose this is all true. How could I honestly think anything else, even as I strain to say something other than the banal or exceptional talk of my age?

My journey has been a particular one, too, of course. Everyone's is. I don't understand much of its significance. It is not over after all. Yet I would venture to say that it is the way I have been given and made time, the way I have come to let time go, the timely way I have begun to be

2. I do not wish simply to conflate the rhetorical move made in this passage of Matthew with the one made in Luke. These are two different texts that happen to be stitched together in the codices of the church and read in its liturgy.

named. Whatever that tiny English pronoun *I* might signify in this case, the thinking and speaking and working attached to it happen here, in this story. And it isn't just my story.[3] I'm not even sure I qualify for a best supporting actor nomination.

It is not insignificant for this story that my hard Scots-Irish ancestors cut their way across an ocean and the rivers and forests of a forbidding New World to reach for the promises they'd heard were hidden under the cruel Appalachian Mountains of eighteenth-century Virginia, or the cruel Ozark Mountains of mid-nineteenth-century Arkansas, or the cruel hills of late nineteenth-century Oklahoma; it is not insignificant that both my parents were raised in abject poverty by single mothers in the Great Depression's dust bowl; that I am an only child; that I attended nine schools before I went away to college; that I was eighteen in 1968; that in the summer of that year, while reading the book of Acts in the desert Southwest, I became a pacifist; that the theologians I first threw myself into were Søren Kierkegaard and John Wesley—no theologians at all, some people tell us; that I have spent my life among Holiness people; that I still think about the lyrics to Bob Dylan's "A Hard Rain's A-Gonna Fall"; that I am an ordained deacon and not an elder; that I have been married thirty-six years, have three children and five grandchildren; and that I have had already a long career as a professor in four private, self-consciously evangelical universities.

Perhaps it is all of that which inclines me on a crisp spring morning to make my way to some tall, broad, clear window and there to dream of the open road—though I am obligated to stay put these days. Perhaps it is all of that which inclines me as well in the morning, afternoon, or night of any and every day to make my way to some tall, broad, clear window of the church—an icon "written" canonically across salvaged planks of wood, or a page of its Holy Scriptures or creeds, or the histories of its martyred mothers and fathers, or the liturgy of the eating and drinking of the Eucharist—and there to dream of God.

3. Anymore than this address is an autobiography.

And When I Saw Him, I Fell at His Feet as Dead

A dream of God is no ordinary dream, nor night terror, as Daniel and John the Revelator teach us. It is an *apocalyptic vision*. As such it makes manifest things respectable people do not want to see, perhaps cannot see. It manifests above all that there is a tomorrow that no yesterday can dictate. But it does so with the ambiguity that accompanies every call to revolution. "The Reign of God is coming," it says, "and it is coming for *you!*" As a member of one of the world's more comfortable socio-economic classes, I should recoil with horror from this word. "Woe to you rich!" Jesus, the apocalypse of St. Luke, declares (Luke 6:24). And yet, perhaps stupidly, I find myself drawn to the apocalyptic literature of God. It is bewildering, a terrifying mystery story, but somehow fascinating.

Not all mysteries are fascinating, of course, especially if, like this one, they are irresolvable. The exact numeric value of pi is a mystery to which is attached neither *tremendum* nor *fascinans.* Those mysteries that most commonly fascinate us are those that we expect with some effort to solve. They are intellectual challenges—mountains that we set out to conquer, even if only because they are there. They remain fascinating only so long as they simultaneously resist and yield to us. Once they are resolved, we move on to something else. We might wax proudly nostalgic as we recount the thrills of our victories, but to remember a *former* mystery is not to *face* a mystery.

Those of us who have been struck by an apocalyptic vision of God would tell a different story. To be thus God-struck is to face what Kierkegaard's pseudonym, Johannes Climacus, points to when he says that the passion of the thinker is to think what cannot be thought.[4] God is an irresolvable, engaging mystery that won't let us go, that won't ever let us rest in peace (cf. Ps 139:8 and 1 Pet 3:19). God revealed is God hidden, and "how unrestingly active God is in all [God's] creatures, allowing none of them to take a holiday."[5] Further, the engagement of this mystery is absolute. It calls for each of us to stand up to it with the whole heart, soul, mind, and strength, as Wesley never tires of reminding us.

4. Kierkegaard [Johannes Climacus], *Philosophical Fragments*, 37.

5. Luther, *De Servo Arbitrio*; the direct quotation is found on 234.

Neither Wesley nor Kierkegaard is an escapist mystic, however. They are both children of the earth, practical people who (unlike Luther) love the book of James, who love the way a command of God takes shape in the concrete evenings and mornings of ordinary women and men. Kierkegaard has a better eye for the ambiguity of all human works; Wesley has the better eye for their definiteness as they become good news, particularly for the poor. But the earthy concreteness of the work to which they both give themselves is inspired by a vision of the *New* Earth that we cannot see without the miracle of new eyes. Kierkegaard may stress the "cannot" of this miracle and Wesley its "new eyes," but in doing so they both bear witness to the impossible event in which we come to yield to an Other who simply will not become our property. Indeed, as we perform the works that bear witness to this Other, Kierkegaard and Wesley would have us let go of those works as well, as *formerly* rich young rulers who, without grieving, follow Jesus through the eye of a needle (Mark 10:18–27). To *keep* the works of love, the works we have done, to *hold onto* them as our property is to be poisoned by them, sickened unto death.[6]

If We Have Been United with Him in a Death Like His, We Will Certainly Be United with Him in a Resurrection Like His

I am a theologian. The works I do are mostly academic and intellectual, the works of words. Just about every day I face the challenge of gathering my thoughts before a classroom of students or a blank computer screen. And I have a lot of thoughts, having read too many books and articles, attended too many lectures, listened in too many senior seminars, spent too many hours—way too many hours—before movie and television screens and loudspeakers, pondered too long the words and deeds of my family and friends and enemies, and found out too many

6. Wesley, *A Plain Account*, in *WJWJ*, 11:440; idem, "The Repentance of Believers," in *WJW*, 2:352 (III.4); idem, "Original Sin," in *WJW*, 2:182–85 (III.1–5); idem, "The New Birth," in *WJW*, 2:188–94 (I.1–II.5); idem, "The Good Steward," in *WJW*, 2:296–98 (IV.1–4). Kierkegaard [Anti-Climacus], *The Sickness Unto Death*, 18; Kierkegaard, *Works of Love*, 40–43, 246–63.

times that I had gotten it all wrong and had to begin again from the beginning.[7] That means that I have many possessions, intangible though they may be—or at least that's what I hear. The question for me, then, is only a slightly different version of the one that went through the man of Mark 10, the man whom Jesus loved. "You lack one thing, Craig; go, sell what you own, and give . . . to the poor, and you will have treasure in heaven; then come, follow me" (Mark 10:21, sort of).

Now, I could look at Jesus' command as an investment opportunity. "Treasure in heaven" sounds like a pretty profitable return. The problem is that when "treasure" gets attached to "heaven," everything gets up-ended. "Heaven" signifies "mystery" (here is that word again!).[8] "Our Father who art in heaven" says chiefly that the God we meet through Jesus is cloaked in mystery.[9] "Treasure in heaven" is, then, a very strange treasure, one I cannot enter into a calculator, one that does not add to my net worth. And so, I'm left, having received the command of Jesus, with an unimaginable promise. It is a positive promise—that I do gather from the passage—but it is one that I have trouble objectifying enough to covet. I suspect that even Husserl would have had trouble conceiving of such a treasure. I am commanded by Jesus to give up all my property for the sake of a most unsettling impropriety. To be honest, it all sounds to me like one big expropriation manifesto. And yet again and again and again the question rings in my ears—"Craig, son of James, do you love me more than these?" (John 21:15–17, sort of). And something stirs in me and I want to say, "Lord, you know everything; you know that I love you" (John 21:17).

How do I *not* go away grieving? How do I feed his sheep? I'm a thinker, and not a very good one at that. Am I to become more ignorant than I am already? Am I to become thought-poor? Is this a call to some Jungian *sacrificium intellectus*? *How* do I not go away grieving? The answer—like the yes of a child to the voice of the mother who calls her name—rises insolubly before the mystery precisely of the evoca-

7. Perhaps that simply shows that even when one has gotten it all wrong, one might still pray. See Barth, *CD* III/3, 265.

8. Von Rad, "*ouranos*, Old Testament," 5:507; Traub, "*ouranos*, New Testament," 5:520–21, 525.

9. See Gundry, *Matthew*, 106.

tive *gospel*. "When I came to you, brothers and sisters, I did not come proclaiming the mystery of God to you in lofty words or wisdom. For I decided to know nothing among you except Jesus Christ, and him crucified" (1 Cor 2:1–2). The mystery before which I am to give up all my intellectual possessions is the mystery of the crucifixion of Jesus Christ.

But this sacrifice of the intellect—and that is the right, though non-Jungian, phrase—is no suicide. The mystery of the gospel is that Jesus Christ gives himself to the coming of the "God not of the dead, but of the living" (Mark 12:27), the coming of the *living* God. The mystery of the gospel is that Jesus' Holy Father, alive in heaven, is made manifest in *life*. The mystery of the gospel, indeed, is that the forsaken death of the carnal Son makes the Holy Father manifest, but that it does so through the *resurrection* of his dead and damned body. The mystery of the gospel is that it is into his *glorified* dead and damned body that *we* are called to move; that it is in that life that we come alive, that we are saved; that there we repeat (derivatively) his life rhythm of crucifixion/resurrection—through the liturgy of baptism and Eucharist—because his body is nothing but the life rhythm of crucifixion/resurrection. The mystery of the gospel is that our evenings and mornings become a kind of dance of death . . . swallowed up in life, that resurrection life is so alive that even death is no contrast to it.)

It is into this liturgy that Peter and I are called. We are called to Jesus' sheep—standing wide-eyed as they do in this world God so loves—to offer them the *food* that is precisely this body into which we have been incorporated. We hear, Peter and I, we hear and believe that to *eat this body* is oddly not for it to be incorporated into us, but for us to be incorporated into *it*—and thus for us to repeat (derivatively) the rhythm of crucifixion/resurrection. It is in this way that we are to *live*—together, as "a *living* sacrifice" (Rom 12:1), one performed again and again and again, pouring out what is freshly given to us, as might a spring that gives water only as it is replenished with the gift of unearned rain)(John 4:9–14).[10] That is the mystery of the *gospel*.

As a theologian, one who hears and believes, I am indeed to gather my thoughts, but only in order to give them away. Had the rich young

10. Cf. Wesley, "The Great Privilege of Those That Are Born of God," in *WJW*, 1:434–36 (I.8–II.1), 442 (III.2–3).

ruler not departed grieving, had he indeed followed Jesus, he, too, would have gathered his property in order to dispose of it. But doing so is never dropping the ballast of worldly goods in order to soar into some higher "spiritual" realm, that is, in order to get out of this world. Following the crucified/resurrected Christ *is* the work of giving away our goods. However, it is performed precisely as an act of plunging into the world, the world hallowed when the carnal body of Christ is glorified in the glorification of the Father on Easter Sunday morning. It is precisely the glorified carnality of the body of Christ that calls to us, Peter and me, renews us in the image of God that is Christ, awakens in us sacramental works of mercy, and grants to us the mind of Christ.[11] Therefore, on the day new goods come into our hands, on that day our hands do not become unclean. How could they, since they have been hallowed by the nail-pierced hands of Jesus? Rather, they are gifted—gifted with a gift that will not become property. And a gift that does not become property is there to be unhanded. To follow Christ, to have the mind of Christ, is with him perpetually to be emptied (Phil 2:5–8; cf. John 4:14).

But how am I, a theologian who has no trouble remembering that he is a human being, to pull this off? The answer in our tradition is a simple one marked by a simple Latin phrase: *sola gratia, sola fide*. It is pulled off by grace alone through faith alone, and faith, as Ephesians 2 reminds us, is itself a gift of God; otherwise, believing would make us haughty. It is finally all grace. This is something Wesley learned from Arminius, the quite non-Pelagian renegade of the Dutch Reformation. But it held true prior to Wesley and Arminius, prior to Holland, prior even to Europe—and will have held true long after Europe and all the world's nation-states it spawned have joined Wesley and Arminius in the grave—that "for mortals it is impossible, but not for God; for God all things are possible" (Mark 10:27).

To say this grace and faith is to say Trinity. God the Father moves out through God the Son in God the Spirit to a world that first and last covets its riches. The Trinity calls to this world from the depths of hell and gathers it into the body broken and left to rot there, the body of Christ in whom the Spirit glorifies the Father. By entering into the body of Christ, the discarded bits of decaying tissue that litter hell are

11. Cf. Wesley, "On Zeal," in *WJW*, 3:308–21.

stitched together to make that body's vital organs, and there partake of its glory—the holiness, the love of the Father—and move in the Spirit into the same world that treated them so badly. My calling as a theologian is to do my word-work down this path, too, as one body part of a journeying body, praying without ceasing, in everything giving thanks, rejoicing evermore, moving back and forth from this groaning earth to the earth eschatologically redeemed, from the earth eschatologically redeemed to this groaning earth. To stand before a classroom full of students or to sit before a blank computer screen is in this way to pray, give thanks, and rejoice in the mystery of the gift.

The Gospel to the Poor

There is another dimension to Jesus' call to the rich young ruler, to Peter, and to me, one no more detachable from it than is depth from a geometrical solid. The rich young ruler is commanded to disperse his goods to the *poor*. How am I to obey this command, I who profess God before classrooms full of students with the resources to attend expensive, private universities?

If I held the opinion that Jesus' attention to the poor in this narrative and elsewhere is to be sublimated into a generic concern for other people ("aren't we all poor in some sense?"), then I would have no problem at all. And it is true that all my students are given to me by God to be served. However, there are actually hungry people in the world—people like my parents were when they were hungry little children—people who are having the life sucked out of them day in and day out by the forces of what we so calmly describe as globalization. As long as I remember that God emptied the tomb of the crucified Jesus; as long as I remember that God made Adam out of the dust of the earth; as long as I remember that it is the *body* of Christ that is salvation; as long as I remember that the church is constituted by the eating and drinking of the Eucharist; as long as I remember that Jesus fed the hungry; as long as I remember that "the whole tenor of Scripture" bears witness to God's prevenient grace, particularly for the poor, I cannot reduce them to one more item on a uniform list of those for whom we are to care.

We are to care for the poor in particular and above all. We are to care for the poor in particular and above all, because God cares for them in particular and above all. God's grace is not an abstract "decision" not to punish those who deserve punishment. God's grace is God's movement out into the world to save it, that is, to sanctify it. The grace of God is the Spirit of God, the Spirit that raised Jesus Christ from the dead. The Spirit is explosive, holy life. She is the wind of a storm, the pounding current of a raging river. And God's grace rushes particularly to the poor. We know that because she rushed particularly to the poor man Jesus, laid out on a cold slab in a cold tomb. If we pray to enter into that grace, we pray that we will be carried on its current particularly to them, to people with faces, dirty, hungry faces, faces I know all too well. That is what I hear in Jesus' call to the rich young ruler and to me.

This, of course, means that he and I are to spend our resources directly for the poor. However, there is in Jesus' command a specific question addressed to me and to people like me, a question that has specifically to do with the word-work of a theologian. It seems so bloodless and distracted and insensitive, but I am a theologian and I am compelled to ask it right out loud: what does it mean for me, a theologian, a word-worker, to obey the call of Jesus to give to the poor?

I do think that in part it means that I am to remember and hope for the poor with my words. I am to give my thoughts away before people who are not hungry for the sake of those who are. I am to teach in the direction of the poor, unhanding my intellectual goods for them, calling my students to unhand theirs goods, and confessing my own unworthiness to take such words on my lips, praying that I, too, will hear the words I am given to say, that I will hear them and obey. But there is more to the call of Jesus than this. To turn to the poor in obedience to the command of Jesus is not to give them a hand up, to teach them to fish, to give them the business skills to begin the steady climb into the middle class. All that already trembles before the principalities and powers we call capitalism. To turn to the poor in obedience to the command of Jesus does not even require that one not be poor. The poor, too, are called to the poor. And we, rich and poor alike, are called to stand in solidarity with them—without demanding that they cease being poor. Doing so is a means of grace not only for them, but particularly for us.

Grace comes particularly where calculation has come to an end. And does anyone doubt that standing in solidarity with the poor without demanding that they cease being poor requires an act of trust, of hope before an incalculable mystery? Not to go away grieving signifies that in the word-work I do I am to take up the task of Isaiah 6 and Mark 4, to be situated like a surd in that social-political-economic field that *makes* people poor. It is to name the beast that devours them and with them to look it in the eye, unafraid. That is, for me to give my goods away to the poor is for me to face the freedom of the God who raised Jesus Christ from the grave, a freedom that does not need sound economic policies, that does not need the system of acquisition, private property, productivity, fixed and circulating capital, investment and return, commodification, supply schedules, derived demand, profit and loss, competition, division of labor, markets, wages, and debt. To give my goods away to the poor is among other things to bear witness to an economy of giving and forgiving, an economy of impropriety, an economy that remembers the hope of the resurrection of the Crucified. That is, to give my goods away to the poor is to live and speak and write before the mystery of God's holy love, a love that comes as an unsettling holiness that will never be a line item on an asset management tally sheet.

This Is My Body That Is Broken for You

Trinity, crucifixion/resurrection, church, the poor—this is the mystery I strain so hard to say when I stand before a classroom full of the children of good people. My task, as a theologian, is to think it and say it again and again and again.) That is what *meta-noia* quite literally means, in particular in my particular case. My task is to think-after, in pursuit of, the way of God into the world. My task is to take whatever thoughts I can find and let them loose before a classroom or a reader or a banquet hall in the liturgy of the Eucharist, the liturgy in which the broken body and shed blood of Jesus are manna, food that is to be eaten, not stockpiled.

It may be that one day Alzheimer's disease will have rotted away all of my thoughts and that there will be effectively nothing there that a professor might give, and no professor there to give it. And yet I will not be alone in that place either. Among the wonders of the gospel is that Jesus is there as well—shining with the light of God's glory. Still, as long as I have eyes to see, I am called on each new day to look for the small round things that God has placed on the face of the wilderness where I sojourn, to pick them up and eat them, to hold out in the freedom of grace the works they enliven me to do, and to say right out in public with the plagiarizing Wesley,

> I come, [Sovereign], to restore to thee what thou hast given; and I freely relinquish it, to enter again into my own nothingness. For what is the most perfect creature in heaven or earth in thy presence, but a void capable of being filled with thee and by thee; as the air, which is void and dark, is capable of being filled with the light of the sun, who withdraws it every day to restore it the next, there being nothing in the air that either appropriates this light or resists it? O give me the same facility of receiving and restoring thy grace and good works! I say, *thine*; for I acknowledge the root from which they spring is in thee, and not in me.[12]

12. Wesley, *A Plain Account*, in *WJWJ*, 11:441. These words are a part of a larger passage that Wesley calls "Farther Thoughts on Christian Perfection." That passage ends with an eight-page section that Wesley has adapted from the work of Jean Duvergier's posthumously published *Lettres Chrétiennes et Spirituelles* (1645). (Randy Maddox, Private Correspondence, April 14, 2006.) The details of Wesley's editing and use of Duvergier's work will be laid out in Maddox's editorial comments to vol. 12 of *The Works*, to be published in the near future.

Bibliography

Alioto, Anthony M. *A History of Western Science*. Englewood Cliffs, NJ: Prentice-Hall, 1987.

Althaus, Paul. *The Ethics of Martin Luther*. Translated by Robert C. Schultz. Philadelphia: Fortress, 1972.

Anselm of Canterbury. "An Address" (*Proslogion*). Translated by Eugene R. Fairweather. In *A Scholastic Miscellany: Anselm to Ockham*, edited by Eugene R. Fairweather, 69–93. New York: Macmillan, 1970.

———. *Proslogion*. Translated by M. J. Charlesworth. In *Anselm of Canterbury: The Major Works*, edited by Brian Davies and G. R. Evans, 82–104. New York: Oxford University Press, 1998.

Aquinas, Thomas. *Summa Contra Gentiles*. Book 1: *God*. Translated by Anton C. Pegis. Notre Dame: University of Notre Dame Press, 1955.

———. *Summa Contra Gentiles*. Book 2: *Providence, part II*. Translated by Vernon J. Bourke. Notre Dame: University of Notre Dame Press, 1975.

Athanasius. *Orations Against the Arians*. In *The Christological Controversy*, edited and translated by Richard A. Norris Jr., 83–101. Philadelphia: Fortress, 1980.

Augustine. *The City of God*. Translated by Henry Bettenson. New York: Penguin, 1972.

———. *Confessions*. Translated by F. J. Sheed. Indianapolis: Hackett, 1993.

———. *The Nature of the Good Against the Manichees*. In *Augustine: Earlier Writings*, edited and translated by J. H. S. Burleigh, 326–48. Philadelphia: Westminster, 1953.

———. *On Christian Teaching*. Translated by R. P. H. Green. New York: Oxford University Press, 1997.

———. *The Soliloquies*. In *Augustine: Earlier Writings*, edited and translated by J. H. S. Burleigh, 23–63. Philadelphia: Westminster, 1953.

———. "The Trinity" (Sermon 52). In *The Works of Saint Augustine: A Translation for the Twenty-First Century*. Pt. 3, *Sermons*, vol. 3. Translated by Edmund Hill. Edited by John E. Rotelle. Brooklyn: New City, 1991.

———. *The Trinity*. Translated by Stephen McKenna. Washington, DC: Westminster, 1963.

Barth, Karl. *Anselm: Fides Quaerens Intellectum*. Translated by Ian W. Robertson. Richmond: John Knox, 1960.

———. *Epistle to the Romans*. 2nd ed. Translated by Edwyn C. Hoskyns. New York: Oxford University Press, 1933.

———. *Evangelical Theology: An Introduction.* Translated by Grover Foley. Grand Rapids: Eerdmans, 1963.

———. *The Humanity of God.* Translated by John Newton Thomas and Thomas Wieser. Atlanta: John Knox, 1960.

———. "Rudolf Bultmann: An Attempt to Understand Him." In vol. 2 of *Kerygma and Myth.* Translated by Reginald Fuller. Edited by Hans-Werner Bartsch. London: SPCK, 1962.

Bauckham, Richard. *The Theology of the Book of Revelation.* New York: Cambridge University Press, 1993.

Betteridge, Harold, editor. *The New Cassell's German Dictionary.* New York: Funk & Wagnalls, 1971.

Bird, Phyllis A. "Sexual Differentiation and Divine Image in the Genesis Creation Texts." In *The Image of God: Gender Models in Judaeo-Christian Tradition,* edited by Kari Elisabeth Børresen, 5–28. Minneapolis: Fortress, 1991.

Blanchot, Maurice. *The Writing of the Disaster.* Translated by Ann Smock. Lincoln: University of Nebraska Press, 1986.

Bornkamm, Günther. "Christ and the World in the Early Christian Message." In *Early Christian Experience,* translated by Paul H. Hammer, 14–28. New York: Harper & Row, 1969.

———. "On Understanding the Christ Hymn: Philippians 2:6–11." In *Early Christian Experience,* translated by Paul H. Hammer, 112–22. New York: Harper & Row, 1969.

Børresen, Kari Elisabeth, editor. *The Image of God: Gender Models in Judaeo-Christian Tradition.* Minneapolis: Fortress, 1991.

Brown, Raymond E. *The Gospel According to John.* 2 vols. The Anchor Bible 29–29A. Garden City, NY: Doubleday, 1966.

Brueggemann, Walter. "The Book of Exodus: Introduction." In vol. 1 of *The New Interpreter's Bible: A Commentary in Twelve Volumes.* Nashville: Abingdon, 1994.

———. *Genesis.* Atlanta: John Knox, 1982.

———. *Theology of the Old Testament: Testimony, Dispute, Advocacy.* Minneapolis: Augsburg Fortress, 1997.

Buber, Martin. *I and Thou.* Translated by Walter Kaufmann. New York: Scribner's, 1970.

Burrell, David. *Faith and Freedom: An Interfaith Perspective.* Malden, MA: Blackwell, 2004.

Calvin, John. *Institutes of the Christian Religion.* Translated by Ford Lewis Battles. Edited by John T. McNeill. Philadelphia: Westminster, 1960.

Catherine of Siena. "Prayer 10." In *The Prayers of Catherine of Siena,* edited and translated by Suzanne Noffke. Ramsey, NJ: Paulist, 1983.

Cavanaugh, William T. *Torture and Eucharist: Theology, Politics, and the Body of Christ.* Malden, MA: Blackwell, 1998.

Claiborne, Robert. *The Roots of English: A Reader's Handbook of Word Origins.* New York: Times Books, 1989.

Cobb, John B., Jr. *Liberal Christianity at the Crossroads.* Philadelphia: Westminster, 1973.

Cummings, Owen F. "John Wesley and Eucharistic Ecclesiology." *One in Christ* 35:2 (1999) 143–51.

Danto, Arthur C. "Persons." In *The Encyclopedia of Philosophy,* edited by Paul Edwards, 6:110–14. New York: Macmillan, 1967.

Derrida, Jacques. *"Différance."* Translated by Alan Bass. In *Deconstruction in Context*, edited by Mark C. Taylor, 396–420. Chicago: University of Chicago Press, 1986.

———. "'Eating Well,' or the Calculation of the Subject." Translated by Peter Connor and Avital Ronell. In *Points . . . Interviews, 1974–1994*, edited by Elisabeth Weber, 255–87. Stanford: Stanford University Press, 1995.

———. *The Gift of Death*. Translated by David Wills. Chicago: University of Chicago Press, 1995.

———. *Given Time: 1. Counterfeit Money*. Translated by Peggy Kamuf. Chicago: University of Chicago Press, 1992.

Descartes, René. *Meditations on First Philosophy*. Translated by Donald A. Cress. Indianapolis: Hackett, 1979.

Dupré, Louis. *Passage to Modernity: An Essay in the Hermeneutics of Nature and Culture*. New Haven: Yale University Press, 1993.

Eliot, T. S. "Choruses from 'The Rock.'" In *The Complete Poems and Plays, 1909–1950*. New York: Harcourt, Brace & World, 1971.

Eusebius of Caesarea. "Oration on the Thirtieth Anniversary of Constantine's Reign." In *The Early Church and the State*, edited and translated by Agnes Cunningham, 45–62. Philadelphia: Fortress, 1982.

Feuerbach, Ludwig. *The Essence of Christianity*. Translated by George Eliot. New York: Harper & Row, 1957.

Fitzmyer, Joseph A. *The Gospel According to Luke*. 2 vols. The Anchor Bible 28–28A. Garden City, NY: Doubleday, 1970.

Foltz, Bruce. *Inhabiting the Earth: Heidegger, Environmental Ethics, and the Metaphysics of Nature*. Atlantic Highlands, NJ: Humanities Press International, 1995.

Fortman, Edward J. *The Triune God: A Historical Study of the Doctrine of the Trinity*. Grand Rapids: Baker, 1972.

Frei, Hans. *Theology and Narrative: Selected Essays*. Edited by George Hunsinger and William Placher. New York: Oxford University Press, 1993.

Gorringe, Timothy J. "Atonement." In *The Blackwell Companion to Political Theology*, edited by Peter Scott and William T. Cavanaugh, 363–76. Malden, MA: Blackwell, 2007.

Green, Joel B. *The Gospel of Luke*. Grand Rapids: Eerdmans, 1997.

Gregory of Nazianzus. *The Theological Orations*. Translated by Charles Gordon Browne and James Edward Swallow. In *Christology of the Later Fathers*, edited by Edward Rochie Hardy and Cyril C. Richardson, 128–214. Philadelphia: Westminster, 1954.

Gregory of Nyssa. *Against Eunomius*. In *The Nicene and Post-Nicene Fathers*. Second Series. Edited by Philip Schaff and Henry Wace. Vol. 5, *Select Writings and Letters of Gregory of Nyssa*. Translated by William Moore and Henry Austin Wilson. Grand Rapids: Eerdmans, 1994.

———. *On the Holy Spirit*. In *The Nicene and Post-Nicene Fathers*. Second Series. Edited by Philip Schaff and Henry Wace. Vol. 5, *Select Writings and Letters of Gregory of Nyssa*. Translated by William Moore and Henry Austin Wilson. Grand Rapids: Eerdmans, 1994.

———. *On the Holy Trinity*. In *The Nicene and Post-Nicene Fathers*. Second Series. Edited by Philip Schaff and Henry Wace. Vol. 5, *Select Writings and Letters of Gregory of Nyssa*. Translated by William Moore and Henry Austin Wilson. Grand Rapids: Eerdmans, 1994.

———. On "Not Three Gods." In *The Nicene and Post-Nicene Fathers*. Second Series. Edited by Philip Schaff and Henry Wace. Vol. 5, *Select Writings and Letters of Gregory of Nyssa*. Translated by William Moore and Henry Austin Wilson. Grand Rapids: Eerdmans, 1994.

Grillmeier, Aloys. *Christ in Christian Tradition*. Vol. 2, *From the Council of Chalcedon (451) to Gregory the Great (590–604)*. Pt. 2, *The Church of Constantinople in the Sixth Century*. Translated by John Cawte and Pauline Allen. Louisville: Westminster John Knox, 1995.

Gundry, Robert H. *Matthew: A Commentary on His Literary and Theological Art*. Grand Rapids: Eerdmans, 1982.

Gutiérrez, Gustavo. *A Theology of Liberation*. Translated by Caridad Inda and John Eagleson. Maryknoll, NY: Orbis, 1973.

Harnack, Adolf von. "Correspondence with Karl Barth." In *The Beginnings of Dialectical Theology*, edited by James M. Robinson, 161–87. Richmond: John Knox, 1968.

Hauerwas, Stanley. *The Peaceable Kingdom: A Primer in Christian Ethics*. Notre Dame: University of Notre Dame Press, 1983.

Hegel, G. W. F. *Phenomenology of Spirit*. Translated by A. V. Miller. New York: Oxford University Press, 1977.

Heidegger, Martin. *Being and Time*. Translated by John Macquarrie and Edward Robinson. New York: Harper, 1962.

———. *Discourse on Thinking*. Translated by John M. Anderson and E. Hans Freund. New York: Harper & Row, 1966.

———. *Introduction to Metaphysics*. Translated by Gregory Fried and Richard Polt. New Haven: Yale University Press, 2000.

———. "Language." In *Poetry, Language, Thought*, translated by Albert Hofstadter, 185–208. New York: Harper & Row, 1971.

———. "On the Essence of Truth." Translated by Albert Hofstadler. In *Basic Writings: From* Being and Time (1927) *to* The Task of Thinking (1964), edited by David Farrell Krell, 111–38. San Francisco: HarperSanFrancisco, 1993.

———. "The Origin of the Work of Art. " Translated by Albert Hofstadler. In *Basic Writings: From* Being and Time (1927) *to* The Task of Thinking (1964), edited by David Farrell Krell, 139–212. San Francisco: HarperSanFrancisco, 1993.

———. *What Is Called Thinking?* Translated by J. Glenn Gray. New York: Harper & Row 1968.

Hepburn, Ronald W. "Nature, Philosophical Ideas of." In vol. 5 of *The Encyclopedia of Philosophy*. Edited by Paul Edwards. New York: Macmillan, 1967

Jaeger, Werner. *Paideia: The Ideals of Greek Culture*. Vol. 2, *In Search of the Divine Center*. Translated by Gilbert Highet. New York: Oxford University Press, 1943.

Jenkins, Philip. *The Next Christendom: The Coming of Global Christianity*. New York: Oxford University Press, 2002.

Jonge, Marinus de. *Christology in Context: The Earliest Christian Response to Jesus*. Philadelphia: Westminster, 1988.

Jüngel, Eberhard. *God's Being Is in Becoming: The Trinitarian Being of God in the Theology of Karl Barth: A Paraphrase*. Translated by John Webster. Edinburgh: T. & T. Clark, 2004.

———. "Humanity in Correspondence to God: Remarks on the Image of God as a Basic Concept in Theological Anthropology." In *Theological Essays*, translated by John B. Webster, 124–53. Edinburgh: T. & T. Clark, 1989.

──────. "The Truth of Life: Observations on Truth as the Interruption of the Continuity of Life." Translated by Richard W. A. McKinney. In *Creation and Christ: Studies in Honor of T. F. Torrance*, edited by Richard W. A. McKinney, 231–36. Edinburgh: T. & T. Clark, 1976.

Kant, Immanuel. *Critique of Pure Reason*. Translated by Norman Kemp Smith. New York: Macmillan, 1958.

──────. *Grounding for the Metaphysics of Morals*. Translated by James W. Ellington. Indianapolis: Hackett, 1981.

Käsemann, Ernst. "Ministry and Community in the New Testament." In *Essays on New Testament Themes*. Translated by W. J. Montague. London: SCM, 1964.

Keen, Craig. "*Homo Precarius*: Prayer in the Image and Likeness of God." *Wesleyan Theological Journal* 33 (1998) 128–50.

Kelly, J. N. D. *Early Christian Doctrines*. 5th ed. San Francisco: HarperSanFrancisco, 1977.

Kelly, Walt. *Potluck Pogo*. New York: Simon & Schuster, 1955.

Kierkegaard, Søren. *Concluding Unscientific Postscript to* Philosophical Fragments. 2 vols. Edited and translated by Howard V. Hong and Edna H. Hong. Princeton: Princeton University Press, 1992.

──────. *Fear and Trembling*. In *Fear and Trembling/Repetition*. Edited and translated by Howard V. Hong and Edna H. Hong. Princeton: Princeton University Press, 1983.

──────. *Philosophical Fragments/Johannes Climacus*. Edited and translated by Howard V. Hong and Edna H. Hong. Princeton: Princeton University Press, 1985.

──────. *The Sickness Unto Death: A Christian Psychological Exposition for Upbuilding and Awakening*. Edited and translated by Howard V. Hong and Edna H. Hong. Princeton: Princeton University Press, 1980.

──────. *Works of Love*. Edited and translated by Howard V. Hong and Edna H. Hong. Princeton: Princeton University Press, 1995.

LaCugna, Catherine Mowry. *God For Us: The Trinity and the Christian Life*. San Francisco: HarperSanFrancisco, 1991.

Lash, Nicholas. "Considering the Trinity." *Modern Theology* 2:3 (1986) 183–96.

Lavely, John H. "Personalism." In *The Encyclopedia of Philosophy*, edited by Paul Edwards, 6:107–10. New York: Macmillan, 1967.

Leibniz, Gottfried. "On the Active Force of Body, on the Soul and on the Soul of Brutes (Letter to Wagner, 1710)." In *Leibniz: Selections*, edited and translated by Philip Wiener et al., 125–29. New York: Scribner's, 1951.

Leith, John H., editor. *Creeds of the Churches: A Reader in Christian Doctrine from the Bible to the Present*. 3rd ed. Atlanta: John Knox, 1982

Levinas, Emmanuel. *Of God Who Comes to Mind*. Translated by Bettina Bergo. Stanford: Stanford University Press, 1998.

──────. *Otherwise than Being, or, Beyond Essence*. Translated by Alphonso Lingis. The Hague: Martinus Nijhoff, 1981.

──────. *Totality and Infinity: An Essay on Exteriority*. Translated by Alphonso Lingis. Pittsburgh: Duquesne University Press, 1969.

Liddell, Henry George, Robert Scott et al., editors. *A Greek-English Lexicon*. 9th ed. New York: Oxford University Press, 1996.

Locke, John. *An Essay Concerning Human Understanding: The English Philosophers from Bacon to Mill*. Edited by Edwin A. Burtt. New York: Modern Library, 1967.

Löwith, Karl. *Meaning in History*. Chicago: University of Chicago Press, 1949.

Luther, Martin. *Commentary on St. Paul's Epistle to the Galatians.* Translated by Philip S. Watson. In *Martin Luther: Selections from His Writings,* edited by John Dillenberger, 99–165. Garden City, NY: Doubleday, 1961.

———. *De Servo Arbitrio.* Translated by Philip S. Watson. In *Luther and Erasmus: Free Will and Salvation,* edited by E. Gordon Rupp and Philip S. Watson, 100–334. Philadelphia: Westminster, 1969.

———. *On Christian Liberty.* Translated by W. A. Lambert. Revised by Harold J. Grimm. Minneapolis: Fortress, 2003.

———. "Preface to the Complete Edition of Luther's Latin Writings." In *Martin Luther: Selections from His Writings,* edited by John Dillenberger, 3–12. New York: Anchor, 1962.

———. "Secular Authority: To What Extent It Should Be Obeyed." In *Martin Luther: Selections from His Writings,* edited by John Dillenberger, 363–402. New York: Anchor, 1962.

———. "Two Kinds of Righteousness." In *Martin Luther: Selections from His Writings,* edited by John Dillenberger, 86–96. New York: Anchor, 1962.

Maddox, Randy. *Responsible Grace: John Wesley's Practical Theology.* Nashville: Kingswood, 1994.

Marion, Jean-Luc. "The Blind Man of Siloe." Translated by Janine Langan. *Image: A Journal of the Arts and Religion* 29 (2000) 59–69.

———. *La Croisée du Visible.* Paris: Presses Universitaires de France, 1996.

———. *The Crossing of the Visible.* Translated by James K. A. Smith. Stanford: Stanford University Press, 2004.

———. *God Without Being: Hors-Texte.* Translated by Thomas A. Carlson. Chicago: University of Chicago Press, 1991.

———. "They Recognized Him; and He Became Invisible to Them." Translated by Stephen E. Lewis. *Modern Theology* 18:2 (2002) 145–52.

Marshall, I. Howard. *The Gospel of Luke: A Commentary on the Greek Text.* Grand Rapids: Eerdmans, 1978.

Maugham, W. Somerset. *The Razor's Edge.* New York: Vintage, 1972.

McCormack, Bruce L. *Karl Barth's Critically Realistic Dialectical Theology: Its Genesis and Development, 1909–1936.* New York: Oxford University Press, 1995.

McNeill, William. "Porosity: Violence and the Question of Politics in Heidegger's 'Introduction to Metaphysics.'" *Graduate Faculty Philosophy Journal* 14:2–15:1 (1991) 183–212.

Meredith, Anthony. *The Cappadocians.* Crestwood, NY: St. Vladimir's Seminary Press, 1995.

Meyendorff, John. *Christ in Eastern Christian Thought.* Crestwood, NY: St. Vladimir's Seminary Press, 1987.

Moberly, R. W. L. "'Holy, Holy, Holy': Isaiah's Vision of God." In *Holiness Past and Present,* edited by Stephen C. Barton, 122–40. New York: T. & T. Clark, 2003.

Moltmann, Jürgen. *The Crucified God: The Cross of Christ as the Foundation and Criticism of Christian Theology.* Translated by R. A. Wilson and John Bowden. New York: Harper & Row, 1974.

———. "The Crucified God and Apathetic Man." In *The Experiment Hope,* edited and translated by M. Douglas Meeks, 69–84. Philadelphia: Fortress, 1975.

———. *Jesus Christ for Today's World.* Translated by Margaret Kohl. Minneapolis: Fortress, 1994.

Niebuhr, H. Richard. *Christ and Culture.* New York: Harper, 1951.

Nietzsche, Friedrich. *Beyond Good and Evil.* Translated by Walter Kaufmann. New York: Vintage, 1966.

———. *Thus Spoke Zarathustra.* Translated by Walter Kaufmann. New York: Viking, 1954.

———. *The Will to Power.* Translated by Walter Kaufmann. New York: Vintage-Random, 1967.

Norris, Richard A., Jr., editor. *The Christological Controversy.* Philadelphia: Fortress, 1980.

Origen. *On First Principles.* Translated by G. W. Butterworth. Gloucester, MA: Peter Smith, 1973.

Otto, Rudolf. *The Idea of the Holy.* Translated by John W. Harvey. New York: Oxford University Press, 1958.

The Oxford English Dictionary. 2nd ed. New York: Oxford University Press, 1989.

Panayiotis, Nellas. *Deification in Christ: The Nature of the Human Person.* Translated by Norman Russell. Crestwood, NY: St. Vladimir's Seminary Press, 1987.

Pannenberg, Wolfhart. *Anthropology in Theological Perspective.* Translated by Matthew J. O'Connell. Philadelphia: Westminster, 1985.

———. *Basic Questions in Theology.* Vol. 1. Translated by George H. Kehm. Philadelphia: Fortress, 1970.

———. *Faith and Reality.* Translated by John Maxwell. Philadelphia: Westminster, 1977.

———. *Jesus—God and Man.* Translated by Louis L. Wilkins and Duane A. Priebe. Philadelphia: Westminster, 1968.

———. *Systematic Theology.* 2 Vols. Translated by Geoffrey W. Bromiley. Grand Rapids: Eerdmans, 1991.

———. *Theology and the Kingdom of God.* Edited by Richard John Neuhaus. Philadelphia: Westminster, 1969.

Parmenides. "Fragments." In *The Presocratics,* edited and translated by Philip Wheelwright. New York: Odyssey, 1966.

Pelikan, Jaroslav. *The Christian Tradition.* 2 vols. Chicago: University of Chicago Press, 1971.

Plato. *Complete Works.* Edited by John M. Cooper. Indianapolis: Hackett, 1997.

Polt, Richard F. H. *Heidegger: An Introduction.* Ithaca: Cornel University Press, 1999.

Pseudo-Dionysius. *The Divine Names.* In *Pseudo-Dionysius: The Complete Works,* translated by Colm Luibheid and Paul Rorem, 47–132. New York: Paulist, 1987.

Rad, Gerhard von. *Genesis: A Commentary.* Translated by John H. Marks. Philadelphia: Westminster, 1972.

———. *Old Testament Theology.* Vol. 2. Translated by D. M. G. Stalker. New York: Harper & Row, 1965.

———. "*ouranos,* Old Testament." In *Theological Dictionary of the New Testament,* edited by Gerhard Kittel, translated by Geoffrey W. Bromiley, 5:502–9. Grand Rapids: Eerdmans, 1967.

Rahner, Karl. *The Trinity.* Translated by Joseph Donceel. New York: Herder & Herder, 1970.

The Razor's Edge. Directed by John Byrum. Columbia Tristar, 1984.

Rorem, Paul. "Foreword." In *Pseudo-Dionysius: The Complete Works,* translated by Colm Luibheid and Paul Rorem, 1–3. New York: Paulist, 1987.

Ruether, Rosemary Radford. *Sexism and God-Talk: Toward a Feminist Theology.* New York: Paulist, 1993.

Runyon, Theodore. *The New Creation: John Wesley's Theology Today.* Nashville: Abingdon, 1998.

Schmemann, Alexander. *The Eucharist: Sacrament of the Kingdom.* Translated by Paul Kachur. Crestwood, NY: St. Vladimir's Seminary Press, 1988.

———. *For the Life of the World: Sacraments and Orthodoxy.* Crestwood, NY: St. Vladimir's Seminary Press, 1973.

———. *Introduction to Liturgical Theology.* Translated by Asheleigh E. Moorhouse. Crestwood, NY: St. Vladimir's Seminary Press, 1966.

Schmidt, K. L. "Ekklesia." In *Theological Dictionary of the New Testament,* edited by Gerhard Kittel, translated by Geoffrey W. Bromiley, 3:501–36. Grand Rapids: Eerdmans, 1965.

Schnackenburg, Rudolf. *Jesus in the Gospels: A Biblical Christology.* Translated by O. C. Dean Jr. Louisville: Westminster John Knox, 1995.

Schüssler Fiorenza, Elisabeth. *But She Said: Feminist Practices in Biblical Interpretation.* Boston: Beacon, 1992.

Schweizer, Eduard. "Sarx, Sarkikos, Sarkinos." In *Theological Dictionary of the New Testament,* edited by Gerhard Kittel, translated by Geoffrey W. Bromiley, 7:98–151. Grand Rapids: Eerdmans, 1971.

Seitz, Christopher R. *Word Without End: The Old Testament as Abiding Theological Witness.* Waco: Baylor University Press, 2004.

Simon, Paul. "The Boy in the Bubble." From *Graceland.* 1986, Warner Brothers 925447-2.

Song, C. S. *Jesus, the Crucified People.* Philadelphia: Fortress, 1990.

Stafford, Thomas. *Christian Symbolism in the Evangelical Churches.* Nashville: Abingdon-Cokesbury, 1942.

Staples, Rob. *Outward Sign and Inward Grace: The Place of Sacraments in Wesleyan Spirituality.* Kansas City: Beacon Hill, 1991.

Stoeffler, F. Ernest. "Tradition and Renewal in the Ecclesiology of John Wesley." In *Traditio–Krisis–Revovatio aus theologischer Sicht: Festschrift Winfried Zeller zum 65. Geburtstag,* edited by Bernd Jaspert and Rudolf Mohr, 298–316. Marburg: N. G. Elwert Verlag, 1976.

Tannehill, Robert C. *Luke.* Nashville: Abingdon, 1996.

Tertullian. *Against Praxeas.* In *The Ante-Nicene Fathers.* Edited by Alexander Roberts and James Donaldson. Vol. 5, *Latin Christianity: Its Founder, Tertullian.* Translated by Peter Holmes. Buffalo: The Christian Literature Co., 1885.

———. *The Prescription Against Heretics.* In *The Ante-Nicene Fathers.* Edited by Alexander Roberts and James Donaldson. Vol. 3, *Latin Christianity: Its Founder, Tertullian.* Translated by Peter Holmes. Buffalo: The Christian Literature Co., 1885.

Tillich, Paul. *The Courage to Be.* New Haven: Yale University Press, 1952.

———. *Dynamics of Faith.* New York: Harper & Row, 1947.

———. "Religion and Secular Culture." In *The Protestant Era.* Translated by James Luther Adams. Chicago: University of Chicago Press, 1957.

———. *Systematic Theology.* 3 Vols. Chicago: University of Chicago Press, 1951–63.

Traub, Helmut. "*ouranos,* New Testament." In *Theological Dictionary of the New Testament,* edited by Gerhard Kittel, translated by Geoffrey W. Bromiley, 5:497–502. Grand Rapids: Eerdmans, 1967.

Wainwright, Geoffrey. *Doxology: The Praise of God in Worship, Doctrine and Life.* New York: Oxford University Press, 1980.

Webber, Robert. *The Secular Saint.* Grand Rapids: Zondervan, 1979.

Weekley, Ernest. *An Etymological Dictionary of Modern English.* Vol. 1. New York: Dover, 1967.

Wesche, Kenneth Warren. "'The Defense of Chalcedon in the 6th Century: The Doctrine of 'Hypostasis' and Deification in the Christology of Leontius of Jerusalem." PhD diss., Fordham University, 1986.

Westermann, Claus. *Genesis 1–11: A Continental Commentary.* Translated by John J. Scullion. Minneapolis: Fortress, 1994.

Wolff, Hans Walter. *Anthropology of the Old Testament.* Translated by Margaret Kohl. Philadelphia: Fortress, 1974.

Young, Robin Darling. *In Procession before the World: Martyrdom as Public Liturgy in Early Christianity.* Milwaukee: Marquette University Press, 2001.

Index

Index